Social Work Intervention

Second edition

EDITED BY TREVOR LINDSAY

Series editors: Jonathan Parker and Greta Bradley

SAGE | LearningMatters

Los Angeles | London | New Delhi
Singapore | Washington DC

Learning Matters
An imprint of SAGE Publications Ltd

1 Oliver's Yard
55 City Road
London EC1Y 1SP

SAGE Publications Inc.
2455 Teller Road
Thousand Oaks, California 91320

SAGE Publications India Pvt Ltd 150
B 1/I 1 Mohan Cooperative Industrial Area
Mathura Road
New Delhi 110 044

SAGE Publications Asia-Pacific Pte Ltd
3 Chuch Street
#10–04 Samsung Hub
Singapore 049483

Editor: Luke Block
Production Controller: Chris Marke
Project Management: Deer Park Productions,
Tavistock
Marketing Manager: Tamara Navaratnam
Cover Design: Code 5 Design Associates
Typeset by: Pantek Media, Maidstone, Kent
Printed by: MPG Printgroup, UK

First edition published in 2009.
Second edition published in 2013 by SAGE/
Learning Matters.

British Library Cataloguing in Publication Data

A catalogue record for this book is available from
the British Library.

ISBN: 978 1 44626 665 6 (pbk)
ISBN: 978 1 44626 664 9

Contents

About the editor and contributors

Dr Anne Campbell is a senior lecturer in social work at the Queens University, Belfast. Her practice background is in community and youth work.

Huw Griffiths is a senior lecturer in social work at the University of Ulster. He has a practice background in child protection and mental health. He currently practises as a mediator with Relate and Family Mediation NI on a sessional basis.

Cathy Jayat was formerly a lecturer in social work at the University of Ulster and is currently a principal social work practitioner. She has worked in a variety of practice settings including family and childcare, youth justice and adolescent mental health. She is registered as a Systemic Psychotherapist/Family Therapist with UKCP.

Irene Lindsay was a part-time lecturer at the University of Ulster and an independent practice educator. She has extensive practice experience in the probation service, as a psychiatric social worker, a trauma counsellor and as a university counsellor.

Trevor Lindsay was a lecturer in social work at the University of Ulster. His practice background is in the Probation Service, specialising in groupwork and group care. He is the lead author of another book in the Transforming Social Work Practice series: *Groupwork Practice in Social Work*.

Mary McColgan is Professor of Social Work and Head of Sociology and Applied Social Studies at the University of Ulster. Her practice experience is in family and child care and medical social work. She has continuing involvement in community development and family support projects.

Emma McGinnis is a lecturer in social work at the University of Ulster. She draws on practice experience in family and child care, child and adolescent mental health and youth justice. She is a trained family group conference co-ordinator and parent trainer. She maintains the currency of her practice through sessional work in youth justice and residential childcare.

James Marshall is an associate lecturer in the University of Ulster and also works as an independent social worker and trainer. His practice background is in statutory family and child care work. His special interests are child protection social work and evidential interviewing of children for criminal courts.

Aisling Monds-Watson is Lecturer in Social Work at the University of Ulster, having previously practised in both community mental health and in family and child care social work, with a particular focus on social work with mothers experiencing mental health difficulties.

Acknowledgements

The writing team would like to acknowledge the helpful advice of Series Editor, Jonathan Parker, Helen Fairlie and Kate Lodge of Learning Matters in the preparation of this book.

The editor would like to thank his partner and life-long friend Irene for her help and support.

Preface to the second edition

A second edition of this book is timely in view of the publication of the Munro Report at the end of 2011 (Munro 2011). The report recognises that services have become overly bureaucratised and that social workers need to move from a culture of compliance to *one that values and develops professional expertise* (page 6). It is the contention of the editor and contributors that the first edition of this text already went some way towards equipping beginning social workers with the knowledge that would help them to develop their expertise, as the report demands. This edition has been updated in the light of the report, in particular with the addition of two new chapters: Aisling Monds-Watson has contributed a chapter on advocacy; and there is an additional chapter from Trevor Lindsay on working with groups. The original chapters have been revised and updated; in particular, Huw Griffiths has added a new section to his chapter on mediation approaches, in which he discusses working with cultural, ethnic and religious differences. The book has also been updated in line with the Professional Capabilities Framework for Social Work.

Introduction

This book is written following what seems a long period during which the helping role of the social worker in face-to-face work with clients has contracted significantly. In the face of changes in social work practice brought about by a shift influenced by management set outcomes, performance indicators, market considerations and a preoccupation with the assessment and management of risk, the role of the social worker as a helper has been eroded. These changes are not in themselves necessarily to be condemned, but it can be argued that they and other legal and policy changes have altered the nature of the role of the social worker, moving it perceptibly towards bureaucratic and proceduralist function-alism. Increasingly, in this new world, as the teachers of new generations of practitioners, we wonder if the subjects taught on social work courses are still relevant. What is the need for theory and the skills and values of social work for people who are entering a workforce where these seem to be diminishing in usefulness? Nevertheless, we take heart and agree with Parton and O'Byrne (2000) that face-to-face work with clients remains at the core of the work. Furthermore, we feel that we have an important role in promoting in our students an enthusiasm and energy for working with clients, with a view to facilitating positive change. In this work social workers need a toolbox of methods and techniques for the work. It has been said that if all you have is a hammer, you tend to see everything as a nail. The purpose of this book is to provide you with a variety of tools to equip you to deal with the demands of a variety of different jobs.

Book structure

We struggled with the title of this book. We started with *Methods of Intervention in Social Work* but did not like either *methods* or *interventions*, one term implying a little more sci-ence and the other a little more intrusion than we cared for. Then we considered *Social Work Interventions: Ways of Helping*, but this did not fit with the style of the series and so the subtitle was dropped and with time the plural just disappeared. The point of all this is that we wanted to write a book which was about doing things *with* clients rather than *to* them and that we wanted it to be about helping people to help themselves rather than intruding unhelpfully into their lives. The title will have to do as we can think of no other.

The structure of the book is simple and self-explanatory. Each chapter in turn deals with a way of working with clients. In terms of the order of the chapters, a word of explanation might be required. In thinking about the order in which we should present the chapters, we had two considerations in mind. On one hand we wanted to produce each method in roughly the order that it developed chronologically. This was because some methods are born either out of or as a reaction to another that came before. So, person-centred work was created out of a concern about the directiveness and power of the worker in psychotherapy; task-centred work came about as a result of evidence that suggested that short methods of work were as effective as the longer methods that preceded it. Consequently, some chapters needed to precede others. However, another consideration was that we wanted to run a case study about the same family throughout the book. This was because we wanted to make a point in the book that the reality of social work practice is that most workers do not rigidly follow one method of working but in fact pick and choose techniques and methods from a substantial menu as they go along, depending on the circumstances, needs and wishes of the client and sometimes the demands of the agency. The story of the Cartwright family dictated that some methods should come before others. Had we been following a strict chronological order, we would have had the cognitive behavioural approach much earlier, probably as Chapter 2 or 3, but the Cartwrights determined that other methods had to come first; again this reflects the reality of practice.

As far as it has been possible we have tried to keep the same format for each chapter, including something on the applicability to social work practice and the advantages and limitations of each method. Where relevant, we use research summaries to provide you with the available evidence for the effectiveness of each of the approaches being discussed. However, there are a few points that we need to make to help you more fully appreciate some of the issues around this information.

Most research into methods of intervention occurs in rather specialised settings, where practitioners are highly trained and experienced in the method and adhere closely to the theoretical model. This is so that the researcher can be sure that they are researching the model in a pure form; it is not contaminated. Therefore, while the research evidence is useful to social work practitioners, its usefulness is somewhat limited, since it is not truly reflective of social work practice. In social work the method is usually applied in a somewhat diluted form by people who have not been extensively trained in it and who frequently apply it in a way where it is mixed in with one or more other methods (we will discuss eclectic and integrative approaches in a later chapter). A number of the methods we will discuss have come about as a result of combining two or more methods that preceded them; it is difficult to make comparisons, since it is impossible to tell which part of which method is making or not making a difference.

Research into methods of intervention tends to take one of two directions – outcome research and process research. Outcome research is interested in the effectiveness of an approach in terms of the benefit to the client; that is, it addresses the question: 'Looking at a group of clients who have experienced this approach, is there a difference in how they are before and after the experience?' A problem with outcome research is that it tends to lack specificity. It does not tell us what works with a particular individual with a particular problem. Process research, on the other hand, has as its focus the identification and measurement of elements in the approach that result in change occurring. These are important differences to bear in mind as you read the research summaries in the book.

Learning features

As with the other books in this series, this book is interactive. You are encouraged to work through the book as an active participant, taking responsibility for your learning, in order to increase your knowledge, understanding and ability to apply this learning to practice. You will be expected to reflect creatively on how your learning needs can be met in respect of using methods of intervention and how your professional learning can be developed for your future career.

In this book, as stated earlier, it was a deliberate decision to use a single case study of a family throughout the book, so as to emphasise that social work practice tends to be eclectic, drawing techniques from a number of different approaches as seems fitting. Activities that require you to reflect on experiences, situations and events will help you to review and summarise learning undertaken. In this way your knowledge will become deeply embedded as part of your development. When you come to your practice in an agency, the work and reflection undertaken here will help you to improve and hone the skills and knowledge needed for your work with clients. Suggestions for further reading will be made at the end of each chapter.

Terminology

In Chapter 10 you will be introduced to the idea that language is not neutral: through language we construct our reality. Language carries powerful meaning and we must use it with care. In this book we refer to the people we work with as *clients*. There has been continuing controversy over what term should be used in practice. A number of terms have come and gone; most recently *client* became unpopular due to its connotation of passive recipient and *service user* was accepted as the preferred term. In fact dictionaries define the term *client* as *someone who uses the services of a professional person or organisation* (Collins online dictionary, 2008), which seems to be apt and not much different in sense from the term *service user* which replaced it. All the terms that have been used are problematical, not least *service user* (McLaughlin 2008). Consequently we decided to use *client* in this book, partly because it is a little more elegant and partly for practical reasons. It is the term most commonly used in counselling and psychotherapy; since we will be making reference to a number of texts from those disciplines, it seemed preferable to use one common term rather than keep switching between *client* and *service user* depending on the situation. Nevertheless, other than where it would not make sense, we have used *worker* and *social worker* throughout, partly to make a distinction between the roles of social worker and counsellor/therapist and partly to relate the content to the task of social work as closely as possible.

This book has been carefully mapped to the new Professional Capabilities Framework for Social Workers in England and will help you to develop the appropriate standards at the right level. These standards are as follows.

- **Professionalism**

    Identify and behave as a professional social worker committed to professional development.

- **Values and ethics**

    Apply social work ethical principles and values to guide professional practice.

- **Diversity**

    Recognise diversity and apply anti-discriminatory and anti-oppressive principles in practice.

- **Rights, justice and economic well-being**

  Advance human rights and promote social justice and economic well-being.

- **Knowledge**

  Apply knowledge of social sciences, law and social work practice theory.

- **Critical reflection and analysis**

  Apply critical reflection and analysis to inform and provide a rationale for professional decision-making.

- **Intervention and skills**

  Use judgement and authority to intervene with individuals, families and communities to promote independence, provide support and prevent harm, neglect and abuse.

- **Contexts and organisations**

  Engage with, inform, and adapt to changing contexts that shape practice. Operate effectively within your own organisational frameworks and contribute to the development of services and organisations. Operate effectively within multi-agency and inter-professional partnerships and settings.

- **Professional leadership**

  Take responsibility for the professional learning and development of others through supervision, mentoring, assessing, research, teaching, leadership and management.

References to these standards will be made throughout the text. You will find a diagram of the Professional Capability Framework in Appendix 1, and relevant extracts from the subject benchmark for social work in Appendix 2.

Chapter 1
Psychosocial approaches

Trevor Lindsay

Introduction

While, in this book, we will be discussing social work interventions, many of the approaches also feature prominently in counselling methods. There is some confusion around the differences and similarities between social work and counselling. Feltham and Dryden (1993) identify a number of areas of overlap and Brearley (1995) argues that counselling and social work *are not two separate entities; they have much in common* (p1). Although, as McLeod (2003) argues, it is not particularly helpful to draw strict lines of demarcation between the professions, such as suggesting that social workers never engage in counselling, it is important to be aware of what distinguishes one from the other. The British Association of Counselling and Psychotherapy provides this definition of counselling on their website (BACP 2008):

Counselling takes place when a counsellor sees a client in a private and confidential setting to explore a difficulty the client is having, distress they may be experiencing or perhaps their dissatisfaction with life, or loss of a sense of direction and purpose. It is always at the request of the client as no one can properly be 'sent' for counselling.

By listening attentively and patiently the counsellor can begin to perceive the difficulties from the client's point of view and can help them to see things more clearly, possibly from a different perspective. Counselling is a way of enabling choice or change or of reducing confusion. It does not involve giving advice or directing a client to take a particular course of action. Counsellors do not judge or exploit their clients in any way.

Counsellors are not social workers and social workers are not counsellors. Although, as we shall see, counselling and social work have a common history and share many values, skills and areas of knowledge, they are quite distinctive professions. Looking at the BACP definition, we can identify the following areas of difference.

- First, we see that counselling takes place in a private and confidential setting. This is not always the case for social work. Social work occurs in a variety of places that are not always either private or confidential, for example the courts, hospitals, day centres and so on.

- *It is always at the request of the client as no one can properly be 'sent' for counselling.* Social work is not always at the request of the client. Many people become involved with social workers, in child protection, compulsory admission to mental health care, at the order of the criminal courts, for example, when really they would rather not. This points to a major difference. Social work always takes place, voluntary or statutory, fieldwork or group care, within a legal framework, and the boundaries of the work are governed by legal mandate. These can and do frequently change and so social workers need to be aware of the current statutes, regulations, policies and procedures that apply to the area of work.

- *It does not involve giving advice or directing a client to take a particular course of action.* The legal responsibilities of social work mean that at times, for example where we encounter risk, we may have a responsibility to direct. Social work also does involve giving advice, for example about the law, rights and resources. Social workers have a body of knowledge which it may, at times, be appropriate to share, for example in terms of stages of child development. Of course, we need to be very careful that the advice we give is accurate and also that it is desired and timely.

There are some other differences of which we need to be aware.

- Generally speaking, counsellors are employed only to provide counselling. Social workers, on the other hand, engage in a greater range of tasks, from finding resources to taking legal action, sometimes in relation to the same person.

- Social workers have different qualifying education and training, and practise under a different set of professional standards.

Nevertheless, social work and counselling share very similar roots (Brearley 1995) and it is not therefore surprising that there is a large number of similarities. Most importantly, they have in common a considerable body of knowledge, values and skills. The quote above provides some evidence of this. Both deal with personal difficulties, distress and dissatisfaction. The communication skills used in social work are the same skills as are used in counselling. Both involve *listening attentively and patiently* and both involve seeing things from the client's point of view and helping them to see things more clearly. Both aim to enable choice, positive change and reduction of confusion. They share principles of being non-judgemental and non-exploitative. However, does it go further than this? As Brearley (1995) argues, the extent to which counselling influences social work practice depends very largely on the practice context. Some areas of practice depend only on the skills of counselling, while in others counselling methods form a significant part of the work. McLeod (2003) makes a useful distinction between being a **counsellor**, in which there is a *formal counselling contract and the counsellor has no other role in relation to the client* and **counselling**, where this is *offered in the context of a relationship that is primarily focused on other, non-counselling concerns* (p9).

McLeod (1993) cites Karasu (1986) as having identified more than 400 distinct models of counselling and psychotherapy, most of which have developed in the last half century. In spite of the large number of different models of counselling and psychotherapy, most owe their origins to one or more of three approaches – psychodynamic; person-centred; and cognitive behavioural therapy (CBT). In this chapter, we will discuss the first of these, introducing psychodynamic counselling generally and following this with a discussion of social casework, which was its first manifestation in social work practice.

Psychosocial approaches

In order to understand the psychosocial model we first need to be familiar with psychodynamic theory, from which psychosocial social work originates. Psychodynamic theory is primarily concerned with the inner person – their thoughts and feelings – and considers external factors only from the client's view. The psychosocial approach borrows from both psychodynamic theory and ego psychology but adds social, economic and practical considerations, hence **psychosocial**. Within social work, a purely psychodynamic approach is rare. However, it forms the basis of psychosocial work and is the starting place for a number of other interventions that we will discuss later in this book. It is important, therefore, that it should also be our starting point in this book. Psychodynamic approaches have been highly influential in social work practice generally, providing essential understanding of:

- the unconscious and how it affects our behaviour and relationships;
- the influence of past experiences on the present;
- defence mechanisms;
- transference and counter-transference.

Psychodynamic theory

The psychodynamic approach encompasses all the theories in psychology that understand human behaviour in terms of the interaction of an individual's drives and urges. Freud's theory of psychoanalysis was the original theory but this has been built upon by a number of others, for example Jung (1963), Adler (1927), Erikson (1965), Klein (1932) and Freud's daughter Anna Freud (1966). The origins of psychodynamic counselling lie in Freud's ideas of the unconscious and his theory of the construction of the personality.

Freud believed that the human mind was divided into the conscious and the unconscious. The conscious is the part of which we are aware. It may involve our thoughts, emotions, perceptions, sensations, moods, dreams, and our self-awareness. The unconscious, on the other hand, represents those areas of which we have no awareness. It contains our instinctual desires and needs. Imagine the human mind as a personal computer. You may think you have deleted data entirely but it can remain on the machine for a long time without your being aware of it and perhaps causing problems and conflicts. So, too, with some of our memories and past thoughts; we may think that they have gone for ever, insofar as they are no longer in our conscious, but they may in fact live on in our unconscious without our awareness. The unconscious can act as a sort of warehouse for our memories, some of which may be very painful. In this way it protects our conscious mind from more emotional pain than is bearable. But these memories can be so strong that they refuse to remain in the unconscious for ever and can come so close to the surface that they affect our emotions and behaviour in the present.

The idea of the unconscious is an important one for social work practice. Firstly because we need to be able to understand where strong emotions in our clients are coming from or what is causing what can seem to be very irrational behaviour. We also need to be able to understand how past painful experiences, such as the withdrawal of affection by a parent, are affecting present behaviour. We also need to be open to and understand the origins of our own emotions, especially those that threaten to overpower us as we react to the experiences and pain of our clients.

Freud understood the personality as being constructed of the *ego*, the *id* and the *super-ego*. In brief, the *id* represents the basic, animal drives – the drive to reproduce, to survive, but also attraction and desire, rage and hatred. It is self-centred, without morality and is ruled by the pleasure–pain principle. It has no use for logic but is primarily sexual and emotionally childlike. The *super-ego* acts as the conscience. It represents our moral sense. It develops in childhood as the child internalises the values, rules and prohibitions of the parents and later teachers and other authority figures. The *ego* is the thinking, deciding, planning part of the personality, the part that relates to reality. The ego is the 'self', I, Me. The ego has a big job to do as it mediates between the id, the superego, and the outside world. Constantly it is protecting itself from external dangers – threats to personal safety, competition, aggression from others – at the same time as controlling the instinctive drives and satisfying the exacting standards of the superego. This internal struggle is reflected in the term 'psychodynamic'. Childhood experiences determine the development of these parts of the personality and this can result in underdeveloped or overdeveloped ego, superego or id. An overdeveloped superego might result in an extreme prudishness or excessive guilt while an underdeveloped one could lead to anti-social behaviour, insensitivity to others, etc. A weak ego can result in an uncertain or inconsistent idea of 'self', low self-esteem and poor self-efficacy, poor self-control or overwhelming feelings of anger, guilt, inadequacy and so on. A large part of the mind operates at the level of the *unconscious*. While the greater part of the ego, but not all, can be conscious, most of the superego and id are unconscious. The child whose parents have failed to provide affection may not have any conscious memory of this but it may have had a large impact on its unconscious, where as an adult they feel that they are unlovable. A child who has witnessed violent arguments between their parents may, as an adult, unconsciously fear close relationships. This, therefore, is an important concept for social workers to bear in mind.

The inner tensions, inherent in the struggle between the ego, superego, id and reality, cause anxiety, which threatens the ego further. The ego deals with anxiety by employing a number of *defence mechanisms*. The function of the defence mechanisms is to keep emotional reality safely at bay. However, these can lead to psychological disturbance (Smith 1996). A major contribution to Freudian psychology was the itemisation of these mechanisms by Anna Freud (1966), some of which have found their way into common parlance. We list the most important.

- **Denial** is the blocking of unwelcome or threatening information from awareness. Consequently, it is possible to refuse to acknowledge that a situation exists. The person behaves as if this were, indeed, the case. A teenager refuses to accept that she is pregnant, in spite of all the evidence to the contrary. A person who is recently bereaved cannot accept that the loved one is dead.

- **Rationalisation** is when we find a logical explanation for behaviour for which we have feelings of guilt or regret. For example, a person buys an expensive car and explains that the purchase was necessary because of more advanced safety features.

- **Repression** is the blocking of unwelcome thoughts, ideas or memories from awareness. A person who was sexually abused as a child has no conscious recollection of it happening.

- **Reaction formation** is turning unacceptable thoughts into the opposite. A four-year-old demonstrates great affection for a younger sibling of whom they are intensely jealous.

- **Regression** is a form of retreat; the person goes back to a time when they felt safer and the stresses were absent. A person in grief curls up into a foetal position.

- **Displacement** is the shifting of impulses on to a different (safer or more available) target. A person is verbally abused by their manager, goes home and shouts at their partner, who scolds the child, who kicks the dog.

- **Sublimation** is finding an acceptable substitute for socially unacceptable but desirable behaviour. Someone who is very angry with their partner aggressively cleans the floor, beats the carpets.

- **Projection** is attributing qualities or behaviours to others that you find objectionable in yourself. A person having an extramarital affair begins to suspect their partner of being unfaithful.

Some, or indeed all, of the defence mechanisms summarised above will probably be familiar to you already. A total of 44 defences have been identified (Milner and O'Byrne 1998). These include clowning, eating and drinking, falling ill, ritualisation, whistle in the dark, acting out, avoidance and passive aggression. What other defence mechanisms do you think there may be?

ACTIVITY 1.1

Try matching defence mechanisms to the situations below.

1. Bill does not see a problem with his drinking, saying, 'I can drink two bottles of wine per night and I never have a hangover.'

2. Gloria is reprimanded for poor practice by her line manager. On arriving home she launches a verbally abusive attack on her partner.

3. Cynthia has no memory of having been sexually assaulted when she was 14.

4. Yasmin is unsuccessful in an interview for a job in a child protection team. She declares that she did not stand a chance as the chair of the panel has always been against her.

5. Thomas is gay but has had a number of heterosexual relationships and is very vocal in his condemnation of homosexuality.

6. Mary, who has a deep-seated need to exercise control and impose order, becomes an achieving social services manager.

7. James is sexually attracted to Fiona. Then he accuses her of flirting with him.

8. Alec, aged six, starts to wet the bed shortly after his baby sister is born.

COMMENT

1. Bill is in *denial* about the effects of his heavy drinking on his health, marriage and social life.

2. Gloria is engaging in *displacement*, turning anger at her manager on to the safer target of her partner.

3. Cynthia has *repressed* the painful memory of abuse.

4. Yasmin is *rationalising* the reasons for her failure in the interview.

5. Thomas's heterosexual activity and expression of anti-gay views shows evidence of *reaction formation*.

6. Mary is *sublimating* her obsessive need to exercise control and order into an area of work where it is acceptable.

7. James is *projecting* his sexual desires on to Fiona.

8. Alec has *regressed* to a former stage of development.

CASE STUDY

The Cartwright family

Aisha is in her first year of practice in a Community Mental Health Team. She has been allocated a new case, a woman called Brenda Cartwright. Because Brenda had taken an overdose, an urgent psychiatric assessment was carried out which advised short- to medium-term social work intervention and antidepressants.

Aisha writes to Brenda suggesting a date when she will visit. The following day she receives a telephone call from Brenda in which Brenda says she can't possibly wait for the visit (in two days time) and asks if Aisha can visit that afternoon. Aisha explains that she has other people to see and that the earliest she can visit is the day of the appointment. Before she has finished speaking Brenda launches into a tirade, very angry, saying that she cannot wait that long, things are desperate, she can't cope. She accuses Aisha of being 'no help at all' and incompetent and ends up by slamming the phone down. Aisha is very taken aback, wonders if she was a bit slack about getting the appointment letter out, decides that she wasn't, wonders if she should reschedule her visits so that she can see Brenda this afternoon and talks to her team leader, who says 'For goodness' sake, Aisha, she has survived this long, another two days isn't going to make a big difference and can you let your other clients down?'

Some weeks later in their contact Brenda and Aisha discuss this episode. Brenda explains how very anxious and desperate she was feeling. She felt that she had so many problems she couldn't bear it any longer. She felt panicky and couldn't stay on top of her thoughts at all. She didn't know why she took it all out on Aisha; she didn't mean to when she phoned; she just couldn't help herself when Aisha said she couldn't come to see her straight away. Aisha said it sounded as if Brenda was dumping all her anxiety and panic on to her and Brenda said that she certainly felt a lot better afterwards. Aisha said that it certainly helped her to get some understanding of what Brenda was experiencing; after the phone call she had felt incompetent, panicked and at a loss as to what to do.

COMMENT

In psychodynamic terms Aisha was encountering emotions in Brenda which were arising out of Brenda's unconscious. When faced with this level of hostility we can respond to it negatively, perceiving it as defensiveness or hostility and respond to it in kind. Adopting a psychodynamic approach, however, we might instead understand it as arising out of strong feelings from the past, manifesting themselves now in the present, and react by trying to reach an understanding of what is causing this sort of outburst. In this example, from a psychodynamic perspective, we see a number of defence mechanisms coming into play. Brenda is so overwhelmed by her difficulties and the emotions attached to them that she (her ego) can no longer cope. Her ego has to protect itself by dealing with all this ungovernable emotion somehow and so it is 'dumped' on to Aisha – a combination really of displacement and projection. The feelings which are unacceptable to Brenda are displaced on to Aisha and at the same time her feelings of incompetence and being unable to cope ('no help at all') are also shifted from Brenda to Aisha. No wonder Aisha felt overwhelmed. In social work practice, we often have to take the brunt of what clients are feeling. These psychodynamic insights help us to understand what first seems irrational.

Other important concepts in psychodynamic counselling are those of *transference* and *counter-transference*. Transference occurs when a person unconsciously transfers the emotions and desires originally associated with one person, for example a parent or sibling, on to another person, often the worker. Counter-transference, in its widest definition, refers to the worker's conscious or unconscious emotional reaction to the client, but is more usually used to refer to either the worker's feelings about the client that stem from the worker's own life experiences, or which are a reciprocal reaction in the worker to transference in the client. An example might be where the client behaves towards the worker as if they were their parent and the worker reacts by taking on a parenting role with the client. Counter-transference can be useful, if the worker is able to recognise it, as it provides further insight into the client's emotional life and unconscious. If not recognised, however, it can be dangerous, in that it can lead to blind spots and inappropriate behaviour on the part of the worker.

CASE STUDY

The Cartwright family

According to the referral information, Brenda is 39 years old and is married to David, aged 40, who has a tool hire business. The couple live on a modern development. Their family comprises Brian, aged 20, Sandra, aged 16 and Philip, aged 14. Brenda has been suffering from depression and anxiety attacks for the past 18 months. She is not able to identify any particular cause. She had a similar episode eight years ago. A social worker had been briefly involved but Brenda had responded well to medication and the case was closed.

Aisha arranges to see Brenda at home. Brenda reacts to Aisha's visit in a very aggressive and defensive way, refusing to answer questions and questioning her on her role, to the point of almost being abusive. Aisha can feel herself becoming angry, but bites her tongue and manages to keep the anger under control. Aisha is very confused by how Brenda is behaving. As the interview progresses, Brenda expresses a great deal of ambivalence about Aisha's involvement with her, appearing to want help and simultaneously to want nothing to do with her. Aisha discusses this in supervision. Her supervisor informs her that the social worker who visited Brenda previously was a rather abrupt, insensitive person. Aisha realises that perhaps Brenda sees her as being the same as the previous social worker.

COMMENT

Had Aisha studied psychodynamic counselling on her social work degree, she might have understood what happened in terms of one explanation – that Brenda was transferring emotions from her contact with the previous social worker on to her. She might have wondered if Brenda had experienced a similar relationship in her earlier life, perhaps an insensitive parent. She might have understood her own emotions of anger, as she responded in turn to Brenda, as counter-transference.

There is a close relationship between defence systems and ego strength. The stronger the ego, the less it needs to be defended. There is a clear role for social workers in helping clients build on the ego strength. A person with a strong ego will need to be less well defended, have greater maturity and rationality and will be in a better position to manage both their inner self and the external world.

You may well be familiar also with Freud's theory of human development in which he suggested that children grow through oral, anal and genital stages. We mention this in the interests of completeness but it does not add much to our understanding in terms of social work practice and has come under much criticism for reinforcing gender stereotypes. Students generally find Erikson's (1965) theory of the stages of personality and moral development and Bowlby's (1951) attachment theory more useful. We are assuming that you will be familiar with these theories already.

The basic assumptions of the psychodynamic approach then are:

- all behaviour has a cause;

- the major causes of behaviour are to be found in the unconscious;

- behaviour has its origins in instinctual drives;

- the different parts of the mind are in constant struggle;

- we cope with anxiety caused by this struggle by use of defence mechanisms;

- adult behaviour can be understood in terms of earlier (usually childhood) experiences;

- problems can arise for people if earlier experiences have prevented them from developing a sufficiently strong ego or sense of self. A strong ego is helpful in dealing with inner tension and relationships with the external world.

ACTIVITY *1.2*

Identify a situation where you had a difficult relationship with someone. Make brief notes about the ways in which the relationship was difficult. What happened? What emotions did it raise in you? Now analyse the situation in terms of psychodynamic theory. What might have been the psychodynamic processes for this person and for you, which made for the difficulty? Make a list of learning points that come out of the situation in terms of how you might behave in the future.

COMMENT

The goal of approaches based on psychodynamic theory is to create the situation where the individual is more aware of what is going on in their unconscious, so that they are less likely to be driven by forces and impulses of which they have limited awareness. They then can take control of the feelings aroused by these in a more satisfying way. In this way they gain insight.

Social casework: The psychosocial approach

Now, having some understanding of psychodynamic concepts we can move on to consider the related psychosocial approach and its manifestation within social work as *social casework*. The term 'psychosocial' has been used to refer to a number of theories, which combine concern with psychological development and the interaction between the individual and the social environment. This contrasts with psychodynamic theory, where the external world is important only in terms of how it is viewed by the client. Early social workers had to work with the interventions that were available to them at the time. Until the 1960s, this was largely limited to the psychodynamic approach. Social workers, however, then as now, spent a large amount of their time working with people who were disadvantaged. Social workers could see that, while psychodynamic approaches were useful in understanding behaviour, their application, as previously conceptualised, tended to be limited. They needed to take into account not just the psychological state of the client but also the social and economic pressures that are the reality of most clients' lives. Out of this situation came social casework, a psychosocial approach, marrying these concerns and working on not only the inner world of the thoughts and feelings of the individual but also the external world of issues and problems that arise out of the environment, social and material life. Florence Hollis (1907–1987) is the person most closely associated with this approach. Social casework was the first theoretically based method commonly used in social work and it dominated teaching and practice from the 1950s until well into the 1970s. The psychosocial approach differs from the psychodynamic approach in two significant ways.

Firstly, while the quality of the client–worker relationship is a key element in both approaches – with shared principles of client self-determination and a non-judgemental, accepting approach – the psychosocial method calls for much warmer and involved worker attitudes and behaviour. A neutral, uninvolved approach is not likely to be effective. It is acceptable for the worker to offer advice and guidance (see below). Effectiveness depends on *the clients' confidence in the worker as an expert or, particularly in persuasion and active intervention, as a person of authority* (Hollis 1964, p237).

Secondly, while the psychodynamic approach concerns itself exclusively with the inner person and is interested in external factors only insofar as they have an influence on this, the psychosocial approach places some emphasis on the external world as also being an appropriate area for intervention. Hollis borrowed terms from Richmond (1922) to refer to the work concerned with the inner person as *direct* treatment and the work concerned with the external world as *indirect treatment*. This allowed her to include knowledge from a number of other disciplines, in particular, sociology and systems theory.

Direct treatment

Hollis (1964) created a six-category typology of techniques used in direct treatment.

Sustainment techniques

These are techniques that build the worker–client relationship and at the same time sustain the ego. Hollis (1964) argued that these were *perhaps the most basic and essential of all casework activities, for without them it would be extremely difficult even to explore the nature of the client's difficulties* (p89). Both verbal and non-verbal techniques are involved and include activities such as communicating interest, understanding, confidence in the client's capacity, acceptance, realistic reassurance, encouragement and in modern parlance 'being there for the person'. In these ways the client feels safe in the relationship and is happy for it to continue.

Direct influence

This involves the giving of advice and guidance. Hollis (1964) placed these activities on a continuum:

- making tentative suggestions ('Maybe Sandra would prefer to be alone with her friends');

- giving advice ('You know, teenage children are at a stage where it is important that they are able to develop strong relationships with friends');

- being directive ('You really must let Sandra have some private time with her friends').

Exploration, description and ventilation

Here Hollis refers to two concepts – the client describing their situation and ventilating, that is bringing out the feeling and emotions associated with the situation, those of anger, hatred, guilt and anxiety. These two in combination lead the social worker to a better understanding of the issues, but are also beneficial for the client in terms of offloading the feelings and thereby allowing the ego to focus more clearly on problem-solving. We need to take care, however, to ensure that the client does not become overwhelmed by their emotions, or that the focus of the work becomes stuck on the expression of emotion at the expense of movement forward.

Person-situation-reflection

Here the social worker encourages the client to reflect upon their current situation. Hollis (1964) was able to subdivide reflection as follows.

- Understanding of others, one's own health or any aspect of the external world.

- Understanding one's own behaviour in terms of its impact upon others or one's self.

- Awareness of the nature of one's own responses, thoughts and feelings. This may include bringing into consciousness thoughts and feelings of which one has not previously been aware. ('Sometimes, mothers can feel quite jealous of their teenage daughter's youth and lifestyle.')

- Understanding of the factors contributing to one's own behaviour when this is related to interactions with others. ('You are very upset about your relationship with your eldest sister who left home when so young. Do you think this might be influencing you in trying to protect Sandra?')

- Evaluation of one's own behaviour. This is in terms of beliefs about right and wrong, values, principles, preferences, image of self. ('Which is more important to you, knowing that Sandra is safe or her having the opportunity to develop as a young adult?')

- Awareness and understanding feelings about the worker and the treatment process. This involves an appreciation of the thoughts and feelings that are provoked in the worker–client relationship and the reasons for this, especially where these mirror feelings aroused in other relationships in the client's life. ('You seem very angry with me today. Is that because you think I am supporting Sandra in her attempt to be independent of you?')

Pattern-dynamic reflection

Here the worker and the client focus together on the *underlying dynamics of his personality* (Hollis 1964, p125). In this the purpose is to throw light on the reasons that the client feels or thinks in particular ways in certain situations and how their thoughts and emotions work. Attention may be given to making links between past (especially early life) experiences, and current patterns of thinking, behaving and feeling. ('You spoke of the sudden death of your sister when you were young; do you think that may be influencing you in how you try to protect Sandra'?) The worker may encourage the client to identify and recognise defence mechanisms. ('Do you realise that every time we talk about Sandra, you try to turn it into a joke'?) The client develops a greater understanding of themselves.

Developmental reflection

Developmental reflection is about change. Here the worker will try to influence the client towards more healthy or profitable ways of acting by helping them to understand the origins of unhelpful behaviour. Again this can involve making links with the past or identifying less useful defence mechanisms but may also involve confrontation, for example in the form of pointing out inconsistent or inappropriate behaviour. ('How much freedom did you have when you were growing up? You say that you want Sandra to grow into an independent young woman, but you protect her from situations where she might have to begin to act like an adult.')

Indirect treatment

Hollis (1964) recognised that not every situation experienced as problematic by the client could be helped by direct treatment – that is, by changes from within the person. Often the problem would lie in the environment, which needed to be changed or required a response which would ameliorate or remove negative effects. Sometimes this would be at the same time as the work with the inner person and sometimes on its own, recognising that there is not always a clear separation between the two. Problems in the environment could be causing problems in the inner person. For example, an addiction to substances might arise out of unfulfilling life opportunities associated with poverty, poor education and deprivation. One consideration here is whether it is better for the worker or for the client to tackle the environmental problem. The more the client is able to do for themselves, the more the ego is strengthened. However, there are some situations where the power and the expertise of the worker are likely to be more successful and prevent failure and consequent ego weakening on the part of the client. Hollis (1964) argued that the skills needed to bring about change in the client's environment are in many respects identical to those needed in direct treatment. Sustaining procedures are important in establishing a relationship with someone who holds the key to needed resources. Direct influence is important in arguing a client's case; exploration–description–ventilation skills are useful in getting someone to express deeply rooted feelings about the client. Reflective discussion helps others in understanding the client's position or the worker's intention or motivation.

Hollis (1964) understood indirect treatment primarily in terms of resources and categorised a number of roles.

- The social worker is a *provider* of resources, as either an advocate or source of knowledge or as a person who has access to the resources of the agency, for example, residential and day care services, foster care, substance misuse services, etc. The worker also has a role in expanding the service available, perhaps by initiating support groups not previously available or by arguing for the introduction of provision of debt counselling.

- Secondly, the social worker may be a *locator* of resources. This may depend on the worker's existing knowledge of the local community or it may involve them in some research, asking around, checking the internet or register of charities, for example.

- The social worker may be a *creator* of resources. This may be through influencing other agencies to provide additional resources, for example demonstrating the need for a medical practice to employ a counsellor, persuading a community centre to provide a room for some activity, or by recruiting and training volunteers or mentors.

- Another role may be as an *interpreter*, that is, in the sense of interpreting the client's needs or position to others so that they may have a better understanding and so behave differently towards the client. A good example here might be of a youth justice worker arranging to see an employer to try to persuade them to take on a young offender or by agreeing to give a talk on local radio in an attempt to dispel some of the popular stereotypical ideas about young offenders.

- Next Hollis (1964) discusses the role of the social worker as *mediator*. This would be where there has been some conflict or tension between the client and another person or agency representative. Mediation may involve working with the client in an attempt to improve their understanding of the other person's position, with the other to advocate on the client's behalf, or more usually a combination of both. Recent moves towards restorative approaches, either in terms of family group conferences or restorative justice are good examples of social workers adopting this role. Chapter 12 provides an introduction to mediation.

- Adopting a role as an *aggressive intervener* is a form of case advocacy, similar, in some respects, to the role of mediator, but with the inclusion of the use of force or threat of force. In adopting this role, social workers need to be careful that they continue to act ethically. It would not be permissible to advocate any form of violence against property or person. However, social workers do have other forms of power available, either in terms of the legal powers available to them – for example, taking care proceedings to protect a child – or as citizens, where they can invoke human rights legislation, or legislation that protects minorities.

Ego-oriented casework

Goldstein (1984, cited in Kenny and Kenny 2000) developed a form of psychosocial counselling, influenced by ego-psychology, which he called 'Ego-oriented casework'. From an ego-psychology perspective the role of the social worker is to support the ego. This is achieved though the use of the relationship to bolster the ego, using direct educational methods and identifying obstacles to ego development, including unhelpful behaviour and unrealistic ideas. Ego-oriented casework has three stages.

- **Assessment** The client and worker work together to identify difficulties and stresses in the client's current situation, resources available externally and in terms of internal capacities that may be drawn on to deal with these problems.

- **Defining the problems** The client and worker decide which particular aspect to work upon. This could be to focus on inner capacities, external conditions or the fit between the two. It will include a review of previous successful and unsuccessful strategies and identification of new ways of dealing with problems.

- **Action** Employing the strategies as above.

RESEARCH SUMMARY

Process research into psychodynamically based therapy cannot tell us if it makes people better but it can tell us something about the accuracy of the underpinning theory. McLeod (2003) cites two such studies: research by Luborsky et al. (1986) supported Freud's postulation that transference occurring in the therapeutic relationship mirrors the way in which the client characteristically relates to other people; Crits-Christoph et al. (1988) demonstrated a correlation between the extent to which a therapist was able to make accurate interpretations as regards transference and client benefit in therapy.

Application in social work practice

We mentioned earlier that pure forms of the psychodynamic approach, where the external world is considered only from the client's point of view, are found only rarely in social work. We need, nevertheless, to have a grounding in these concepts in order to be able to understand psychosocial approaches and other methods which draw on psychodynamic theory. Psychosocial casework has clear origins in psychodynamic theory but adds to this a concern with the interaction between the client and the external world.

Strengths

A psychosocial approach can be useful in any situation where there is a significant emotional agenda. With its emphasis on the development of ego strength, it may also be appropriate for use with people who have personality disorders, who lack confidence or have problems asserting themselves. Some understanding of psychodynamic theory is essential for some other methods of intervention, for example crisis intervention and transactional analysis.

The idea that people's behaviour arises from past experiences and unconscious inner tensions, influenced by environment factors, all beyond their control, allows us to adopt a non-judgemental approach to our work with all types of people. A 'there but for the grace of God go I' attitude enables us to work with people who have behaved in all sorts of ways that may be considered reprehensible, something we might not otherwise be able to do.

The psychosocial approach has strengths at each point in the social work process. Perhaps the most significant contribution that it makes to social work practice lies with the importance it places upon the client–worker relationship. Whenever two people come into contact for any significant period of time a relationship develops. For productive work to take place the relationship itself must be positive. Much of what we know about forming and maintaining successful relationships with social work clients comes from this body of knowledge, with its emphasis on attentive listening, accepting, being non-judgemental and taking care in giving direction. An understanding of transference and counter-transference can help us to understand and find appropriate ways of responding when we are faced with client reactions that seem irrational and possibly threatening. In any of our work with clients we must strive for the best working relationship possible. There are clear and obvious links between many of the core values of social work and the principles of the psychosocial casework relationship. This provides a foundation for any approach to the work. Even if we do not set out to intervene using a psychosocial method, it nevertheless provides us with useful knowledge and techniques at each stage of the social work process.

Assessment

Insights from this approach provide us with a framework for understanding how personality is formed, the effect of past and present relationships and experiences, the connections between these and both the internal and external experience. Some of the ideas have been so attractive that they have become a part of the common knowledge. Concepts such as the unconscious, ego strength, defence mechanisms and transference have been generally accepted as part of folk wisdom, even if they may not be known by these terms. To some extent, this allows for a shared body of knowledge that enables us to work alongside clients to find a common understanding of the factors that are causing unwelcome or unhelpful behaviour.

Nathan (1997) argues that the managerialist, pragmatic, 'check-list' approach which has developed over recent years in social work, while providing procedures that are fair, rational and explicit, cannot deal with the highly charged emotional situations in which social workers often find themselves. Insights and understanding from psychodynamic theory are of more value in these situations. In this way we can begin to make sense of behaviour. We can understand current behaviour in terms of past experience and how people impact emotionally on each other. We are better able to recognise anxiety and stresses, to identify their sources and to assess people's coping skills and ego strengths. All this puts us in a better position to assess risks and areas of strength and vulnerability and to understand how effectively people are relating to their environment.

Intervention

We noted earlier the importance of the relationship throughout our contact with the client. However, in psychosocial casework, the relationship takes on even greater significance and becomes a means in itself of promoting and fostering positive change. All the work takes place within the context of the client–worker relationship, as it were, 'in the room'. Within this context the client and worker try to find a common understanding of the client's problem, what it is, what causes it, how it is linked to other emotional and behavioural factors in the client's life. Kenny and Kenny (2000) suggest that when clients and workers are able to make sense together, they can find common understanding and new perspectives on the work in hand. We have seen earlier how the approach provides us with a number of techniques, which support and challenge clients, and how it identifies a number of different roles we can adopt when working with other agencies and professionals.

Evaluation and review

Reflection on our practice forms an important part of evaluation. During reflection we need to think about not only what happened or did not happen, but also our inner world. This will include the emotions that were raised in us and how this influenced our work. Developing an understanding of ourselves is an important part of the work. We need to understand where these emotions came from and how they relate to other feelings and experiences. Concepts such as the unconscious and how it relates to how we are motivated, and transference, particularly in the unequal worker–client relationship, are invaluable to us when we come to reflect upon our own practice.

Limitations

We should remember that casework was in its heyday at a time before concerns about power and oppression had much prominence in social work thinking. The approach is characterised by ideas which assume white, middle-class heterosexual values and ideas as the norm and anything else a form of deviance. It has difficulty in responding appropriately to difference. The approach assumes a consensus in society, where values and norms are shared and where there is a common culture. The failure to recognise that this is not the case results in an approach that at best marginalises some groups and at worst is stigmatising and oppressive. It fails to take account of the experience of people who have been subjected to the abuse of power in ethnic and/or cultural terms. The focus on early childhood experiences to explain current difficulties tends to put the blame on the caregiver, who is usually a woman, and is therefore inherently sexist. It is perhaps unfortunate that within social work the approach withered in the face of these criticisms; it might have been possible for practitioners and academics to find ways of adapting the method to resolve these problems but this did not happen.

Any approach that focuses on individual pathology is potentially oppressive. As with the medical model, the client is seen as being sick and therefore in need of treatment. Although writers such as Hollis (1964) included ideas taken from other social sciences, there remained an overall assumption of deficit – that the users of social work services had shortcomings of one type or another that social work intervention would address. For the most part, these shortcomings were thought to have their origins in the client's past. Where the deficit was in terms of practical resources the client needed to be helped to obtain better access to these. The focus is therefore on what is wrong with the client and the intervention is to work with the client to make them better. There is little understanding of the scarcity of resources or of how these are denied to less powerful groups. Because the deficit is understood as being mainly with the client, there is little interest in the promotion of social reform.

Following on from this, the worker is the expert, the professional. The client is not capable of curing themselves. The worker makes an assessment of the client's situation and decides whether it is helpful of not to share this assessment with them. There is therefore an inherent imbalance of power. The worker assesses the client and decides on the appropriate remedy. The client need not be involved in this process. The approach is very deterministic. It leaves little room for personal choice or decision-making.

The purpose of the contact is to establish a working relationship with the client, so that the client and worker can discover the underlying causes of the client's problem. In this way the client acquires *insight*. Having gained insight the client will improve naturally. In fact, there is little evidence that the gaining of insight necessarily leads to positive change. A further problem may be that at the point of insight the worker may decide that the work is done, or that further problems are attributable to the client's desire to remain unchanged.

This is a 'talking cure' where the client is able and willing to become actively involved in the therapeutic process and has some capacity for self-reflection. It is not likely to be an appropriate method, therefore, to use with involuntary clients or with people with under-developed conceptual ability or poor verbal skills.

Psychosocial approaches are also criticised for being without time limits. Contact between worker and client can go on for months or even years. For some clients regular contact over an extended period can be efficacious for as long as it lasts but without creating any improvement in coping capacity or lasting positive change. Furthermore, in these circumstances, where the relationship with the counsellor is so important, there is a danger of increasing client dependency. In the current climate of value for money and cost effectiveness, long-term interventions such as psychosocial casework do not fare well.

Psychosocial approaches are very difficult to evaluate for effectiveness. Many of the central concepts, such as the unconscious, are subjective and so cannot be tested. Research has to rely upon measures of the client's perception of improvements in quality of life issues – better able to cope, better relationships – that are difficult to measure.

CHAPTER SUMMARY

- Although counselling and social work share common roots, knowledge, skills and values, they are different professions with different professional standards, roles and responsibilities. Nevertheless, they have influenced each other and continue to do so.

- Psychodynamic theory is based on Freud's theory of the personality, which emphasises the unconscious and the struggle between the ego, id and super-ego.

- This struggle causes anxiety that the person attempts to relieve through the use of defence mechanisms.

- Features of the therapeutic relationship are transference and counter-transference.

- Skilled workers can help the client to achieve a greater understanding of their unconscious and the underlying causes of their psychological problems. Having achieved this insight, people are in a better position to cope.

- Social casework derives from the psychodynamic approach, adopting and adding to psychodynamic counselling techniques and including a concern with the demands of the external world. Ego-oriented casework focuses on strengthened ego resources through improving capacity, working to remove external obstacles or improving the fit between capacity and the environment.

FURTHER READING

Milner, J and O'Bryne, P (1998) *Assessment in social work*. Basingstoke: Palgrave.
This book contains an accessible chapter on psychodynamic approaches in assessment.

Coulshed, V and Orme, J (2006) *Social work practice*. Basingstoke: Palgrave Macmillan.
This text contains a brief account of psychosocial social work.

Dryden, W (ed.) (2007a) *Dryden's handbook of individual psychotherapy* 5th edition. London: Sage.
This contains three chapters, each of which deals with a separate approach within the psychodynamic approach – Freudian, Kleinian and Jungian.

Dryden, W and Mytton, J (1999) *Four approaches to counselling and psychotherapy*.
London: Routledge.
This has a succinct and accessible chapter on the psychodynamic approach.

Chapter 2

Person-centred approaches

Trevor Lindsay

Introduction

Many social work texts pay relatively little attention to person-centred theory and practice, perhaps only giving a nod in its direction in the course of discussion about the social work relationship. Here we give it a fat chapter to itself. This is because of the fundamental insights it provides for all social work practice, extending beyond our work with clients to how we behave towards our colleagues and the sort of relationships we strive for in contacts with other people and agencies. You will have a degree of familiarity already with some of the content of this chapter. A good deal of what is here was known before Carl Rogers formulated his person-centred theory. However, his unique contribution was to recognise the centrality of the client–worker relationship in the facilitation of positive change. Although, in recent years, social work practice has become increasingly functionalist, *very defensive, overly proceduralised and narrowly concerned with assessing, managing and insuring against risk* (Parton and O'Byrne 2000, p1), the relationship remains at the core of the work. We will see later, in the final chapter, that this aspect of our work is the most significant single factor in determining its outcome.

Person-centred counselling was developed by Carl Rogers (1902–1987) during the 1940s and 1950s as an alternative to the two theories dominant at the time, psychodynamic theory and behaviourism (see Chapters 1 and 7), both of which are deterministic (all human behaviour is inevitably determined by what has happened before and therefore there is no such thing as free will). This new approach became known as 'the third force'. Rogers had started his career as a psychotherapist very much in the psychodynamic tradition. However, from his practice experience he soon came to realise that:

> *It is the client who knows what hurts, what direction to go, what problems are crucial, what experiences have been deeply buried. It began to occur to me that unless I had a need to demonstrate my own cleverness and learning, I would do better to rely upon the client for the direction of movement in the process.*

(cited in Thorne 2007, p145)

Therefore, he started to develop ideas that led to the therapy that he originally called *the non-directive approach*. Rogers' work is often placed in the context of the American cultural values of the time *such as distrust of experts and authority figures, emphasis on method rather than theory, emphasis on individuals' needs rather than shared social goals, lack of interest in the past and a valuing of independence and autonomy* (McLeod 2003, p30). It is not surprising, therefore, that the person-centred approach embodies these values, emphasising the client rather than the counsellor as the expert on themselves, a focus on *how to be* with the client rather than a concern for any complex theory, a concern with what is happening now rather than the origins of problems, a non-directive methodology and, in line with the *American Dream*, a belief in the inherent potential of each individual.

In this chapter, we will look at some of the key ideas in person-centred work that have applicability to social work.

- Everyone has strengths that they can develop in the right circumstances and the capacity to develop and grow. A key notion in social work is that people can change, so that they may lead more satisfying lives.

- Every person is a person of worth and entitled to be treated as such.

- The nature of the relationship that develops between the social worker and the client is crucial in whatever work takes place. Essential qualities of the worker are genuineness, empathic understanding and acceptance.

- The client–worker relationship should be one of collaboration, based on equality.

Theory and practice

Rogers (1957) shared Maslow's ideas of *self-actualisation* which Maslow (1943) defined as the:

desire for self-fulfillment [sic], namely the tendency for him [the individual] to become actualized in what he is potentially. This tendency might be phrased as the desire to become more and more what one is, to become everything that one is capable of becoming.

(p380)

The person-centred approach views clients as being fully capable of attaining their own growth potential. However, it recognises that this can only occur when conditions are favourable. A potato in a dark cellar will grow but it will not reach its potential until it is brought into the light and given nourishment. Similarly, a person will not grow to their full potential if they are denied the required conditions for growth. Rogers argued that when a person is denied acceptance and positive regard from others – or when that positive regard is given only on condition of behaving in particular ways – they take on board a view of themselves based on that experience – 'I am not a worthwhile person', 'I am only lovable when I do what others want'. Consequently, they lose their sense of 'self' and what their own experience means for them. This then becomes an obstacle in their journey to reach their potential. They view themselves in that way, rather than in the way they actually are. They see themselves as a 'person who never argues back' or 'who always puts the needs of others first'. It either becomes a matter of this or risk losing the positive regard of significant people. Rogers argued that the person becomes *incongruent* and therefore fails to reach their full potential. Rogers would have argued that it is not reasonable to expect a young offender who had never experienced being treated with respect to respect others. It is not surprising that some parents who did not experience love and affection as children may have difficulty in showing love and affection to their own offspring. Rogers believed that an individual could recover their potential for growth through the relationship with the counsellor (or for that matter another person). While other counselling methods accepted the importance of certain qualities in the worker–client relationship, Rogers insisted that these qualities are both *necessary* and *sufficient* for personal growth. Nothing else was required. Rogers (1957) summarised the six necessary and sufficient conditions in a brief and simple article, sometimes known as the *Core Conditions Paper*.

No other conditions are necessary. If these six conditions exist, and continue to exist over a period of time, this is sufficient. The process of constructive personality change will follow. (p96)

You can find the conditions here with some explanatory notes.

1. *Two persons are in psychological contact.*

   Both the counsellor and client need to be actively present, in both the physical and the psychological sense. Rogers said little about this condition other than that it is satisfied when the client and counsellor are aware of being in personal contact. However, this is an important point to consider in relation to social work practice, where in some cases, in fact, there may not be even a minimal relationship, at least in the sense that

Rogers intended – a minimally positive relationship. In this situation, person-centred work cannot take place. Implicit in this condition is the idea of the client giving permission for the work to take place.

2. *The first, whom we shall term the client, is in a state of incongruence, being vulnerable or anxious.*

Incongruence refers to a situation where there is a discrepancy between how a person sees themselves and what they are experiencing. For example, someone may see themselves as being honest but regularly cheats on their expenses at work; a person may think of themselves as articulate but find that other people become very confused about what they are saying. It would be a mistake to think of incongruence in any pejorative sense, as is perhaps implied here. We all need to be incongruent at times to survive socially. You may have seen the Jim Carrey film *Liar*, where Carrey plays the role of someone who cannot lie, with disastrous and, of course, hilarious results. Being incongruent is not in itself an 'unnatural' way to be. We all need different faces for different situations. This is not what Rogers is referring to here. It is where a client is so unavoidably incongruent – where there is such a gap between how they see themselves and how they are experiencing life – that they are vulnerable or anxious, that the second condition is satisfied. It seems clear that in most cases, social work clients are in a state of incongruence. There are, of course, some exceptions; we regard people wishing to become foster carers or adoptive parents as clients and look for a state of congruence in them.

3. *The second person, whom we shall term the therapist, is congruent or integrated in the relationship.*

There is no 'edge' to the counsellor. What you see is what you get. The counsellor is genuine, open and honest. The counsellor is 'together', that is they are *freely and deeply themselves* (p98), are in touch with themselves, their feelings, thoughts and attitudes. If you cannot accept yourself, you are not in a position to accept the client. You do not put up any façade, either to the client or to yourself. Rogers said that this could mean your being yourself in ways not ideal for psychotherapy; for example, if you are frightened of the client or repulsed by them. Nevertheless, if you are able to 'own' these feelings, then the third condition is met. It is not necessary for you to convey overtly your state of congruence to the client, but neither should you try to deceive the client about yourself.

Congruence is an important factor in the client being able to trust the social worker, the client knowing that the response they will get will be open and honest. The client will also be able to see the worker as a human being, with weaknesses as well as strengths; someone who may make mistakes and acknowledges that they have done so. This allows the client to feel more accepting of the weaknesses in themselves and so, eventually, perhaps, more tolerant of weakness in others. Furthermore, genuineness on the part of the worker sets a climate for the contact, making it more likely that the client will respond in kind. Once again, you will sometimes find yourself in a position where it is impossible to be congruent; for example, where you are the guardian of information that the client wishes but cannot have, such as in child protection work.

4. *The therapist experiences unconditional positive regard for the client.*

In social work, we tend to use the term *acceptance* rather than unconditional positive regard but the intention is the same. The worker has total acceptance of the client, in all their fullness, missing nothing out: this is without conditions. It is not a question of accepting them if they behave in a certain way, but of accepting them in whatever way they may behave. It is not acceptance of them in terms of what they have the potential to become, but as they are now, regardless of desirable or undesirable attributes and qualities. It involves unreserved respect for the individual, valuing them as a unique human being, without judgement. It involves caring for them, being concerned about them and wanting the best for them. It includes feelings of warmth towards the person. This is not to say that the social worker should condone behaviour or attitudes on the part of the client that run contrary to our professional values or responsibilities. As social workers we often come up against behaviour that is not acceptable in terms of our values and responsibilities. This topic has attracted much attention and debate in the literature. Fleet (2000) suggests that in these circumstances the social worker conveys separation of acceptance of the person, as someone of worth, from the behaviour. In other words, the worker accepts the person but not the behaviour. Lietaer (1984) suggests dealing with the dilemma by accepting the behaviour as *something that is there 'for the time being'* and *keep on valuing the deeper core of the person, for what she basically is and can become* (p47). This dilemma is more fully discussed by Lindsay and Danner (2008) in relation to working with the perpetrators of hate crime.

Make a list of all the people for whom you currently have unconditional positive regard.

COMMENT

How many did you get? Did you include your partner? Your children? Perhaps you did. If so, you will know what is meant by the term. How many were outside of your immediate family? Probably not many, if any. Were there clients in there? Let's face it – some clients are easier to accept than others are and there will always be occasions that test the limits of our unconditionality. Rogers recognised this dilemma and saw unconditional acceptance as an ideal and here (1957, p98) makes the position clear.

From a clinical and experiential point of view I believe that the most accurate statement is that the effective therapist experiences unconditional positive regard for the client during many moments of his contact with him, yet from time to time he experiences only conditional positive regard – and perhaps at times negative regard, though this is not likely in effective therapy.

Nevertheless, the more we are able to convey genuine unconditional positive regard for the client, the greater are the chances of success. There are a number of reasons why unconditional positive regard is so central to the person-centred approach. It is well worth setting them out here.

- Many clients believe that they will only be accepted if they behave in accordance with the conditions of others. 'John will only be able to love me if I never argue with him.' Acceptance is conditional. The client does not see themselves as being intrinsically acceptable. The communication of unconditional acceptance contradicts this. The client finds that in this relationship it is possible for the worker to accept them as they actually are, without conditions.

- The inability to be self-accepting becomes a self-fulfilling prophesy. The individual behaves in accordance with their image of themselves as lacking worth. They may be overly defensive, withdrawn, aggressive – qualities which result in a negative reaction in others and further non-acceptance. Unconditional positive regard on the part of the worker breaks into this cycle, as the worker consistently responds to the client as someone to be valued.

- Since there is now no reason to be self-protective in the presence of the worker, the client is able to open up more during contact and delve more deeply into personal experiences and their effect.

- As the client continues to experience the unconditional acceptance of the worker, they become more accepting of themselves. At this point, the client is able to begin to move forward.

ACTIVITY **2.2**

The following exercise is adapted from one in Mearns and Thorne (2007). Go through the following list. Use a score of 1 to 5 to reflect upon how much you feel you would be able to show unconditional positive regard for the individuals described.

- *A client who is poorly dressed, unkempt and smells badly.*
- *A woman who has neglected her baby to the point that it requires hospitalisation.*
- *A man who has repeatedly battered his wife.*
- *A heroin addict whose habit is funded by selling drugs to schoolchildren.*
- *An Evangelical Christian who keeps telling you that you need to let Christ into your life.*
- *A gay man.*
- *A lesbian woman.*
- *A person who swears and blasphemes a lot.*
- *A person who holds and forcibly expresses anti-gay views.*
- *A rioter who boasts of assaults on police officers.*
- *A police officer who boasts of assaults on rioters.*
- *A young man who has tied up an old woman in her house, physically assaulted her and robbed her.*
- *A Muslim who supports acts of political violence.*

ACTIVITY **2.2** *continued*

- *An Irish Republican who supports acts of political violence.*

- *A millionaire who has made his fortune by buying up housing property and letting it out to people who do not have enough points to be housed by the local authority.*

- *A man who has repeatedly abused his female children.*

- *His wife who has been aware of this but has done nothing to stop it.*

- *A man who has never worked in his life but is claiming benefits for children whom he is not supporting.*

COMMENT

This exercise should help you to identify some of your personal values and perhaps your prejudices. Our values influence our ability to show unconditional acceptance and we need to be aware of them and think about their origins. We may have been socialised into them or they may have arisen out of personal experience. The difficulty in accepting some clients at some times belongs to us, not to the client. It may be that we need to discuss this in supervision, so that we are in a better position to empathise and develop an accepting attitude.

5. **The therapist experiences an empathetic understanding of the client's internal frame of reference and endeavours to communicate this experience to the client.**

We know that empathy involves being able to put oneself in the shoes of another. Rogers (1957, p99) puts it succinctly. *To sense the client's world as if it were your own, but without ever losing the 'as if' quality – this is empathy ... To sense the client's anger, fear, or confusion as if it were your own, yet without your own anger, fear, or confusion getting bound up in it ...*

Mearns and Thorne (2007) use a four-point scale for possible levels of empathy.

Level 0 There is no evidence of empathy – perhaps a response that bears no relationship to the client's feelings.

Level 1 There is evidence of some understanding of the client's surface feelings.

Level 2 There is evidence of understanding of the thoughts and feelings expressed by the client. This is *accurate empathy*.

Level 3 There is not only evidence of understanding of the feelings being expressed but also of underlying feelings, of which the client may not even themselves be aware, a *depth reflection*.

Accurate empathy is particularly important in the person-centred approach.

- It indicates to the client that the worker understands their situation and this in itself may help with self-image.

- It suggests to the client that the worker is sufficiently interested in them to strive to understand them.

- It may help to dispel alienation, since it is difficult to maintain personal alienation when someone is demonstrating understanding.

- The focus of the worker on achieving accurate empathetic understanding can provoke the client to become more aware of their underlying emotions and feelings and when this understanding is communicated to the client, there is a tendency for the client to be able to delve deeper and become more aware.

6. *The communication to the client of the therapist's empathetic understanding and unconditional positive regard is to a minimal degree achieved*.

Rogers' logic here is straightforward and simply put.

> *Unless some communication of these attitudes has been achieved, then such attitudes do not exist in the relationship as far as the client is concerned, and the therapeutic process could not ... be initiated.*

(1957, p99)

Having considered Rogers' core conditions you may find the following statement cited in the Munro Report (Munro 2011) to be obvious and self evident:

> *Helpers who are cold, closed down and judgemental are not as likely to involve clients as collaborators as are those who are warm, supportive and empathetic.*

(Knei-Paz 2009)

Acquiring the qualities of congruence, unconditional positive regard and accurate empathetic understanding requires considerable work on the part of the worker. Communicating our unconditional positive regard and empathy to the client is another dimension. How do we do this? Let us spend a little time considering this in respect of each condition in turn, since this is what this book is about – how do you do it?

Developing worker congruence

We can start from the position that the reason you are working with this person is that they have dissatisfactions or problems in their lives that arise out of feelings of worthlessness or incongruence. This follows from the conditionality of their relationships with others. It is reasonable to assume that in these relationships they will have experienced people who have been dishonest with them, who have manipulated them and given them contradictory messages. It will be understandably difficult for them initially to accept that you are not going to be like this in your relationship with them and also it will be difficult for you to be this congruent person. It is not what you are used to, no matter how nice you are. Maybe you think it will be OK so long as you are only saying positive constructive things to the client, but if you do not actually mean them, the client will soon see through you – your non-verbal communication will give you away – and the client will learn that you do not mean what you say. It will also be very scary for you to say things that the client may not want to hear – that you do not like what they have done, that you are feeling bored or that you find it hard to like them at times. Perhaps the first step in achieving this congruence is to recognise that you, not the client, are responsible for these feelings. The client is not making you feel this way. This is to do with your inner self, your values, your socialisation. You need to become aware of the reasons you have these feelings. Where do they come from?

Lack of worker congruence can occur in two ways. First, it may be that we are simply not fully aware of what we are experiencing and so cannot accurately communicate this. Second, it may be that we are aware but decide not to give any indication of what we are experiencing, because we do not want to upset someone or we fear an angry reaction. Earlier, we suggested that, at times, it is impossible to be congruent in our daily lives. We are probably able to be more congruent in situations with people we trust – immediate family, friends and close colleagues – than in others. In a way, we turn our congruence up and down, like the sound on the television, to match different situations. We cannot do this in the client–worker relationship. We need to try to be as congruent as possible, all the time. Perhaps we can take some comfort in the fact that all workers make mistakes. The congruent worker recognises this and is able to admit the mistakes to the client. In this way the client–worker relationship is able to develop. Consequently, we do not need to be frightened of our mistakes. Of course, we want to make as few as possible, but we also want to be open about those we do make and to learn from them.

Being congruent does not mean that you blurt out everything you are feeling in the social work session. To do so would be to meet your needs and not the client's. Mearns and Thorne (2007) make this very clear:

> When we talk about being 'congruent' … we are referring to the counsellor giving expression to responses she has that are relevant to her client and that are relatively persistent or striking. (original emphasis)

Mearns and Thorne (2007, p142)

Mearns and Thorne (2007) suggest two ways in which we can develop our congruence. We can expand our experience of the human condition. We can identify and reflect upon the situations in which we may find it difficult to be congruent and upon the types of people with whom we may find it difficult to be congruent. Perhaps we find the concept of death hard to handle and so have difficulty in being congruent with people who are terminally ill. Perhaps we find it hard to be congruent with people who are of a very different culture. Increasing our self-awareness and our empathetic understanding can help here. The other way we can develop our congruence is by trying out different aspects of ourselves in the counselling session. This may be about getting in touch with different parts of ourselves and using this. In working with an angry client, it can help to remember how you felt when angry. Getting in touch with your feelings of bereavement may help you to be more congruent when dealing with someone who has experienced a major loss. This is not the same as empathy. You cannot say, 'Oh, I know exactly how you are feeling, the same thing happened to me' because the client's experience will be different. Nevertheless, being aware of these parts of yourself will help you to become more congruent.

Developing and communicating unconditional positive regard

Acquiring and communicating unconditional positive regard can be one of the most difficult areas for us. Could you have unconditional positive regard for a serial killer or for someone who has sexually abused children? The posing of such questions reveals a misunderstanding. Unconditional positive regard does not involve identifying with or approving of unacceptable behaviour. Nevertheless, it is possible to care for that person and to try to understand them. It is these aspects that are unconditional.

In order to develop unconditional positive regard you need first to accept yourself. This is a personal journey which is never-ending and on which you have to find your own way. As a social work student you should already have started. There are a number of resources available to you that should help you on your journey. First are those who are closest to you and who can provide you with honest feedback. Next are the professionals to whom you have access – tutors, practice teachers, possibly counsellors or facilitators, who can provide feedback. Finally, there is yourself. Meditation and self-reflection can be helpful.

Do not attempt a person-centred approach, unless you believe the underpinning theory to be correct. If you do not believe in the core conditions as set out by Rogers (or, as later developed, Bozarth 1998a; Lietaer 1993; Mearns 1994) do not do it. However, if you believe that people need to experience unconditional positive regard in order to grow and that you can provide it, good, but accept also that your capacity is limited. Identify where those limits lie and strive to expand them. Again, this will be a personal journey and how you make it is for you to decide.

Now you must suspend judgement. Adopt the view that had you had the same experiences as the client you might well be in the place where they are now. Any discomfort you experience in your relationship with this person is down to you, not them. You must also, as Rogers put it, 'look at the sunset'. You do not try to change the sunset; you accept that it is beautiful as it is and that although it will change, it will do so in its own way and in its own time. Finally, acknowledge how fortunate you are to have the opportunity to be in contact with this other person.

Having achieved some measure of unconditional positive regard, you may find communicating it comes much more easily. Communicate warmth as you may do with others for whom you feel unconditional acceptance – your children, your partner. Meet them when they arrive, shake hands, smile, look them in the eye, attend closely to what they are saying, show interest in them and touch them, if you feel it is welcome and appropriate. Mearns and Thorne (2007) give some guidance on the use of touch to convey this warmth. First, we need to be aware of and respect differences in cultural norms. Secondly, we need to be very sensitive to whether touch is welcome or not. Thirdly, we need to distinguish between touching as a genuine expression of regard and touching to meet a need of our own. Use of appropriate touching, a brief connection with shoulder or wrist, or even the sincere offer of a hug, can be very helpful but, as with all our work, we need to be respectful and appreciative of how it is experienced. As Mearns and Thorne suggest, there is no escape from this dilemma. Nevertheless, to take the position of never touching *is to withdraw our humanity from our work* (Mearns and Thorne, 2007, p110).

The concept of being non-directive throws up a number of challenges in social work practice. Although Rogers initially called his approach *non-directive therapy*, he did not use this term after 1951, preferring *person-centred therapy*. This has led to much controversy. For writers such as Lietaer (1990) this has meant an evolution of the theory away from non-direction while others (Bozarth 2000; Brodley 1997) argue strongly that following the core conditions inevitably results in being non-directive.

> *Non-directivity is part and parcel of client-centred therapy and practice and, as well, a behavioural result of adhering to the central conditions of client-centred therapy. For those who believe the critical foundation of client-centred theory, i.e. that the client is his or her own best expert about his or her life, non-directivity is a natural stance that emerges from the theory.*

> (Bozarth 2000)

Brodley and Schneider (2001, p157, cited in Mearns and Thorne 2007, p115) insist on a non-directive approach on the grounds that

> *Unconditional positive regard is ... communicated by the absence of communications that display challenge, confrontation, interventions, criticisms, unsolicited guidance or directive assurance or support. Whether it is intended or not, all of these omitted types of communication, if expressed, are likely to be perceived as the therapist's expression of conditional approval or explicit disapproval.*

Mearns and Thorne (2007) take issue with this insofar as it proscribes the worker's behaviour. They suggest that so long as the worker continues to accept that the client is the expert in their situation, a number of options, in terms of direction, are available and that which one of these is employed will depend on the client. A client with a very poor sense of self will need a non-directive approach. With a person who is sufficiently secure in themselves that they experience greater equality in the client–worker relationship, the worker can afford to be more directive, safe in the knowledge that the client will be able to take it or leave it on their own terms. Realistically, social workers do not have the luxury of being non-directive in every situation. In some situations it is possible, for example in problem-solving and enabling; in others it is less so, for example in child protection work or in situations where confrontation is required.

Developing and communicating empathetic understanding

Shulman (1992) suggests we can communicate empathy by *displaying understanding of the client's feelings* which *involves indicating through words, gestures, expression, physical posture or touch (when appropriate) the worker's comprehension of the expressed effect* (p126).

Brink and Faber (1996, cited in McLeod 2003) analysed Rogers' empathetic responses as follows.

- Providing orientation. Rogers would start the session by providing an opportunity for both the client and himself to settle down – getting comfortable, suggesting a brief period of silence and reflection.

- Affirming attention. Showing interest, leaning forward, head nodding, saying 'm-hm, m-hm'.

- Checking understanding.

- Restating. Mirroring back to the client what they had said, briefly summarising what the client has been saying, making reflective statements.

- Acknowledging unstated feelings. Shulman (1992) points out that there may be times when the client *stops just short* of expressing an emotion, perhaps because they are not sufficiently sure of the feeling to be able to express it or because they are not sure that it is acceptable to express it. Tentatively completing the expression for them can be helpful and also conveys empathy.

- Providing reassurance.

- Confronting, where a client appears to be avoiding a painful or difficult area.

- Direct questioning, for example to encourage a client to explore an issue further.

- Self-disclosing.

- Accepting correction, where the worker's understanding has been inaccurate and the client points this out.

CASE STUDY

The Cartwright family

In her supervision session, Aisha reflects on her initial contact with Brenda. She can see that she made a number of mistakes. She was under a lot of pressure on the day in question and did not tune in. She reacted badly to Brenda's anger, taking it as a personal affront and responding with her own anger. She was left confused by Brenda's ambivalence and now finds that she is no closer to understanding what Brenda has been experiencing than she was before the visit. Aisha arranges another appointment with Brenda and, before going, tunes in. She reminds herself about depression, its causes and how it manifests itself, by talking to colleagues and by reading relevant articles and texts.

She reads Brenda's file and discovers some rather pejorative remarks left by the previous social worker. She reflects on herself, her attitude to mental illness, her experience of her sister's depression and the disabling effect it had on her and those around her. She thinks about the times she herself has been very anxious, remembering how difficult it made it to focus on anything, how tired she was through lack of sleep and how very irritable she became. Her reading up on practice reminds her of person-centred counselling and she decides to draw on that approach when she next sees Brenda.

Aisha is feeling anxious on the day of the visit but is careful to make a friendly start, waits to be asked to sit and adopts an open posture. She starts the interview by apologising to Brenda for how she was last time they met. The beginning of the interview goes like this.

Aisha   I was a bit taken aback last time by your questions about why I was here. I sort of took it personally and reacted badly to you. I should have been better prepared and more understanding. I am sorry and I hope we can start again. I can understand you perhaps being worried about why I am here and what I will be like. I really want to take my lead from you, to listen to what, if anything, is troubling you and to be with you in it as much as I can. Would you like to start or is there anything you would like to ask me?

Brenda   (Looking relieved) *Oh, I am so glad you said that. I have been worrying about it. I had a bad time with the last social worker and I kind of took it out on you. I thought I would never see you again. I am so fed up. So much is going wrong. I don't know what to do. I wish I could walk out and never come back.*

Aisha   You feel overwhelmed and it is getting you down badly.

The interview continues with Aisha and Brenda discussing a number of issues that Brenda has been worrying about. Brenda and David are going through a rough patch in their marriage. David's tool hire business is not doing well. He is out all the time working and comes home too exhausted for there to be much communication between them, other than about money problems. David's mother, aged 79, lives nearby; her health has been poor and she has recently been diagnosed as suffering from Alzheimer's. Although Mrs Cartwright is looked after by David's sister, the situation is nevertheless worrying. Brenda and David's sex life is suffering as a result of all the stress. Brenda is worried about her eldest son, Brian. Having dropped out of university, he cannot get a job and has a number of debts outstanding from his time at university. Brenda has been finding it difficult to control both Sandra and Philip's behaviour. Philip has been suspended from school on two occasions, for aggressive behaviour towards other pupils. Sandra has bad eczema, which the family doctor has suggested may be stress related. Brenda thinks Sandra is worried about her forthcoming GCSE exams.

Aisha is careful to develop as much empathetic understanding for Brenda as she possibly can – reading a range of material and also 'tuning in' to herself, particularly to previous feelings that may help her. She immediately demonstrates congruence and respect for Brenda by openly admitting her earlier mistake. Recognising the early stage in their relationship, she adopts a non-directive approach and acknowledges Brenda as the expert in her life. She uses a reflective statement to communicate empathetic understanding.

RESEARCH SUMMARY

Rogers himself conducted extensive research into his method and was able to provide evidence to support his contention that person-centred therapy resulted in a decrease in client incongruence; the gap between the clients' perception of themselves and what they were experiencing becoming smaller as therapy progressed (Rogers and Dymond 1954, cited in McLeod 2003).

The prevalence of the person-centred approach over the past 60 years has resulted in a large number of studies. Truax and Carkhuff (1967) in an early review of research evidence into the effectiveness of psychotherapy concluded, research consistently seems to find empathy, warmth, and genuineness characteristic of human encounters that change people – for the better *(p141). More recently Bozarth (1998b, p1) examined a number of reviews and from this concluded:*

1. Effective psychotherapy is primarily predicated upon (1) the relationship between the therapist and the client and (2) the inner and external resources of the client.

2. The type of therapy and technique is largely irrelevant in terms of successful outcome.

3. Training, credentials and experience of therapists are irrelevant to successful therapy.

4. Clients who receive psychotherapy improve more than clients who do not receive psychotherapy.

5. There is little evidence to support the position that there are specific treatments for particular disabilities.

6. The most consistent of the relationship variables related to effectiveness are the conditions of empathy, genuineness and unconditional positive regard.

Application in social work practice

As with the psychosocial approach, we rarely see a pure form of client-centred social work practice. This is mainly because the authoritarian aspects, which are so often a part of the role, make it difficult to satisfy the core conditions fully. Trevithick (2005) argues that attempts to adapt the approach to resolve this causes further problems as, in moving away from the core conditions, consistency with the philosophy of the approach is lost. Consequently, if you cannot be congruent because you are the guardian of information that you cannot share, or if your role requires you to confront a client about behaviour that is putting others at risk and you are therefore unable to show regard unconditionally, you are not following a person-centred approach. Nevertheless, there are some situations where you can fully adopt the approach, for example supporting women who have been abused, working with bereavement and loss, or in some voluntary work with young people. We also need to remind ourselves that Rogers saw the full implementation of the core conditions as the ideal. When these were present, positive change was bound to occur. He accepted also, however, that this could rarely be achieved but argued that the more fully the conditions were present, the more it was that change would take place (Rogers 1957). We know of no intervention that guarantees a positive outcome in every case. We may need to be content with the knowledge that when we meet the core conditions as fully as possible, we stand the greatest chance of a successful outcome for the client. Person-centred work is probably best regarded as a way of being, rather than a way of doing. In this way, it becomes an important source of guidance in whatever way we decide to work. The core conditions form the basis of all positive worker–client relationships. This, as Sheldon (1995, cited in Seddon 2000) suggests, provides the 'packaging' for other approaches.

Strengths

- Person-centred counselling has wide applicability across a range of client groups and settings. It can form the basis of work with individuals, families, groups and communities. It can inform work which is of a supportive, pedagogic or practical nature. We can apply it in our work with people, regardless of their ages, culture, ethnicity, class or sexuality. With its emphasis on the potential of clients rather than on their deficits, it avoids some of the criticism of individual pathology levelled at other methods.

- Although the person-centred approach focuses on individual changes it is not unresponsive to structural inequality and issues of power and oppression. It does not involve working directly for social change but as Mearns and Thorne (2007, p217) argue, it involves social workers in a *process whereby the experience of relationship, characterised by deep understanding and personal honesty, provokes not only distress but sometimes rage at the rampant injustices and shameless hypocrisy that all too often characterise our political and social environment*. The approach, for them, is *politically radical ... a constant opponent to the societal influences of social control over the individual ... working with the whole person and ... oriented towards the goals of that person rather than the agenda society has for the person*.

- Even though it may be difficult in many social work situations to apply the person-centred approach fully, it is easy to understand and can be adopted as an overall philosophy for our work. The client–worker relationship is the most important aspect of the work. The approach gives strong guidance on what are the qualities of a helping relationship. It is not necessary to make a diagnostic assessment or to employ any particular strategy or technique. Indeed to do so would run contrary to the core principles of the approach.

- The approach is thoroughly positive, being part of the humanist tradition that affirms the dignity and worth of all people. It is non-judgemental. It places worker and client on an equal footing, thereby encouraging a partnership approach based on equal respect. All experience is of value. Clients are the experts on their own lives and emphasis is placed on their inherent potential to find their own way through.

Limitations

- Other than in some voluntary settings, social work involves the use of authority. This runs against the central tenets of unconditional positive regard. It is not always possible for social workers, who have a responsibility to protect not only the client but also other people, to be non-directive, empathetic, unconditionally accepting and congruent.

- The approach demands that the client *perceives himself as faced by a serious and meaningful problem* (Rogers 1961, p285). This means that the approach is not suitable for someone who has not yet recognised that they have a problem.

- It is a 'talking cure' and may not be suitable for use with people whose verbal and/ or conceptual abilities are limited. Some clients may be irritated by the non-directive nature of the approach, preferring and expecting a more directive, concrete approach.

- The non-directive nature of the approach is unlikely to be suitable in work where it is necessary to use confrontation, for example with sex offenders.

CHAPTER SUMMARY

- Carl Rogers argued that people have an innate tendency to reach their potential, provided this has not been thwarted by images they have acquired of themselves, through a history of relationships where they experienced no regard from others or where this was conditional.

- Nevertheless, such people can regain the capacity to reach their potential in a therapeutic relationship that is characterised by three core qualities on the part of the worker. These are worker congruence, unconditional positive regard and accurate empathy. It is necessary that the latter two qualities are communicated to the client to a minimum degree. Where these qualities are communicated, the person will improve. No other conditions are necessary.

FURTHER READING

Mearns, D and Thorne, B (2007) *Person-centred counselling in action.* London: Sage.
An excellent, accessible and comprehensive description of Rogers' original theory and method that also gives new formulations.

McLeod, J (2003) *An introduction to counselling.* 3rd edition. Maidenhead: Open University Press.
This contains a chapter in which the author discusses the development of person-centred therapy from its original formulation to the present day.

Dryden, W and Mytton, J (1999) *Four approaches to counselling and psychotherapy.* London: Routledge.
This provides a concise and accessible account of the approach.

Chapter 3
Crisis intervention

Emma McGinnis

A C H I E V I N G   A   S O C I A L   W O R K   D E G R E E

This chapter will help you to develop the following capabilities from the **Professional Capabilities Framework**:

- **Professionalism**
  Identify and behave as a professional social worker committed to professional development.
- **Knowledge**
  Apply knowledge of social sciences, law and social work practice theory.
- **Intervention and skills**
  Use judgement and authority to intervene with individuals, families and communities to promote independence, provide support and prevent harm, neglect and abuse.

It will also introduce you to the following standards as set out in the 2008 social work subject benchmark statement.

5.1.1 Social work services and clients.
5.1.4 Social work theory.
5.1.5 The nature of social work practice.
5.5.1 Managing problem solving activities.
5.5.3 Analysis and synthesis.
5.5.4 Intervention and evaluation.

Introduction

We turn now to crisis intervention, an approach which has its origins in ego psychology but which also draws on developmental psychology, cognitive behavioural approaches and on systems theory in its most contemporary manifestation. As Payne (2005) points out, the development of the underpinning theory occurred at a time when social work became transformed from a small-scale underdeveloped profession to the more extensive range of services we see today. An important consideration was the method's appeal as a cost-effective, short-term intervention that was easy to understand by practitioners and policy-makers alike, compared to the longer term, rather more esoteric approaches that had existed previously. Crisis intervention offers a way of working that is initially fairly directive, is time limited and seeks to address the individual's priority needs at a critical point in their lives. It is a framework, offering particular skills and techniques, that ought to be based on an understanding of the nature of 'crisis' itself.

Crisis intervention can be considered as an amalgam of theoretical approaches forging together as a means of both understanding and guiding intervention with individuals in crisis. Although, as we will see, at times it has endured criticism, most practitioners have some idea of what 'crisis intervention' is and most will have used a crisis approach, if not having held fast to the model. Arguably the most comprehensive guide to the intervention is offered by Roberts (2005), *Crisis intervention handbook*. As with any method of intervention in social work practice there are key considerations on which to reflect when intervening with people and families. We all occupy intricate social, interpersonal and environmental spaces that often have a substantial bearing on how we are experiencing what is occurring. Thus the challenge to the practitioner is to attend as much to the context as to the intervention, a necessary and recognised component part of most current assessment frameworks in contemporary social work practice. This is the essence of effective social work practice and a constant theme of this chapter.

The first part of this chapter will provide you with an understanding of what crisis is and means. Indeed this will occupy most of the discussion: an understanding of the internal journey of the individual who is facing a crisis. Their efforts, anxieties and perceived failings and inadequacies form a major part of 'working' with crisis. Knowing the process of crisis is prerequisite; the mechanisms of intervention will then follow.

At the end of this chapter you should be able to:

- consider the context in which the intervention is practised; that is, be aware of and recognise your role in attending to the socio-environmental factors impacting on the client, as well as the interpersonal challenges;

- identify situations where crisis intervention represents the most useful approach in helping;

- be familiar with the general model, and the three phases of crises;

- recognise key skills and ethical considerations essential to working in this approach.

ACTIVITY **3.1**

Think of a time in your life that you would identify as having been a time of crisis. Make a note of:

1. *how this felt;*

2. *how it feels to recall it now;*

3. *one single factor or support that you can clearly recall as helpful (that possibly transformed the situation);*

4. *something that wasn't helpful at the time, indeed may have exacerbated the situation.*

Such reflection is vital; Butler (2010) emphasises the importance of reflecting on the feelings component of our personal experiences in practice and in our development as socially and emotionally competent practioners.

COMMENT

The factors that constitute a crisis for you are no more or less valid than those that are significant for another person. The meaning and affective experience – that is, the emotional, practical and potentially physical impact – is what defines the event. Indeed, it may continue to evoke powerful feelings now, when brought to recall.

If we consider a crisis to be a time of extraordinary challenge, difficulty and uncertainty that leads us to question, or indeed challenges, our ability to cope at the most basic level of human functioning, then, by virtue of our humanity, every one of us has experienced crises. Such is life. There is much debate within social work on what actually constitutes a 'crisis'. Popular definitions offer explanations that are generic, applicable to contexts that obviously can't 'capture' exactly the meaning and experience of a crisis situation for the individual or family with whom the social worker may be involved. We may even think sometimes that some clients are in a state of perpetual crisis. Here, however, in addition to being oppressive, we would be misguided. Three fundamental and interconnected theoretical principles are essential to an understanding of what constitutes a 'crisis' situation.

Defining crisis

First, we need to understand crisis as *an upset in a steady state* (Rapoport 1970, p276). This is a little different from earlier ideas of crisis as a disturbance of equilibrium. Rapoport used the concept of 'steady state' to refer to a situation where the individual is responding appropriately and healthily to change, learning from each challenge and therefore growing or developing ego strength. A problem occurs where the person is not able to adapt to an overwhelming challenge. Stress affects all of us; it can be as disabling as it can be productive. If it affects us in a prolonged way, for example if we have an unsettled infant, ongoing financial problems, difficulties at work, we may come to see our lives as chaotic. The key factor here is how we as individuals manage it. Often this is learned through our primary socialisation, whatever that experience might have been. Stress is not crisis, even though the stress may be intense and persistent: for example, managing long-term illness in us and others. Crisis is different in that it is indicated by acute psychological and often physical overwhelm, which most theorists concur can only be short term in nature because as humans we adapt and find our own unique ways and supports in coping. The initial overwhelm – alarm, panic, despair, or all of the aforementioned – lessens into a more tolerable state, dependent on the context. How we cope in the eye of the storm, that is during the intense four- to six-week time frame (Caplan 1965), will largely determine how we will manage similar situations in the future. This is inevitably linked to the coping mechanisms we have learned and adapted, hence the relevance of developmental psychology. Here psychodynamic theory provides a necessary understanding of how we react in our minds. People in crisis are often coping with sudden loss or change; thus many theorists frequently evoke models such as the *Cycle of Grief* (Kubler-Ross 1969). This model has five stages: denial; anger; bargaining; depression; acceptance. These stages are not necessarily sequential; however, knowledge of the emotional and physical impact of these, and the process of coping with loss and change, should provide us with an understanding of appropriate intervention and skill in managing such situations. The stages themselves imply a time of major disturbance and upset. The emotional overwhelm can certainly seem unmanageable, unprecedented and terrifying. Such is often the extent of this that thought processes, sleep pattern, and appetite may be severely affected; a spiral of distress develops and in some cases results in disabling alarm. Navigating the crisis and these stages successfully, although this is a relative term, should equip the individual with some self-efficacy and belief in their own competence in coping with future crises.

Second, a crisis is a subjective experience; that is, our decision to intervene with crisis intervention should always be informed by our having attended to and assessed the intervention as appropriate, based on, above all else, the unique story of the individual or family. Of course, in our assessment of the situation we will have gleaned information from a number of sources, but the intervention must be predominantly informed by the meaning and reality of the situation as experienced and communicated to us, from the position of the client, what Parker terms a *biographical understanding* (2007, p118). Crises are often inextricably linked to life cycle events, those events that occur in the passage of our lives that mark the boundary between developmental stages, and/or times of major readjustment when we are at the very least forced to accommodate the unacceptable; even eventually assimilate the unimaginable (for example a sudden death, or illness, or perhaps an unplanned pregnancy). Thus the human life cycle is a key underlying theoretical consideration in crisis intervention and one with which we should familiarise ourselves.

Third, crises in the lives of people and families happen in all our distinct and complex environments. Here we need to realise how systems theory informs this approach. While a basic understanding of intrapsychic processes in reacting to crisis is essential, so too is a knowledge of the impact on and the function of systems central to the individual or family, for example children, siblings, the potential role of support services. The progression and resolution of a crisis is predictably linked to the person's functioning before the crisis event, which may in itself appear relatively minor compared with previous traumas or challenges. Typically there will have been a build-up or series of stressors. These are known as *precipitating hazardous events* (Caplan 1965). Often it is the case that the crisis is the proverbial 'straw that broke the camel's back', a stressor too far (Johnson and Yanca 2001, p257). Therefore, information on context is vital in determining the intervention; this requires an initial assessment; in-depth historical detail is best avoided; the focus must be about the 'where and how' in moving forward, as opposed to a preoccupation with the 'why'. Worker skill is critical in this model in maintaining focus. Identifying supports in the person's networks, community and family are key to the action. These are all issues we will return to later in this chapter. Within social work practice the reality is that those in receipt of services all too often will be overrepresented in indices of poverty and exclusions. This is a critical issue.

The context of crises

Not to include environmental and socio-economic factors in understanding 'person in environment', and the role of these in creating and maintaining challenge and crises, is to ignore the requirements of governing bodies in terms of standards and assessment tools and formats that rightly aim to address the context as opposed to merely the 'problem'. These codes and standards exist as the working embodiment of the value base of social work, which all social care workers must uphold. Crisis intervention is potentially one of the most directive interventions in social work practice. As we will learn, throughout this chapter, the social worker may have a particularly active, guiding role, particularly in the initial stages of the approach. Crisis intervention requires us to steadfastly adhere to a structured reflective process in examining what we do and why we are doing it if we are to avoid creating an overly dependent and ultimately unhelpful relationship. As with all intervention, no matter how technically proficient we may believe ourselves to be, open and honest review and reflection with self, client and supervisor are fundamental to the task in militating against the potential for oppression in what we do. Developing a mindfulness of the emotional impact on self when working with people in crisis and distress is an essential prerequisite to good practice. Munro (2011) acknowledged the anxiety attached to the role in protecting children; indeed, commentators argued that more 'time' is required to engage families in a voluntary capacity, which ultimately should result in less conflict, rather than the new interventions suggested in the Munro Report (*Community Care*, 2011). The most effective practitioners will place a value on attending to self-care, and having self-compassion and personal responsibility for themselves in this emotionally demanding role.

It is often the case that students will experience some frustration in putting into practice the print version of a method of intervention in social work practice; crises rarely follow a predictable course. However, there are some key points which are important to note while using this intervention; these should orientate you in charting the often chaotic environment and are important to highlight before considering the 'nuts and bolts' of how we might assist in a crisis.

- People manifest overwhelming distress in many different ways. Crisis should not be equated only with extreme outward emotional responses. Anger, overwhelm and depression may be impossible to articulate in extreme situations. The analogy of coping with loss and grief is important in realising the effect and possibly to some extent predicting the path of a crisis. An awareness of environment and culture is critical. The crisis experience is bound by cultural norms and values. As social workers it is incumbent on us to equip ourselves with the knowledge of how an individual's context and culture will determine how crisis manifests and presents itself; this is the essence of culturally competent intervention. Sullivan et al. (2006) succinctly summarised this requirement, stating that:

    Culturally competent crisis intervention requires a contextual approach to understanding the client in crisis. This view recognizes that race/ethnicity intersects with other factors, such as gender, socioeconomic class, immigration status, history, and current oppression, which have import for one's values, perceptions, expectations, as well as help-seeking behaviours and health beliefs. These factors also have import for exposure to stress and coping capacity as well as the individual's perception of being 'in crisis'. (p988)

- We must understand that most will have attempted to find solutions to their situations, and at the point of social work intervention, may feel overwhelming inadequacy and failure. Often the individual will fully believe that they are responsible for the crisis. Attending to people's efforts, and their 'reality' as they perceive it then, is important in providing reassurance of their desire to function and have control in the situation. What may at first appear to be a maladaptive coping mechanism can often be reframed as a positive attempt to restore a balance or state of normality. For example, an individual who feels compelled to visit daily the site of an accident that left them disabled may not so much be morbidly stuck in the past as trying to resolve what has happened in order to move on.

- Related to the above point is the vital issue of attending to the person's story, in their words, in their world. To intervene effectively we must appreciate psychodynamic, psychosocial and systems theory in so doing.

- A crisis can provide the opportunity for change and growth. Beckett (2006, p108) evokes the thoughtful analogy of the metamorphosis from caterpillar to butterfly to encapsulate the disintegration and subsequent regeneration into something which is different and has potentially benefited from the learning and experience.

- As often stated in this chapter, crisis intervention does not offer one single way of intervening with an individual. Crucially we must realise that how an individual copes in a crisis will not necessarily offer an accurate account of how they cope generally. Some level of acknowledgement that the individual is at 'overwhelm' needs to be articulated, at the very least hinted at. There is a distinction to be made between severe psychological distress and crisis. Psychological distress may result in an individual having limited insight into their inability to meet their own basic needs, to the extent that they may present a risk to themselves and potentially others. With crisis the issue is the level of overwhelm inhibiting them from meeting those very needs. If in any doubt about this distinction the worker must ascertain if the client is having, or has had thoughts about, harming themselves or others. Depending on the response, this may need to be explored further; for example, have they thought of an actual plan in either case? Approached confidently and sensitively, this is not an unnecessary intrusion; indeed it may provide an important opportunity for the client to articulate uncomfortable and frightening thoughts and feelings. My own practice experience is that any hint of an indication, should be explored, unapologetically, in the best interests of the client and others.

CASE STUDY

Aisha has been seeing Brenda for about five weeks. Brenda was prescribed antidepressant medication and this now appears somewhat effective in stabilising her mood, along with a psychodynamic counselling approach that was agreed with Brenda and in the supervision process. Brenda and Aisha have included in their discussion the circumstance surrounding Brenda's depression eight years ago, in an attempt to establish any connection between what happened then and Brenda's current emotional state. It transpires that Brenda reacted very badly to the death of her father and was ill for about two years. This was followed by a period of stability which deteriorated again 18 months ago. The situation remains fairly volatile. Brenda is a private person who acknowledges that she has little confidence in making friends and is loath to discuss any of her difficulties with her extended family. Other than her aged mother-in-law and her preoccupied sister-in-law, her nearest relative is over a three-hour drive away. She is using the sessions

effectively to discuss her feelings in relation to ongoing issues in immediate family rela-
tionships. Recently Brenda shared her anxiety regarding an upcoming court case of
her husband David's. This morning Brenda rang in to the office. She was barely able
to communicate; hyperventilating as she attempted to explain to Aisha that David has
received a six-month custodial sentence for fraud. It transpires that David was gambling
heavily and acquired significant debt. The business, in which Brenda is a nominal partner,
and the house may well have to be sold. Brenda has just found out that the household
bills, including the mortgage, have not been paid. She has very little money left for food
and, in her words, the children and she 'are in bits'. Brenda has not slept, can't eat and
'feels like she may go under'. You know from your work with her that her sleep pattern
is disturbed and that she has lost weight as a result of a very poor appetite. She isn't
allowed to visit David until a week's time; however, she isn't sure if she will even go; the
procedure for getting there is way beyond her. Brenda is in shock, she is distraught, and
Aisha can hear 14-year-old Philip and 16-year-old Sandra upset in the background. On
the phone she attempts to encourage Brenda to try and stay calm, reassuring her, and
arranges to see her that day.

Brenda is clearly articulating that she is not coping. Your work with her to date will tell
you that the situation is precarious and she is vulnerable. Consider what you have read
so far in this chapter. What are the identifiable physical, psychological and environmen-
tal factors that might indicate Brenda is in crisis? Make a list under each of these three
headings, before progressing to the next section.

Let us consider below the factors within the previously mentioned three categories that
suggest Brenda is in crisis.

Physical
- Brenda has stated to you that she is not eating and not sleeping. These are symptomatic of severe stress, though in themselves may not indicate crisis.

Psychological/psychosocial
- Brenda is extremely emotional, indeed she has clearly articulated her concern that she believes she won't cope. Her acknowledging that she isn't coping, while uncomfortable, is important.

- Currently she is taking prescribed antidepressant medication which is having some success in managing the worst of her distressing symptoms. You have the advantage in a sense of knowing the context, and recognising that this is an already volatile situation.

- We might assume that Brenda feels misled, even deceived, by her husband and may question this relationship that has defined her role and sense of self for most of her adult life.

- The threat of losing her home represents potentially another loss that is untenable. Her whole environment and that of her children is threatened, in terms of her – and their – life space, and networks. The importance of appreciating the intricate relationship between 'loss' and crisis is critical here.

- Brenda's confidence is low and she does not make friends easily. She feels deeply ashamed about the current situation and her husband being in prison. Brenda believes she has no one to confide in, and stays indoors most of the time.

Environmental

- You know that Brenda has very limited existing networks of support. It's a three-hour drive to her nearest close family member. Contact with extended family is limited and it is unlikely that they are fully aware of the present situation. David's family are not in a position to help.

- You recognise that Brenda is extremely isolated. She has never had to approach agencies or even take care of the routine household bills. Now she risks losing her home and is simply frozen at the prospect of needing to approach the range of financial institutions and utilities companies to sort out the family debts and ascertain if they can keep their home.

- There is no money at present, except to buy the bare essentials. The children are distraught and she in turn feels helpless. As a social worker, poverty and the impact of exclusion should be a predominating concern for you.

- The dynamic threat of losing her home, financial status, the loss of her husband in prison and her emotional response to this, all compound to create a crisis situation.

An obvious advantage in this situation is that Aisha has already completed an initial assessment and is involved in a planned intervention. However, as we know, assessment is an ongoing process, reviewed and updated as a result of changing circumstances. The indicators of an *active crisis* (Golan 1978, p38) are clear; to persist with an approach that doesn't account for this and address immediate issues could potentially mean deterioration in the situation, for all the family. A priority recommendation of the SCIE *Think Parent*, *Think Child*, *Think Family* guidelines, for all professionals working in mental health and children and families services, is the implementation of a 'Family threshold criteria for access to services to take into account the individual *and* combined needs of parents, carers and children' (2009, 3). This evidence-based recommendation recognises the impact of parental mental health difficulties on whole families.

Crisis intervention in action

The remainder of the chapter will present a working framework predicated on the above discussion of what crisis means, a template in which to organise and thus provide a useful planned service to an individual in crisis; that is, to intervene. The skills and knowledge necessary and useful to each stage will be explicitly discussed with relevance to each.

If we understand that the crisis process can broadly be observed as occurring in three phases, often overlapping, certainly not distinct, then we can attempt to apply a template for understanding and intervening within these, with some predictability. In this chapter the succinct and purposeful phases of Beginning, Action and Termination have been adapted as a framework on which to hang the amalgam of theory, skills and knowledge that forge together to create crisis intervention. (For other models see Roberts 2005; James and Gilliand 2001.)

Myer and Conte (2006, p966) point out that the luxury of taking information away and subjecting it to standardisation and testing isn't initially within the realms of this approach. (To this end they offer a very useful triage assessment form to measure clients' presentation in crisis across three domains: affective, behavioural and cognitive. This is within the context of a clinical setting; however, it doubtless has a use in the field to assess severity and plan accordingly.)

Table 3.1 is a summarised framework of the tasks to be achieved, and skills and knowledge necessary at the beginning phase of crisis intervention. Lest we forget: at the core of our job is assessing, and planning to intervene to meet need, including protection needs. The pressures on current practice environments are such that involvement beyond the stage where need is addressed to a satisfactory level is unlikely. Therefore it is incumbent upon us to manage our time and the 'therapeutic space' effectively. Crisis intervention is an active process from our first contact.

Discussion

The reality of the highly individual, relative, and often traumatic experience of crisis is reflected in the theoretical conglomerate of approaches that crisis intervention is hinged upon. Theorists are reluctant to commit to a definitive approach in explaining the subjective experience and perception of the myriad circumstances and lives in which crises occur (see Roberts, 2005 for the definitive guide). However, example is essential as a learning tool to illuminate key principles in the model.

Table 3.1 *Tasks, skills and knowledge framework*

Task	Skill	Knowledge
Assess risk of harm.	Active listening; being present and available through the use of verbal and non-verbal communication.	Crises are time limited.
Gather important information relevant to the 'here and now'; in the case of a new client ascertain supports.	Appropriate and sensitive use of questioning to identify precipitating events and potential risks, 'When did this happen? How did you find this out? What did you do when you found out/heard what had happened?' are examples of questions appropriate to this stage. Avoid over discussing historical detail.	Assessment is an ongoing process throughout; specifically the potential risk of harm, to self or others. All interaction is fluid, and assessment ever evolving in response to new information.
Attend to feelings and provide reassurance.	'I imagine you feel dreadful'; 'From what you're saying it must be hard for you to take in'; 'No wonder you're so upset'; 'It seems you are trying to cope with a great deal'. Gently, reframe the client's perception of self and events into a more realistic understanding of the situation.	Showing acceptance is key to effective relationship building. Non-verbal communication is vital to relaying empathy. All attempts, or non-attempts at resolution to this point are valid, in that they must be framed in the context of the client's efforts to cope with a unique and overwhelming situation.
Outline the use of crisis intervention time frame.	Use clear language: 'From what you have told me it's my view that you may benefit from an approach whereby I work with you closely for about four to six weeks on a number of goals we agree together to help you through this upsetting time. Is this something you would consider to support you through this?'	Be clear in the further discussion and the intervention about the level of contact and duration; remember, this is a time-limited endeavour. Be open about the need to work with other agencies in the best interests of families.
Set realistic goals, even a goal.	Clarifying, probing and paraphrasing to establish goals and task agreement. Solution-focused approaches are very effective (see Chapter 8).	At this stage, which inevitably will last beyond the initial interview, while it's important to acknowledge feelings, try to focus on the thoughts and actions in relation to goal formation and task achievement.
Define individual tasks in achieving set goals.	Being clear, using SMART objectives, negotiating responsibilities, organisational skills.	Work in partnership; be aware of power differentials; work to empower.

The beginning phase may last over a period of up to two weeks. Concrete goals are not going to be established in the first interview, even the first number of interviews. As Beckett (2006, p112) rightly identifies, people in crisis take longer to process information. It is essential to set small goals, which are achievable, that observe the SMART acronym; that is, they are:

Specific

Measurable

Achievable

Realistic and

Time limited.

These will have a valuable function when planned and agreed on together, in that:

- through attainment the goals allow the client some sense of self-efficacy and they may begin to believe that they are able and have some worth;

- by also involving yourself, the worker, in agreed tasks, the client experiences being supported and 'doing with' as opposed to 'doing alone'. As mentioned earlier the risk of doing for and assuming responsibility in this approach is real. The challenge for the professional social worker in enabling change is to truly understand the value of agreed goal setting as a priority. The experiential benefits to the client in achieving a positive outcome as an effect of their action, at a time when they may conceive all their efforts to date as ineffective, can't be underestimated. However, only if we have engaged with the client in attending to their present narrative and skilfully facilitated them to move to a position where they can begin to identify priority needs in their situation, can we begin to formulate goals. Therefore, at this point it is worthwhile revisiting the activity and key skills and knowledge related to the task of the beginning phase.

ACTIVITY 3.3

You have visited Brenda, and have spent some time with her, listening to her account of recent events, and using your skills to attend to and acknowledge her current emotional upset. Let's imagine that you have agreed with her a short period of fairly intensive working together to support her over the next few weeks. From the above discussion on goals make a note of the following:

- *what you assess as the priority goals based on the SMART acronym in each of the areas:* physical, psychological/ psychosocial, *and* environmental;

- *the immediate practical tasks you assess as relevant to goal achievement;*

- *'who does what', in the short term (remember what you have read about the initial phase of the crisis).*

COMMENT

Goals may appear something like those listed below. Financial and mental health issues are undoubtedly the most pressing here. Task setting and goal achievement must address the client's needs; resolution is relative to them. Using the techniques and skill of solution-focused therapy, such as the miracle question *and* scaling questions *(see Chapter 10) will encourage the client to make a paradigm shift in thinking to their preferred future.*

Potential goals

- Clarify issues in relation to home finances.

- Access sources of financial support.

- Address physical symptoms of sleep and appetite.

- Communicate the situation to the children.

Resulting tasks

- Make an appointment for the local social security office to discuss the need for immediate financial help.

- Seek permission to contact a debt/money advice service for an urgent appointment.

- Encourage Brenda to collect/locate all relevant financial documents to take with her.

- Request Brenda to make an appointment with her GP to discuss her appetite and sleep disturbance.

- Enquire about any local community resources on stress management. (This might be an area where you would need to be more directive with Brenda, in strongly encouraging her on the benefits here.)

- Facilitate a 'family meeting' with Brenda and the two children (to help provide information and reassurance and ease Brenda's anxieties regarding their well-being).

There are four basic goals, with six related tasks, that simply seek to address the priority issues in this case. As the social worker, you are addressing the basic needs. However, and this can't be emphasised enough, the effect is in how this is done. Consistently reassuring that the response is understandable and warranted, whilst encouraging goal setting and task achievement as a means of moving forward is the art in this endeavour. This is the essence of your involvement over the next number of sessions. You are a very important resource.

Students typically are confused as to what crisis intervention actually looks like beyond the initial couple of meetings. Motivation for both parties may be high initially; serious challenges are most likely to arise in the middle phase of this approach, what Caplan (1961) described as the recoil stage, when the client's usual coping responses are applied to the situation and simply do not work; thus motivation may be reduced. This is to be anticipated and understood; here the worker has a role in reassuring the client of the process at this stage while encouraging persistence with goals and tasks. This, I believe, represents the most critical stage of intervening in crisis. The worker must stick with the client's efforts, resistance, doubts and disappointments, being aware of their own responses to these. The process is the same as through the initial phase. However, a gradual increase of responsibility must be given back to the person. Each meeting with Brenda therefore needs to attend to the following issues.

- Briefly review the intervening period in terms of the agreed goals, relating them to tasks – an example of how this may be introduced could be, 'So could we talk about how we both have got on this week with our tasks?'

- Reframe goals/tasks not achieved as providing valuable information. Maybe these need to be modified: non-achievement is not the responsibility of either but a wider resource issue.

- Attend to new information and developments but remember to focus on the thinking and doing.

- Ensure that the end 'is in the room' at every session, regardless of whether or not this is a one-off time-limited piece of work or, as in the case of Brenda, a departure from usual practice/intervention in response to a crisis situation.

Solution-focused techniques can be purposeful, particularly at this stage, in giving the client a real sense of what it will be like at the final meeting (see Chapter 10).

Chui and Ford (2000, p45) see the final phase of crisis intervention very much as the doing phase. This is not to say that the client and worker will have managed all the issues, rather that through a process of negotiation, action and modification – and doubtless some frustration – essential building blocks for moving ahead should be in place. A feature of this approach is that these three phases are by no means distinct. This doing phase is next door to ending.

The skills required in this approach are outlined many times in this chapter. Perhaps this phase is better explained in describing what an observer might witness during the process of an interview at this point. Let's imagine it is week three with Brenda and that two more sessions remain following this one. Firstly, the worker would identify a clear structure to the session, where from the beginning the time allocated and purpose of the visit would be outlined, including also a statement on the remaining number of agreed overall sessions left. A brief discussion of the progress and any issues since the previous interview would follow. The process of ongoing assessment should be obvious, partly through reassurance that significant information here would be assimilated if necessary into future task setting, or reconsideration of particular goals. Given that agreeing goals and task setting is so pivotal to this intervention, the work of reviewing tasks should be clearly demarcated in the interview. At this point the worker ought to be seen to explore the thinking and behaviour that resulted in either achievement or non-achievement of tasks for the client. This should be observed as a genuine curiosity or needing to know what were the circumstances that culminated in either outcome, as opposed to any indication of disappointment. Remember this is valuable information and the worker might need to reflect on the achievability of the task. Collaborate on goal motivation with the service user; it is a good opportunity to evidence respect for their expert status.

Let's imagine that Brenda has seen a debt adviser on a number of occasions and a deferment of mortgage payments has been negotiated. Also payment has been made by the local social security agency, therefore the financial pressures that were so exacerbating the stress are reduced. An additional goal of accessing community support is more difficult for Brenda; a task that involved her in attending an information morning wasn't achieved. Through discussion with her, you both understand that one-to-one support will work initially, so she has agreed to some individual sessions on stress management with a community voluntary group.

Here, this information is skilfully used to promote similar behaviour, in this case reinforcing the benefits of action, and to encourage awareness of patterns of thinking and doing that result in less helpful outcomes for the client. In this case you may reflect on how involving herself in a group/community situation might provide essential support and adult company for Brenda in the future (see Chapter 7); an important factor in reducing isolation. This is likely to be a longer term, though crucial goal. Task achievement is rewarding and esteem-building for any individual; it is so crucial in instilling belief in the client's efforts in this intervention.

Within crisis intervention the final session ought to:

- clearly identify this session as being the last in the intervention;

- review progress since the previous session;

- evaluate overall goals;

- identify potential goals for the longer term;

- reinforce supports developed in order for them to be maintained.

Again, this must amplify achievements and instil in the client a tangible sense of change and improvement between 'then' and 'now'. For Brenda we would hope that she might have a more realistic view of the crisis situation in which she found herself and ultimately come to see that she managed by a process of doing through a very challenging time. Here is where an ecological and understanding person in environment approach has its value; helping Brenda to recognise the events as largely external factors, as opposed to personal shortcomings. This is what the worker needs to emphasise: the accomplishment in the process and having reached the final session.

RESEARCH SUMMARY

Much of the research on 'crisis/trauma intervention and work' tends to come from the psychological community and mental health services that, typically, though not exclusively, will have a clinical remit. Discourses on 'trauma' tend to dominate the research agenda in this context. Nevertheless, both theoretical and knowledge bases are consistent in agreeing that the meaning attached to the trauma or crisis by the individual is critical to their resolving and processing of it. The idiosyncratic nature of practice in this area has prompted academics and practitioners to voice the need for future research to attend to individual differences in better predicting who will need post-traumatic stress disorder (PTSD) support and what are the factors that predict resilience in the longer term (Litz, 2008).

A substantial body of research and evidence has developed in relation to crisis and trauma responses with groups and whole communities in managing natural and human disasters and emergencies. On an individual crisis response, much of the research focuses on the vital assessment of crisis and the validity and reliability of measurement tools for identification. This further reinforces the importance of accurately assessing, literally 'on foot', the need to intervene with crisis intervention.

A common interest area of both the psychological and social work community is addressing priority needs in the period of time immediately following a trauma. Bisson (2008) cites a range of research studies supporting a growing evidence base which asserts that, shortly after a traumatic event, immediate practical, social and emotional support should be offered (p510). His guarding against the use of psychological interventions in the immediate aftermath of a trauma, except in the most acute cases, appears further supported by McNally, Bryant and Ehlers (2003), and research conducted by Ehlers and Clark (2003). Indeed Bisson's 2008 article cites National Institute for Health and Clinical Excellence guidelines, which credit the work of Ehlers and Clark in recommending a period of watching and waiting (potentially a one-month period), often of self-observed symptoms of PTSD, followed by cognitive behavioural interventions that include a focus on the traumatic events or incident. A critical finding from the influential research of Ehlers and Clark (2003) is the link between early presentation of post-traumatic symptoms (within the first two weeks) as a predictor of longer term outcomes. The lesson here for social work is the need to be aware of the indicators of PTSD and the timeliness of further interventions and/or referral on to other agencies to meet ongoing needs arising from traumatic and crisis events. Assessment skills and being alert to how a person is coping (as discussed previously) or what may be maladaptive in the context of trauma are vital.

A recent research study by Thompson and Waltz (2008) sought to explore the interesting relationship between self-compassion and post-traumatic stress symptoms. This revealed that participants who had a high rate of self-compassion post trauma were less likely to avoid painful situations, emotions, recall and thoughts regarding this. While the study was limited in terms of target group and size, the authors tentatively suggest that including aspects of self-compassion in treatment might assist in offsetting the blame and self-criticism typically associated with trauma and, one could suggest, crisis. This certainly is consistent with the basic value position of social work, actually giving credence to the practice and skill in crisis intervention of reassuring the individual, along with challenging the pervading tendency of over-responsibility and blame. While the findings might appear obvious, they should lend support to and encourage practitioner confidence of the therapeutic validity and potential outcome in attending to and promoting the client's self-compassion.

Developmental psychology again has influenced social work practice in this area. Attachment theory suggests that the patterns an individual develops in processing experience and information, relate directly to their internalised experiences of close relationships (internal working model). John Bowlby (1980) originally focused his research and ideas in this area on children, whilst acknowledging the implications into adulthood of attachment styles. However, research and development in this area have come to understand *attachment* as a trans-theoretical framework that seeks to explain why some individuals may be more disposed to coping with adversity than others, across the lifespan. Its application now extends beyond its initial preserve of children's services and is seen to contribute heavily to assessment and intervention across a range of service user groups (criminal justice, mental health).

Dykas and Cassidy (2011), propose a theoretical model based on a comprehensive literature review of research studies into how attachment types/styles influence the processing of information over the lifespan. Amongst a number of conclusions, they appear to suggest that where an 'insecure attachment' exists, and the processing of social information/ experiences is likely to cause 'psychological pain', then an individual will 'defensively exclude the information from further processing' (2011, p19). The potential relevance to crisis intervention here is in recognising that a 'crisis' for some is often the end of a process of having tried to avoid extreme psychological and emotional pain. Supporting the 'how' focus of crisis in validating the painful experience, along with helping the individual to see the situation as actually manageable and begin to address it, as opposed to 'excluding' and potentially worsening the crisis, can be seen as encouraging attachment behaviour. It could further assist us in understanding why some service users may appear to continuously seek to avoid painful experiences as a consequence of their internal working model of attachment. Therefore as opposed to suggesting that some with whom we work might 'need' crisis, we might choose to reframe our analysis to accommodate a more informed and empathic understanding of the process by which individuals deal with overwhelming distress. This point is linked to the previous section regarding the need for workers to encourage self-compassion during times of crisis.

Limitations of the approach

The major criticism of this approach is its occasional neglect of structural inequalities. While we know crisis to be a relative experience, the lack of resources available to many to have their most fundamental needs met – for example, adequate housing, financial resources, access to transport and facilities – cannot be reconfigured within individual tasks that are too often helplessly beyond the scope of any micro exercise in goal achievement. For example, Smith and Middleton (2007) state that 20 per cent of women and 18 per cent of men in the United Kingdom live in poverty. This figure rises significantly and in direct proportion to one's ethnicity and disability. In these circumstances it would be fair to assume that those individuals living this experience of poverty will be overwhelmingly represented in any analysis of the socio-economic profile of those in receipt of crisis intervention services. The relationship of poverty and exclusion and the impact of these on coping capacity are central to all practice. Environmental supports and resources have a profound impact on internal resources and capacity for coping.

The body of social work-specific research into this practice area is limited. While it is purposeful and relevant to extrapolate from other disciplines in understanding the anatomy of crisis, there is a void in respect of crucial social and environmental issues that could surely enhance all disciplines' understanding, and thus effectiveness, in this complex practice area.

CHAPTER SUMMARY

- For the purposes of this chapter, crisis intervention is an umbrella term for an approach to intervening as assessed by a worker in partnership with a client. It also represents an increasingly proven and established mode of intervening at times when groups or whole communities are affected by trauma, and its legacy, whatever the cause.

- Crisis is a relative experience; two identifying factors are essential in discerning the appropriateness of the intervention: firstly, that the individual perceives the situation to be extraordinary within their relative context; and, secondly, that they perceive it to be beyond their realm of coping or managing, for them at that time.

- Skills in listening, questioning, paraphrasing, reframing and possibly leading are required, particularly at the initial stage. Agency interfacing and communication is critical in managing risk here.

- Crises are time limited.

CHAPTER SUMMARY *continued*

- Assessment of suicidal ideation and intent, along with assessment of harm to others, may be an essential component of the work in this approach. Agency interfacing and communication is critical in managing risk here.

- Reassurance and attending to the subjective experience of the individual is key; tasks aligned to goal setting must be framed within the resource possibilities and capabilities of the individual, here and now. These ought to consider the experience of deprivation and exclusion: an all too often commonality in the life experience of recipients of social services.

- Solution-focused techniques represent an opportunity for a shift in mindset to 'preferred futures' in task and goal setting.

- Crisis intervention is an active approach: exploration must zoom in on the link between thinking and doing.

- The end is firmly located in the beginning: the approach is time limited and increasingly task focused.

- The client must have follow-up support available in no more that four to six weeks afterwards. This may take the form of a one-off session, or a progression to other therapeutic interventions to address other underlying issues in depth.

FURTHER
READING

Roberts, A (ed.) (2005) *Crisis intervention handbook: Assessment, treatment and research.* 3rd edition. Oxford: Oxford University Press.

This book is the current and comprehensive text for any practitioner engaged in crisis work with individuals, families or groups. It is considered authoritative for those engaged in mental health services specifically, but is a guiding text for anyone engaged in crisis work.

Stepney, P and Ford, D (eds) (2000) *Social work models, methods and theories: A framework for practice.* Dorset: Russell House Publishing.

This text provides a very accessible chapter on crisis intervention; succinctly defining it as well as exploring the process.

Sullivan, M, Harris, E, Collado, C and Chen, T (2006) Noways tired: Perspectives of clinicians of color on culturally competent crisis intervention. *Journal of Clinical Psychology*, 62 (8): 987–99.

In this article, the authors, through their own practice experience, address the crucial need for, and benefit of, cultural competence in crisis intervention, drawing on specific practice work with Black Americans, Latino Americans and Asian Americans.

Parker, J (2007) Crisis intervention: A practice model for people who have dementia and their carers. *Practice*, 19 (2):115–26.

This article is important from a social work perspective in that the author considers crisis intervention from a systemic perspective, accounting for the issues for individuals with dementia and their carers.

Chapter 4
Advocacy

Aisling Monds-Watson

A C H I E V I N G   A   S O C I A L   W O R K   D E G R E E

This chapter will help you to develop the following capabilities from the **Professional Capabilities Framework:**
- **Professionalism**
  Identify and behave as a professional social worker committed to professional development.
- **Knowledge**
  Apply knowledge of social sciences, law and social work practice theory.
- **Intervention and skills**
  Use judgement and authority to intervene with individuals, families and communities to promote independence, provide support and prevent harm, neglect and abuse.

It will also introduce you to the following academic standards as set out in the social work subject benchmark statement.
5.1.1 Social work services and clients.
5.1.4 Social work theory.
5.1.5 The nature of social work practice.
5.5.1 Managing problem solving activities.
5.5.3 Analysis and synthesis.
5.5.4 Intervention and evaluation.

Introduction

Advocacy has historically been considered a core aspect of social work practice (see, for example the work of Hollis (1964) in Chapter 1). Indeed, as well as being designated a key social work role (role 3 of the National Occupational Standards) evidence indicates that skilful advocacy is highly valued by clients from various programmes of care. This was illustrated in the recent major review of UK Child Protection (Munro 2011), where children who had experienced Child Protection Social Work *spoke very highly about advocacy services, which they saw as critical to helping them talk about abuse and harm* (2011, p26).

Similarly, advocacy with older people is considered a critical aspect of adult safeguarding, the Commission for Social Care Inspection (CSCI 2008, p9) states:

...councils, care providers and regulators all have crucial roles to play in ensuring that the essential elements of prevention and early intervention are in place, namely people being informed of the right to be free from abuse; and supported to exercise these rights, including having access to advocacy.

The revised UK mental health legislation (Section 30 of the Mental Health Act [2007]), requires certain *qualifying patients*[1] to have access to independent mental health advocacy (IMHA).

However, despite its central position in descriptors of the profession's role and responsibilities, the literature relating to social work and advocacy is sparse, and few introductory social work textbooks explore it in any depth. This chapter will consider the challenges of defining advocacy and its role in contemporary social work practice. We will explore the dimensions of advocacy as delineated by Wilks (2012), and consider the implementation of advocacy-orientated practice within contemporary social work.

RESEARCH SUMMARY

Although a core aspect of social work, there has been very little formal evaluation of advocacy from the client's perspective. However, a report commissioned by the Department of Health (Harding and Beresford 1996), emphasised the importance of advocacy. The researchers asked clients and carers from a wide range of voluntary and statutory organisations across the UK about the standard and style of social service provision they wanted to receive. There was a high level of consistency regarding the desirability of access to advocacy.

The report considered advocacy as being essential in facilitating the ability of carers and users to say what were their needs and desires, their preferences, anxieties and dissatisfactions.

Defining what 'advocacy' means

The Dictionary of Social Work defines advocacy as simply *speaking up, or being helped to speak up* (Pierson and Thomas 2010, p20), while Brandon (1995, cited in Bateman 2000, p17) offers a more politically orientated, rights-based definition of advocacy as *a device to influence the balance of the needs/rights of the group in the favour of the needs/rights of individuals, especially those on the social margins.*

If you consider 'the group' to encompass accepted social norms and values, essentially the cultural and social 'power base', then advocacy is certainly an issue of activism and empowerment. Therefore, undertaking an advocate role demands that you possess both the inclination and the capacity to challenge the status quo in defence of individual basic human rights, to protect and support the vulnerable, the marginalised and the excluded.

---

[1] For further details see the Independent National Mental Health Development Unit (2009) Mental Health Advocacy: Effective Practice Guide. London: NMHDU available online at: **www.nmhdu.org.uk/silo/files/independent-mental-health-advocacy-effective-practice-guide.pdf**

However, numerous models of advocacy have been described (see Table 4.1), ranging from wide-reaching, rights-based, legislative challenges, to ensuring the personal needs and wishes of individual clients are acknowledged. The notion of advocacy encompasses multiple dimensions, and orientations, depending upon the context within which it is employed.

Table 4.1 *Models of Advocacy (adapted from Forbat and Atkinson 2005 and Wilks 2012)*

Self advocacy	Whereby an individual or group represents their own needs or wishes. Includes collective action (collectivism) via community development groups, civil rights groups, and trade unions. Essentially self-advocacy is where an individual or group campaigns or advocates to have their **own** voice heard or their **own** needs met.
Citizen advocacy	Whereby a citizen (lay person), represents the views, and asserts the rights of another disempowered individual.
Legal advocacy	Advocacy within a formal legal context, which is usually contractually and/or financially constrained.
Issue-based, expert, or case advocacy	Professional advocacy work with individual clients or small groups to help promote their perspectives, and/or articulate their wishes and feelings.
Peer advocacy	Advocacy offered to an individual from within their peer group; i.e. from an individual with comparable experiences, such as the support offered to clients with mental health difficulties from some mental health client groups.

Arguably, although much cited and certainly considered a vital component of social work, actually defining what is meant by 'advocacy' can be somewhat complicated and contested (Brandon and Brandon 2001).

A serviceably inclusive definition, is provided by the organisation Action for Advocacy:

> *Advocacy is taking action to help people say what they want, secure their rights, represent their interests and obtain services they need. Advocates and advocacy schemes work in partnership with the people they support and take their side. Advocacy promotes social inclusion, equality and social justice.*

(Action for Advocacy 2011, p5)

However, although Action for Advocacy's definition captures the aims and ethos of advocacy, it doesn't encompass the various methods of transformation and change, nor does it indicate the wide-ranging application of advocacy approaches. Wilks (2012) proposes a multi-dimensional model, which usefully encompasses the scope and orientation of various advocacy approaches. The model is commensurate with the variety of practice situations you are likely to encounter, and illustrates the flexibility required to effectively promote the interests of clients.

Highlighting four advocacy dimensions, (purpose, perspective, focus and scope), Wilks (2012) demonstrates that the purpose of advocacy can range between 'speaking for' to 'enabling to speak', its perspective can range from 'persuasion' to 'giving voice', while its focus may traverse instrumental (ensuring benefit entitlement) to expressive (representing clients' perspectives) elements, and its scope can encompass individual need to collective concern (see Table 4.2).

Table 4.2 *Dimensions of Advocacy (adapted from Wilks 2012, p24)*

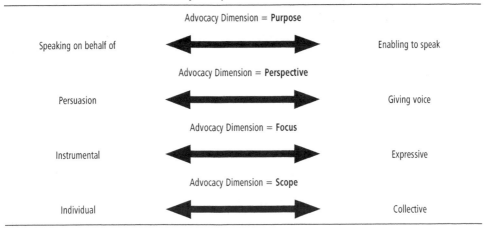

Comment

Note how these characterisations of advocacy move beyond a traditional definition of an advocate as *a person who pleads on behalf of another* (Concise Oxford Dictionary 1988) towards that of an advocate as an enabler – someone who helps others to have their voice heard.

Advocacy, social justice and present-day practice

The relationship between advocacy, social justice and social work is firmly enmeshed. The vast majority of social workers join the profession because they want to help improve lives, and/or to challenge social injustice. Social work's commitment to human rights and social justice is implicit in both its codes of ethics, and within the definition of social work agreed by both the International Association of Schools of Social Work and the International Federation of Social Workers (IASSW 2012):

> *The social work profession promotes social change, problem-solving in human relationships, and the empowerment and liberation of people to enhance well-being. Utilising theories of human behaviour and social systems, social work intervenes at points where people interact with their environments. Principles of human rights and social justice are fundamental to social work.*

While the Barclay Report (1982, p110) on the roles and tasks of social work cautions that:

> *Social workers would be failing in their duty if they did not speak out in the light of their personal knowledge and the evidence amassed from contact with such (poor and disadvantaged) people, challenging ... policy decisions or the way resources are allocated.*

Certainly on both a micro and macro level, and encompassing direct and indirect action, the scope of advocacy in practice is broad (Brandon and Brandon 2001). On a micro (or individual) level, for example, you could be directly engaged in arguing for a client to receive their benefit entitlement in a timely fashion, or be indirectly supporting a group of clients to articulate their concerns about cuts to service provision. On a macro (or community) level, you might be part of a lobby group for improved services to your programme of care (direct advocacy), or ensuring that unmet need is being formally recorded and highlighted to the powers that be, so that gaps in service provision are not ignored (indirect advocacy).

Perhaps one of the most familiar and straightforward examples of social work advocacy is in the area of housing and benefits. Representing clients' needs to other agencies, negotiating on their behalf, accessing resources and utilising social policy and human rights legislation to support claims, appeals and entitlements has traditionally been a core aspect of practice. Similarly, advocacy within the area of safeguarding and protection is easily identifiable. Articulating the need for various supports and securing the resources to protect and support the welfare of the elderly, young, disabled or vulnerable, while meeting their need for protection, care and autonomy are all roles that sit comfortably within the advocacy paradigm.

However, some argue that increasing bureaucracy, managerialism, performance indicators and the fragmentation of services has meant that social work's *tradition of advocacy for social and economic justice has fallen prey to benign neglect* (Mitchell and Lynch 2003, p14). Furthermore, it has been argued that advocacy can only be truly effective when the advocate is *free to act independently on their partner's behalf* (Brooke 2002, p14). Payne (2005) contends that proscribed agency roles in relation to care management and service provision inhibit effective, accurate and comprehensive promotion of client's perspectives. Payne (2005) and others (Brooke 2002; OPAAL 2009) believe that authentic advocacy can only occur when the advocate is utterly independent of agency or statutory responsibility.

> *Advocates should be free of conflicts of interest to ensure that the needs and interests of the advocacy partner remain paramount...*

> (OPAAL 2009, p7)

Social workers rarely engage with clients on an independent basis. Instead they are subject to agency remits and restraints, and must comply with policy, procedure and codes of practice. Therefore, although advocacy is identified as a key role, the reality is that social workers often face major barriers to acting as advocates.

What happens, for example, when the client's self-identified needs and wishes fall outside the remit of the agency, the expertise of the social worker, or are contradictory to those identified via a social work assessment, or the welfare of others such as their family, or their carer? Alternatively, what about those occasions when you want to avoid creating dependency in the client, and want to work in as empowering a manner as possible? In circumstances such as these, the social worker needs to have both working knowledge of others who will advocate independently and ethically on behalf of the client, and/or (when appropriate) the skills to enable, support and empower the client to make their own voice heard. Consider the following scenario in our case study about Brenda and Aisha.

Following David's arrest and custodial sentence for fraud, the family's assets and business bank account have been frozen pending further investigation. With Aisha's support, Brenda is trying to cope with both the emotional and financial implications of the situation; however her psychological state is precarious. Brenda is having difficulty sleeping, and her poor appetite is affecting her physical health. Social isolation and poverty are making life even more difficult and Brenda is finding it very hard to cope.

Brenda contacts Aisha in a very distressed state; she tells Aisha that 16-year-old Sandra has been suspended from school after being overheard by a teacher threatening another girl with physical violence. Furthermore, a letter has arrived from the bank stating that her personal account is 'in arrears' and a hefty charge is being made against her account for four 'bounced' cheques. Brenda asks Aisha if she can speak to both the bank and the school and try to 'sort it out', because she 'can't cope with it anymore'.

ACTIVITY **4.1**

Consider how Aisha might best support Brenda at this time while simultaneously promoting her independence. Is it in Brenda's best interest that Aisha adopts the advocacy role? How can Aisha offer practical support, while maximising Brenda's autonomy and coping capacity?

COMMENT

Brenda is essentially asking Aisha to act as her advocate with both the school and the bank. However, Aisha needs to ask herself if this is in Brenda and her family's best interests. She also needs to consider if advocating for Brenda is likely to be effective, whether it would be ethical; and most importantly, how should she 'go about' making this decision?

It is critical that Aisha recognises that partnership lies at the core of effective and ethical advocacy, and that advocacy is all about endeavouring to ensure that the views of the advocacy partner (the client) are articulated and heard. Brandon (1995, p1) exhorts that the intent and the outcome of such advocacy should increase the individual's sense of power; help them to feel more confident, to become more assertive and gain increased choices.

Advocacy-orientated practice

Alongside the 'obvious' or 'traditional' advocacy that we've already discussed, and with which you are likely to be familiar (safeguarding, advancing claims/appeals/housing), there is frequent need, ample opportunity and ethical obligation for social work practice that employs an 'advocacy orientation' (Freddolino et al. 2004).

Advocacy-orientated practice essentially encompasses those approaches which embrace and involve client empowerment, specifically, *creating supports to enhance functioning and fostering identity and control* (Freddolino et al. 2004, p119). These are approaches which have as their aim, the growth of a client's capacity to make their own voice heard, and to proactively have their own needs met. Wilks (2012, p41) highlights that the *key goal of social work is to find a route to a set of circumstances whereby clients are enabled to speak for themselves.* Consider the unfolding tale of Aisha and Brenda.

CASE STUDY

Aisha arranges to meet with Brenda later that day. She asks Brenda's permission to look at the letter from the bank, and the communication from Sandra's school, and asks Brenda to have them for her when she arrives. When they meet, Aisha asks Brenda to identify which issue she wants to 'look at' first. Brenda prioritises the issue with the school. Aisha is conscious that she is a social worker with the mental health programme of care, and that at this point in time, Brenda does not want the Family and Child Care team involved with her family. Although Aisha knows of a parenting advocacy service, for which she provides Brenda with contact details, they cannot meet with Brenda in the next few days and the school situation needs to be dealt with quickly.

Apparently Sandra has been on the receiving end of numerous nasty comments from a number of her peers since her father's arrest, and had been heard threatening to hit a girl who had been repeatedly taunting her about her father being a 'crook'. Suspension will mean that Sandra misses out on important class coursework in the week before the exams, and the suspension will be permanently recorded on her (previously exemplary), school record.

Aisha helps Brenda on the home computer to find a copy of the school's anti-bullying policy and which teacher is responsible for student welfare. Then they work together to construct a list of reasons that challenge the school's decision to suspend Sandra. Aisha helps Brenda to write a script for a phone call to the school, requesting a meeting with the relevant teacher. When this has been arranged, they write a synopsis of the difficulties Sandra has been experiencing, and review the school's commitment to anti-bullying. Brenda feels better prepared to deal with the meeting. They 'role play' the meeting, and Brenda practises what she wants to say to the school.

In regards to the problem with the bank, Aisha helps Brenda to understand the letter, but realises she has neither the knowledge nor authority to challenge the bank's charges. However, she does help Brenda to arrange an appointment with an independent debt adviser associated with the local Citizens Advice Bureau, who has previously worked with Brenda and who will help Brenda to negotiate with the bank.

COMMENT

Although Aisha hasn't spoken on behalf of Brenda to either the bank or the school, she has acted as an advocate by helping to ensure that Brenda's voice has been heard. This sits comfortably within the 'enabling to speak' dimension of advocacy (Wilks 2012, p24). Furthermore, she has helped Brenda to develop the confidence and skills required to 'speak up and be heard', effectively empowering and advocating for her client.

Advocacy skills

Effective advocacy demands a meaningful and appropriately employed combination of knowledge, skills and sensitivity. As with all social work practice, the relationship between client and worker lies at the core. Without an established rapport, a practitioner is unlikely to accurately understand and interpret the needs and wishes of their client, or be clear of the objectives they wish to achieve.

As a professional social worker you are also in the position of having enhanced 'social clout', which comes via your education, experience and access to resources, other professionals, and agencies; this influence can be exploited to benefit those less powerful, i.e. your clients. However, beyond professional influence, and your fundamental relationship and communication skills, there are additional skills specifically aligned to effective advocacy.

ACTIVITY **4.2**

Thinking again about the totality of Brenda's situation, what skills might Aisha need to be able to advocate more directly on Brenda's behalf?

Bateman (2000) categorises the skills needed for advocacy in health and social care as follows.

- **Interviewing** This should be old ground to you, incorporating skills in listening, questioning, clarifying, understanding non-verbal responses, developing cultural sensitivity, summarising, feeding back and so on.

- **Assertiveness and force** Researching entitlement, setting minimum acceptable outcomes, identifying who has authority, recognising the other side of an argument, arguing for *interest* rather than *demands*, (for example, 'What I am seeking to achieve is a situation where Sandra can continue to benefit from her education', rather than 'I want the bully to be removed'.

- **Negotiation** WEA North West (2011) specifies the following negotiation skills: leading with your strongest argument; being brief and concise; focus on solutions not problems; emotional control; deciding on a minimum 'win'; understanding the other side's position; sticking to your basic needs; pointing out the other side's weaknesses and liabilities; asking for the chance to present additional information later, being prepared to leave while leaving the negotiation open. To this could be added preparation, planning and developing a strategy.

- **Self management** includes use of time, evaluation and review, creative thinking, decision-making and managing stress.

- **Using legal knowledge and conducting research.**

- **Litigation.**

Advocacy in specific practice settings

The range and role of advocacy in various practice settings is diverse; however, there are a number of specific advocacy approaches explicitly aligned to particular programmes of care. These include, amongst others, dementia advocacy, non-instructed advocacy, self-advocacy and statutory advocacy; the following section will briefly consider some of these.

Instructed advocacy and non-instructed/best-interest advocacy

Instructed advocacy is basically 'what it says on the tin'. The advocate engages with their client to establish an agenda of instruction which has been identified and prioritised in partnership with the client. This process is always user led, and can be delineated as:

- **forming** a candid, trusting relationship with the client;

- **determining** what the client wants from the relationship;

- **identifying** objectives and desired consequences from the advocacy process;

- **gathering information** (policy, legislation, research) on behalf of the client;

- **representing** the client's perspectives, needs, and concerns to other parties;

- **reviewing** the process in partnership with the client in relation to achieved objectives and/or redefined goals.

(Adapted from Henderson 2006)

Compared to instructed advocacy, the notion of non-instructed advocacy initially sounds like a bit of a contradiction in terms. How can the wishes of the client be represented if they haven't been heard? However, non-instructed advocacy (sometimes called best-interest advocacy) is essentially advocacy on behalf of an individual who (for whatever reason, perhaps dementia, illness or profound disability), cannot communicate their wishes, or make decisions about their life.

> *Non-instructed advocacy is taking affirmative action with or on behalf of a person who is unable to instruct an advocate due to issues of capacity ... The non-instructed advocate seeks to uphold the person's rights; ensure fair and equal treatment and access to services; and make certain that decisions are taken with due consideration for all relevant factors which must include the person's unique preferences and perspectives.*

(Action for Advocacy 2011, p5)

In essence, this means that when clients 'lack capacity' (under the terms of the Mental Capacity Act 2005), others involved in their care can make decisions on their behalf as long as these are undertaken in the 'best interests' of the client. The Mental Capacity Act provides a 'best interests checklist' to guide this process.

The Mental Capacity Act 'Best Interest' Checklist (NHS, no date)

- Do not make assumptions on the basis of age, appearance, condition or behaviour.

- Consider all the relevant circumstances.

- Consider whether or when the person will have capacity to make the decision.

- Support the person's participation in any acts or decisions made for them.

- Do not make a decision about life-sustaining treatment 'motivated by a desire to bring about his (or her) death'.

- Consider the person's expressed wishes and feelings, beliefs and values.

- Take into account the views of others with an interest in the person's welfare, their carers and those appointed to act on their behalf.

It is imperative under circumstances of impaired capacity that the client is engaged as much as is possible in the process, and that appropriate consultation is undertaken with significant others such as family, friends, and other professionals to ensure that any decisions made reflect the likely wishes of the client. The advocate must also be very aware that 'capacity' can fluctuate depending on a myriad of influences, therefore all decisions must be taken with much sensitivity, consideration and reflection regarding the various factors which may affect their client's situation. Furthermore, great care must be taken to ensure that 'speaking for' doesn't become 'speaking instead of' (Boylan and Dalrymple 2009). Clearly the manner in which the non-instructed advocacy process is established, led and enacted differs considerably from instructed advocacy; and non-instructed advocates are obliged to make decisions based on varying levels of judgement and interpretation (Wells 2006). Lacking clear direction from their client, the non-instructed advocate must judge what the concerns or issues are likely to be, how that client would prefer them to be addressed, and what a successful outcome should look like.

There are a number of advocacy techniques and strategies that can be employed, which endeavour to ensure that the 'best interests' of the client are protected and promoted. These include the following.

- **Rights-based advocacy** The advocate compares and contrasts the services and supports available to their client against clearly defined standards of rights and guidance. Henderson (2006) describes advocates adopting this approach as *'watchdogs/negotiators'*, because their primary objective is to ensure the client has access to agreed and equitable circumstances compared to others, and to seek reparation if required. Although little is required in terms of a relationship between client and advocate, the advocate ensures that their client's basic human rights are promoted and defended.

- **Person-centred advocacy approaches** Via a long-term, meaningful and reciprocally respectful relationship with their client, the advocate forms a perspective about their client's wishes based on their life history, preferences, beliefs, lifestyle etc. Henderson (2006, p6) characterises this type of advocate as a kind of *articulate friend, who tries to ensure that the person is healthy, happy and feels to the extent that it is possible, in control of their own life and circumstances*. Because this kind of advocate has witnessed how their client responds to stimuli in their environment, they are able to establish a sense of what their client values and needs and develop an understanding of their likely inclination. Essentially, the advocate is utilising their capacity to empathise with the client to garner insight to their prospective perspectives and preferences.

- **Observation (or witness) advocacy** Although closely aligned to both person-centred and rights-based advocacy as described above, observation (or witness) advocacy can also encompass those situations whereby an observer becomes aware of such things as unacceptable practice, insufficient service provision, or client disadvantage; and reports these to the relevant parties, so that they can be taken account of and corrected. The advocate has observed (or acted as a witness to) how a client's environment or service provision meets their needs and reported their concerns, however they may not have really engaged with the client in a meaningful manner (Henderson 2007).

• **Whistleblowing** Although distinctive from observation (or witness) advocacy, this is perhaps an appropriate point to mention whistleblowing, and consider how it falls within the remit of advocacy. The GSCC *Code of practice* avows that social workers have a duty to challenge and report abusive or dangerous practice and/or failures in the provision of safe care, specifically they must inform an *'employer or an appropriate authority where the practice of colleagues may be unsafe or adversely affecting standards of care'* (GSCC 2010a, p8).

It follows that if you are reporting concerns regarding the services provided to clients, you are effectively 'speaking on their behalf' and therefore advocating for their best interests. Whistleblowers in the United Kingdom are protected under the Public Interest Disclosure Act 1998, which offers a legislative framework to prevent institutional or agency reprisals (such as bullying, harassment and discrimination), against individuals who follow appropriate procedures to report malpractice. All statutory and voluntary agencies have a formal whistleblowing policy that provides guidance on how to raise concerns in that particular practice setting.

CASE STUDY

Whistleblowing Advocacy: Winterbourne View Care Home scandal

Winterbourne View was a private hospital in South Gloucestershire, England, for adults with learning disabilities and autism; the majority of patients were detained under the provisions of the Mental Health Act 1983. In October 2010 a charge nurse at Winterbourne, Terry Bryan, contacted the management of the facility because he had seen bad practice and poor attitudes, staff ignoring people when they were distressed and threats – staff saying, "If you don't stop banging your head against the wall then you won't see your mum at the weekend"' (Mencap and CBF 2012, p11).

His concerns were passed on to the Adult Safeguarding Team, and then to the Care Quality Commission (CQC, the regulatory body for independent health care and 'watchdog' for patients detained under the Mental Health Act). However, despite a subsequent CQC inspection no action was taken, and there was no improvement in the care afforded to patients in the unit. Terry Bryan then brought his concerns to the attention of the BBC who arranged for an undercover reporter to secure employment as a support worker at the hospital.

Over five weeks, the reporter secretly filmed staff. His film revealed serious abuse of patients and appalling standards of care; staff were filmed tormenting, bullying and assaulting patients. The subsequent Panorama documentary of May 2011 resulted in four CQC inspections, a serious case review, and regulatory action against the owners of the hospital (Castlebeck Care Ltd), which resulted in its closure a year later.

Eleven Winterbourne employees subsequently pleaded guilty to 38 charges of ill-treatment. The Winterbourne scandal prompted unannounced CQC inspections of 145 care homes, half of which failed to meet the standards for essential care and safeguarding (Ramesh 2012).

The limitations of advocacy

Being an effective advocate can be particularly gratifying, one of those rare occasions when you can really feel that you have both *helped someone and righted a wrong* (Bateman 2000, p8). As an advocate in Trevett (2001, p2) comments, *the satisfaction of walking away from a case knowing you have made a difference is priceless!*

Moreover, the advocacy role appears harmonious with the social worker's duty to *promote the independence of service users while protecting them as far as possible from danger or harm including the use of established processes and procedures to challenge and report dangerous, abusive, discriminatory or exploitative behaviour and practice* (GSCC 2010b, p14). This is one crucial aspect of practice, which can occasionally be hard to reconcile with advocacy orientated practice. Barnes and Brandon (2002, p40) emphasise that *advocates do not work in the best interests of service users but work to their direction.* Obviously, promoting the client's wishes or self-identified needs, when these are contrary to what is in their own, or their family's best interests, is going to conflict with the social work role. Instead, a well-informed social worker will be able to direct such clients to appropriate external agencies or independent advocacy groups.

CHAPTER SUMMARY

- Conceptually, advocacy is *a bit of a slippery fish* (Wilks 2012, p19), a single, four-syllable word, which encapsulates a very expansive range of interrelated endeavour.

- Advocacy occupies a central role within practice, however, it is often over simplified and understood only in terms of 'speaking on behalf of'.

- This chapter has offered an overview of the multi-dimensionality of advocacy-orientated practice, and illustrated how social work advocacy is firmly entrenched within the profession's obligation to empowerment and social justice.

FURTHER READING

Given the central component that advocacy plays in social work practice, surprisingly little has been written on the subject. The available literature on advocacy skills is very limited, and that which is available is generally orientated towards the legal professions. There are, however a few texts which explore the area in greater detail.

Wilks, T (2012) *Advocacy and social work practice*. Berkshire: Open University Press

This is a clearly written book which provides an introduction to advocacy in social work. It has a strong focus on the practicalities of the work with the theoretical knowledge required for the advocacy role.

Trevett, A (ed.) (2001) *Taking their side: Fighting their corner; 16 stories demonstrating the difference independent advocacy makes to the lives of people with dementia*. London: The Dementia Advocacy Network. **dan.advocacyplus.org.uk/data/files/Taking_their_side/FINAL_COPY_TAKING_THEIR_SIDE_MARCH_2012.pdf**

Published by the Dementia Advocacy Network, this is a short collection of personal accounts of how advocacy has been used to improve the lives of people with dementia.

Leadbetter, M (2002) 'Empowerment and Advocacy' in Adams, R, Dominelli, L and Payne, M (eds) *Social Work: Themes, Issues and Critical Debates*, Basingstoke, Palgrave in association with the Open University.

This is a thoughtful and useful chapter with an emphasis on the client perspective and empowerment.

Chapter 5
Task-centred work

Mary McColgan

Introduction

In this chapter, we will consider how a task-centred approach can be applied to Aisha's work with Brenda. In preceding chapters, you were introduced to the ways in which Aisha used different approaches such as counselling and crisis intervention. You will have seen how she has been building rapport with Brenda and developing the social work relationship with her and her family. You may have come to realise Brenda's personal strengths while Aisha has been working in partnership with her and her family as they have faced the initial crisis of David's imprisonment. However, Aisha will be engaging with a new set of circumstances in this chapter, some of which arise because Brenda is now on her own caring for her three children and the consequences of David's imprisonment have begun to impact on the family.

The chapter begins with a discussion about the origins of task-centred work and its key principles and processes. This is followed by the application of each of the stages of the task-centred model to the case study.

Description of task-centred model

Origins of task-centred work

While most methods of intervention in social work have their origins in other disciplines, task-centred work stands out as an example that has originated and been developed within the social work profession itself. In the 1960s, psychotherapeutic casework was the dominant model of intervention and there was little emphasis on working in partnership with clients. Knowledge about the benefits of short-term intervention began to emerge through research undertaken by Reid and Shyne in America (1969). They found that when clients were working on agreed problems identified by service users themselves, the short-term focus on agreed goals and actions resulted in more effective outcomes. The worker's role was to discuss and achieve consensus about the priority areas and agree a contract for action with defined tasks. In using this approach, clients were encouraged to take responsibility for deciding what was important to them.

Elements of task-centred approach

The task-centred approach to social work has become an increasingly popular model of problem-solving approaches because of its emphasis on time-limited, focused interventions where tasks are clearly defined, problems are prioritised and clients are encouraged to build their capacity and confidence by achieving agreed goals.

RESEARCH SUMMARY

A study by Reid and Shyne (1969) compared the benefits of short-term intervention with longer-term approaches and found that families who were in receipt of services lasting three months fared better than families who received services lasting up to 18 months. Reid and Shyne's (1969) work illustrated the importance of working on agreed tasks with associated activities, with the purpose of achieving clear goals which clients had set for themselves and agreed with their social worker. Their approach was regarded with great interest because it challenged the well-established methods of social work practice, particularly the psychoanalytic model of casework (see Chapter 1).

Table 5.1 outlines the different stages involved in task-centred approaches as identified by Ford and Postle 2000; Doel 2002; Marsh and Doel 2005; Parker and Bradley 2010; and Wilson et al. 2011.

Table 5.1 *Core elements of task-centred approach*

Ford and Postle (2000)	Phase One: Problem exploration, getting started, initial explanations Phase Two: Selecting and prioritising target problems Phase Three: Setting goals, identifying tasks and making contracts Phase Four: Working to implement the tasks Phase Five: Bringing the work to an end
Doel (2002)	Identifying entry Phase One: Exploring the problem Phase Two: Agreeing a goal – the written agreement Phase Three: Implementing the tasks Exit
Marsh and Doel (2005)	Thirteen elements: • Mandate • Problem and goals • Goals • Exploring problems • Focusing problems • Refining goals • Time limits • The recorded agreement • Tasks and the task role • Task development • Review • Ending • Evaluating
Parker and Bradley (2010)	Four-stage approach: 1. Developing a focus on the problem 2. Reaching agreement: goals and contracts 3. Developing goals into manageable tasks 4. Ending and reviewing the work
Wilson et al. (2011)	Seven stages: 1. Problem exploration 2. Identifying and agreeing the target or selected problems 3. Agreeing the goals 4. Drawing up an explicit agreement 5. Identifying a task or tasks needed to address the problem 6. Carrying out the task(s) 7. Evaluating and termination

Common themes associated with this practice model include:

- clarification of problems experienced;

- identification and prioritisation of agreed problems to be focused on;

- establishing verbal or written agreement about goals and tasks;

- defining manageable tasks to be undertaken, time scales for the work and agreement about responsibilities;

- working through each defined task and reviewing work on a regular basis;

- taking stock of progress and agreeing outcomes.

Refer back to the case studies in the earlier chapters, particularly Chapters 2 and 3. In her crisis work with Aisha, Brenda has managed to sort out the immediate and pressing financial problems; Brenda has seen her GP and has received some medication to help with her appetite and sleep disturbance. She has also attended one session at the community voluntary group for stress management but hasn't gone back, saying it was all just about healthy living and not very useful. Make a list of the problems that may be remaining, remembering that Brenda is anxious not just about her own situation but also about all the family members.

COMMENT

You have probably come up with quite an impressive list.

*   *Brenda and David's relationship was poor and has not been improved by his imprisonment. There will still be a large number of unpaid bills, for example council tax, electricity and gas.*

*   *Mortgage payments were only deferred and will shortly be due again. There are arrears and continuing fears about possible eviction.*

*   *Brian is currently unemployed and has incurred debts because of his period of time studying at university.*

*   *Sandra has recently developed health problems related to anxiety, and problems at school.*

*   *Philip has been suspended from school on two occasions and Brenda is finding it difficult to control his behaviour.*

Stage 1: Clarification of problems experienced

Faced with such a range of problems, Aisha may feel daunted about how to tackle them but may have some ideas about what resources could be available for each family member. However, it is important to remember that Brenda herself identifies the problems, although Aisha has a role to play in helping Brenda clarify the range and nature of the problems she is experiencing. Elaboration skills are important in this phase of work; for example, Aisha may ask probing questions such as 'Can you tell me more about ...?' or 'You have told me you have a large number of unpaid bills, can we discuss what bills you need to pay and when they are due?'

In this first stage, through careful exploration of how Brenda experiences her problems, Aisha recognises that user involvement is paramount. Beresford (2000) is adamant that to avoid being tokenistic, social workers should include client's *perspectives, knowledge and analyses* of their situations. In essence, Beresford (2000) is advocating that client's own views are integral to understanding how their circumstances impact on them. In order to be able to work in partnership, Aisha needs to communicate her understanding through her skills of empathy. Wilson et al. (p123) emphasise the importance of empathy as the basis of developing relationships between clients and social workers. Working with

Brenda, Aisha would use empathy to acknowledge how difficult it is for her to carry the responsibility for her family when her husband is in prison and to offer her an opportunity to talk about how she feels about having to cope with the major changes in her life. Through active listening to Brenda's underlying concerns, Aisha uses empathy to develop rapport and build a relationship with Brenda.

Duffy (2006) suggests this relationship is central to the helping process: *to understand how service users actually feel about the social work process is important, how it impacts on them on every level and what we can do to make the process as supportive as possible* (p37).

Stage 2: Identification and prioritisation of agreed problems to be focused on

This is probably the most important phase of the work because Aisha needs to explore in detail with Brenda the extent of her concerns about the issues she has raised and her motivation to resolve them. Using her tuning in skills, Aisha will recall her knowledge about how change occurs and consider how ready Brenda may feel to undertake certain tasks or to work in partnership with Aisha to find solutions.

Several aspects need to be considered such as Brenda's readiness for change and her ambivalence about taking steps to tackle different issues.

DiClemente and Prochaska (1998) identified a model for considering how change occurs through various stages. In their model, they developed six stages of change (see Chapter 8).

- The pre-contemplation stage occurs when someone is unaware to some extent that there are problems which they need to address. Sometimes this can also happen because they are in denial or feeling depressed or may be feeling defensive. In Brenda's case, she is unable to identify any particular cause for her depression and anxiety attacks at the point of referral to the Community Mental Health Team.

- In the contemplation stage, Brenda may both consider change and refuse to accept that change is necessary or desirable. Miller and Rollnick (2002) refer to this phase as *a kind of see-sawing between reasons to change and reasons to stay the same*. In fact, this also describes the process of ambivalence, which occurs because of Brenda's fears and concerns about the issues she faces. Such feelings are quite normal and if Aisha uses her skill of empathy by understanding Brenda's underlying concerns, she will in fact help to focus on what she actually wants to do.

- The next two stages – determination (to consider options) and action (to address problems) – would involve discussing options and steps to take before Brenda would agree to any particular course of action. According to the authors, when action is agreed the maintenance stage involves supporting and encouraging service users to follow through an agreed plan. Miller and Rollnick (2002) also stress that a change process can often involve unsuccessful attempts which result in relapse, but rather than regarding lack of progress as a sign that the tasks are not relevant or working out as agreed, it is important to regard progress as incremental. In this way, small achievements can be acknowledged and will boost confidence.

Stage 3: Establishing verbal or written agreement about goals and tasks

---

CASE STUDY

Brenda and Aisha agree to draw up an agreement, having identified three goals which are to have priority.

Goals of the contract:

- *Brenda wants to have better management of her debts (see Table 5.2);*

- *Brenda wants to have support for Sandra;*

- *Brenda wants to have help for Philip to cope with his Dad's imprisonment (see Table 5.3).*

Here is what Brenda and Aisha agree.

This agreement is between Brenda and Aisha. We agree that the following problems will be discussed.

(i) Unpaid bills

- *Compile an accurate list of outstanding bills, the amounts due and the dates for payment;*

- *Work out a weekly budget for food, heating, mortgage, school meals, clothes.*

(ii) Support for Sandra

- *Encourage Sandra to follow the regime for treating her eczema;*

- *Discuss with Sandra what support she needs at home and at school.*

(iii) Support for Philip

- *Understand why Philip is acting up at school;*

- *Provide support for Philip to remain at school;*

- *Discuss strategies with the school to support Philip.*

How long will we meet for?	*About 1 hour*
How often will we meet?	*Once a week, normally Thursday at 10.00 a.m.*
Where will we meet?	*Usually in Brenda's house but sometimes we will meet in Aisha's office*

SIGNED: *Brenda and Aisha*

DATE: *9 February 2009*

Table 5.2 *Dealing with unpaid bills and mortgage arrears*

Task	Who	What	When	Where	How
Brenda will gather information about her unpaid bills	Brenda	1. Contact gas and electricity departments 2. Ring council offices to ask for council tax refund forms	Within two weeks, Brenda will have information about unpaid bills	Local offices	Brenda will make appointment with electricity and gas companies
Clarify extent of mortgage arrears and get legal advice.	Brenda	Contact local Citizens Advice Bureau (CAB) office and make appointment to discuss options open to Brenda	Within next week, Brenda will have made appointment	Local CAB office	
Compile list of bills, amounts owed and possible payments	Aisha and Brenda	Develop list with payment amounts	Within four weeks	At Aisha's office	

Table 5.3 Philip's suspension from school

Task	Who	What	When	Where	How
Brenda will speak to Philip about the recent suspension from school	Brenda and Philip	Brenda will suggest time for opportunity to talk with Philip	On Thursday evening after football practice	At home	Get Philip's agreement to talk about school suspension
Aisha will talk through with Brenda what she will say to Philip	Brenda and Aisha	Role play to help Brenda understand Philip's behaviour	Thursday morning	At home	Aisha will ask Brenda to think about time when she was Philip's age
Brenda will contact school and make appointment to talk to Philip's form teacher about his suspension	Brenda	Gather specific information about what happened, what was said, how did Philip react, what do school plan to do?	By next week	At school	Ask school for written report of incident
Aisha will investigate the possibility of referral to 'out of school' club	Aisha	Referral to 'out of school' club	By next week		Aisha will contact Children in Need co-ordinator

Stage 4: Defining manageable tasks to be undertaken, time scales for the work and agreement about responsibilities

Several examples of defined tasks to be undertaken can be found in Tables 5.2 and 5.3. Below are some important points for Aisha to remember.

- Ensure tasks are broken down into achievable steps (bite-sized chunks).

- Ensure that for each of these steps there is a time scale and that the steps can be measured or evidenced in some way. For example, if Brenda agrees to speak to Philip about his suspension from school, there needs to be agreement about the best time to do this. If Brenda is gathering information about her unpaid bills, agreement is needed about how many of these there are and how many will, at the end of three months, be paid in full and how much money will still be outstanding.

- Try to build in early successes so that Brenda can see her progress and achievements. For example, if Brenda has the opportunity to meet a CAB officer and discuss options, she may feel less overwhelmed because she has options to consider and choices to make.

- Several of the tasks involve Aisha in gathering information for Brenda. Although it could be argued that this may not be empowerment in practice, in fact Aisha's role also requires her to act as a broker of resources. As Cree and Myers (2008) point out, in the interests of promoting service users' capacity ... *there will be an expectation that the service user will have a major role in deciding on and undertaking the tasks* (p94). So, the key issue is that Brenda's role in decision-making is crucial. A common tendency that arises when using the task-centred approach is that the worker assumes too much responsibility for defining the tasks. Such practice is disempowering for clients. Sometimes it seems easier to take responsibility for suggesting what tasks need to form part of the contract. Wilson et al. (2011) contend that the experience of using a task-centred approach should *leave the satisfied user more capable of solving subsequent problems without help* (p369). Thus in working towards solving her problems, Brenda learns about coping skills and problem solving approaches which she can use in the future.

Stage 5: Working through each defined task and reviewing work on a regular basis

This includes tasks for the client and tasks for the worker separately and may also involve other people. For example, Aisha will be asking the school to let her have a report about any incidents involving Philip. It may also mean Brenda and Aisha working together on tasks. In the case study example, Brenda and Aisha will be engaging in role play. Aisha cannot assume that Brenda will be willing to engage in role play and in the contract she has suggested that Brenda does some homework in advance of their meeting. Aisha has encouraged Brenda to think about her own experience of being a teenager and growing up. The purpose of this homework is to help Brenda to identify with some of the experiences her son may be having and to remind her of the pressures young people feel, and how difficult it can be for them to express their feelings. However, Aisha needs to explain to Brenda why it is important to 'rehearse' her conversations. Here, Aisha is trying simultaneously to develop Brenda's understanding of how her son is feeling and also to influence changes in her behaviour and interactions with him. Nelson-Jones (2005, p199) suggests that rehearsal skills can promote changes in communication through role reversal, which helps the client to step into someone else's world, or through a process of mirroring, where the client sees themselves as others see them.

Stage 6: Taking stock of progress and agreeing outcomes

A primary goal of task-centred work is to ensure that the process of undertaking defined tasks achieves progress and illustrates to the service user that they themselves have the capacity and ability to find solutions to their problems. However, this is not to suggest that the process always results in successful outcomes. Achieving and sustaining change is often influenced by external factors as well as internal motivation. For example, when Aisha reviews the agreement with Brenda after four weeks, some progress may have been achieved but there may be further action needed. This process of taking stock and being clear about the length of time to accomplish tasks is integral to task-centred work. Cree and Myers (2008) make the point that as the approach is *premised on the motivational impact of deadlines* (p95) the focused nature of the work promotes the client's independence.

CASE STUDY

In the last meeting with Aisha, Brenda makes the following comment: 'I never thought I would be able to see any reduction in my unpaid bills. Money is still very tight but at least if I can buy weekly stamps, I will have some money saved towards the next bill. I am very worried about the cost of gas though; the weather has been so cold, I have kept the heat on and I am expecting a huge bill. How will I ever be able to pay it? With David in prison, I have such a reduced income to make ends meet. This is getting me down.' Initially Aisha feels disheartened by the apparent lack of progress. However, it is easy to minimise the progress that has been achieved, so Aisha asks Brenda about what she has learned from the process of working together and what has been helpful for dealing with future issues.

Table 5.4 *Progress of tasks undertaken after four weeks*

Task	Progress	Future plans
Gather information about unpaid bills	Brenda has submitted application for council tax refund	Submit new application
	Gas arrears have been reduced – only last quarter is outstanding	Buy weekly stamps to budget for next bill

---

What do you think Brenda would identify as her learning? Write down all the learning points you can think of.

COMMENT

Some possible answers would include the following points.

- *Breaking problems down makes each task more manageable.*

- *Having someone to meet with on a regular basis and discuss her concerns helps Brenda to cope.*

- *Writing down the tasks enables Brenda to see the progress she has achieved.*

- *Budgeting her finances and buying savings stamps can help Brenda to deal with future bills.*

- *Learning new ways of solving problems has made Brenda feel empowered.*

Application in social work practice

Task-centred work is a popular method of intervention in social work practice. It does not depend on any complex theory, is down to earth, makes sense and is easy to understand in its application.

Strengths

- Any practice that is based on a mutuality of understanding of the nature of the social work contract is likely to be more successful in outcome. It concentrates on the client's own conception of their difficulties as the key to reaching a solution. It has the potential to create equality between worker and service user.

- Task-centred work promotes empowerment and is also anti-oppressive insofar as the client is encouraged to take control of their own life.

- People's strengths are assessed and therefore self-esteem is enhanced, as are skills in problem-solving.

- The use of time itself can be therapeutic in pushing the process forward.

- If used effectively, this method should increase the client's ability to cope in the near and distant future.

- From the very start of a 'contract', the end is in view because all parties are fully aware of the tasks they have set.

- It is an optimistic approach, which moves away from a focus on the person to finding ways of dealing with problem situations. It is a strengths-based approach, which assumes that the client has the capacity to overcome the problems with support.

Limitations

- As a method that deals only with the issues raised and prioritised by the client, it can leave underlying problems unaddressed – for example, emotional problems.

- It is an approach that depends on a level of cognitive functioning that makes it less effective with people who do not have a good enough level of ability, for example due to mental illness or learning difficulties.

- It may not be as effective with involuntary clients.

- Some people may be so overwhelmed by problems that they don't have the energy to work on them. Alternatively, it is possible that problems are so enmeshed with and exacerbating of each other that dealing with only one or two has no impact on the overall situation.

- The idea of contract may leave inherent power differentials between client and worker ignored.

- It may not take account of factors that arise out of structural oppression, for example, poverty, poor health, unemployment, racial or gender oppression.

CHAPTER SUMMARY

- Task-centred work came about as a response to the need to find more time-limited and effective methods of social work intervention.

- There are a number of different models but common themes are the need to clarify and prioritise problems, to draw up agreements between worker and client on the tasks required to solve the problems, to work on the problems and review progress.

FURTHER READING

Marsh, P and Doel, M (2005) *The task centred book.* London: Routledge/Community Care.
This text has detailed chapters on the task-centred approach, particularly the agreement and defining of tasks.

Trevithick, P (2005) *Social work skills: A practice handbook.* 2nd edition. Buckingham: Open University Press.
This has a very useful appendix which details how task-centred work is undertaken.

Chapter 6

Cognitive behavioural approaches

Trevor Lindsay

Introduction

Cognitive behaviour therapy (CBT) is concerned with the thoughts, images, beliefs and attitudes that we have (our cognitive processes) and how these impact upon and influence our behaviour. As we shall see later in this chapter, it is one of the best evidenced approaches in terms of effectiveness. Although it is often treated as one therapeutic approach its origins are twofold – behavioural therapy and cognitive therapy, these two having their roots in related but different sets of theoretical concepts. We could even go further and subdivide behavioural therapy into three, those which derive separately from *classical* or *respondent*, *operant* and *observational* learning. Not satisfied with this categorisation we could go yet further and identify a huge number of different but related methods of working which can be considered as cognitive behavioural. It is clear that this is not possible in this short chapter. We will work through each of these types of learning – *classical*, *operant*, *observational* and *cognitive* – with just one or two examples of how this translates into practice in each case. A major focus then will be on rational emotive behaviour therapy, which will be used as an illustration of cognitive approaches.

Classical or respondent conditioning

Classical conditioning was first described by Pavlov (1849–1936) who knew that when a dog was presented with meat it would salivate. Pavlov discovered that when the meat was consistently presented to a dog along with another stimulus, for example a bell, the sound of the bell itself would provide sufficient stimulus to provoke salivation on its own. This was a *conditioned response*. For example, the author found that the experience of being attacked, during a caravan holiday, by a man who first knocked on the caravan door, resulted in a fear reaction to the sound of someone knocking on the door, for some time afterwards. The fact that this response occurred regardless of the type or location of the door, meant that this conditioned response had become *generalised*.

Systematic desensitisation

Systematic desensitisation is an intervention, based on classical conditioning, which can be helpful in work with people who are experiencing phobias and avoidance reactions. Desensitisation involves first teaching relaxation techniques so that the individual is better able to manage their anxiety. This is then followed by the client identifying a hierarchy of anxiety, related to the phobia. Someone with a fear of spiders may come up with seeing a photograph of a spider, a spider on a television programme, a real spider on the floor, in the bath, on the bed, feeling it on the hand, running across their face and so on. In treatment, the person, while practising the relaxation technique, is asked to imagine each scenario in turn, until the associated anxiety subsides. Imagined scenarios are followed by the person facing the fear in real-life situations. This is a common enough intervention on the part of clinical psychologists but is not usually practised in social work.

Operant conditioning

While in classical conditioning the organism is passive and learns what to expect from the environment, in operant conditioning the organism is active and learns how to get what it wants from the environment. Skinner found that rats in a box would learn that when they pressed a certain lever they would be rewarded with a pellet of food or that they could be taught to avoid other behaviour which resulted in a shock. The application of this in practice is easy to see, for example when working with parents who are having problems with their children's behaviour. You have often seen the situation where a child wants something, perhaps a sweet, the parent refuses, the child then screams, the parent capitulates. In so doing the parent rewards the screaming behaviour and makes it more likely that the child will behave in this way in the future.

CASE STUDY

Things have settled down a little and Brenda and Aisha have made good progress with the main tasks that they identified. However, with David away, Brenda is finding it increasingly difficult to control Sandra, aged 16. She will not come home at a reasonable time at night, is difficult to get up in the morning and is irritable and verbally abusive to Brenda. Brenda also suspects that Sandra has been stealing money from her purse. Aisha and Brenda discuss the possibility of using a star chart to modify Sandra's behaviour. The idea is that Brenda will use a calendar on which she will stick a star every time Sandra comes home before 11 p.m. When Sandra has ten stars she will receive a reward. Brenda and Aisha meet with Sandra, who agrees to the idea, and together they decide that the reward will be a trip to the disco on a Friday night, when she will be able to stay out until 1 a.m.

COMMENT

Social workers can work with parents, carefully discussing situations that have proved difficult, analysing what happened and suggesting more appropriate parental responses for the future. Trying to control a child's behaviour by shouting at them works only for a time; eventually the child becomes accustomed to the shouting and this stimulus becomes ineffective. Operant conditioning forms the basis of reward schemes for children, as in this example of a star chart. Brenda rewards the behaviour that she sees as desirable – Sandra coming home at a reasonable time. Note that Sandra is involved in the decision-making, in particular the nature of the reward, thus ensuring that she is best motivated.

Other examples of operant conditioning are chaining and backward chaining, used to teach behaviours to people with learning difficulties or stroke survivors.

Chaining and backward chaining

Chaining involves breaking a task, such as getting up in the morning, into its component parts – A,B,C,D, – so that the client is taught to do A, then A+B, A+B+C and so on until they can complete the whole task. Get out of bed – get out of bed and take off sleepwear – get out of bed, take off sleepwear, have a shower, etc. Backward chaining starts from the other end, so that the worker performs all the elements except Z, leaving that for the client, then Y+Z, then X+Y+Z, and so on. For example, on the first occasion the social worker accompanies the client to the doctor's surgery, sees the receptionist and sits with the client until they are called but the client makes their own way to the doctor's consulting room. The next time the client makes their way to the waiting room and waits for the doctor to call them. On the third occasion the client lets the receptionist know they have arrived, goes to the waiting room and waits. The advantage of backward chaining is that it always finishes with a reward for the client – the achievement of the task, in this example seeing the doctor.

Observational learning

Bandura (1977), however, believed the relationship between the individual and the environment could not account for all learning. He argued that there must also be a social element and was able to demonstrate this from observing children in an experimental situation. The children were found to reproduce aggressive and non-aggressive behaviour according to how they had observed adults' behaviour towards a large doll.

Bandura (1977) identified four key processes of observational learning.

Attention In order to learn you need to pay attention. Anything that distracts you will reduce your capacity for observational learning. Conversely, dramatic, interesting or novel aspects in what you observe will increase your capacity for learning. Observing someone with whom you identify or whom you admire is likely to grab your attention.

Retention You must be able to retain, that is remember, what you have observed. How successful we are in retaining the memory will depend on our ability to code or structure the information. This process depends on our ability to put it into language or to imagine it again in the form of mental images, so that we can reproduce the behaviour later ourselves.

Reproduction Having observed and retained the behaviour you also must be capable of reproducing it. However, this may involve the use of skills that you do not yet have and which you must first acquire. Practice of the behaviour leads to improvement and skill advancement.

Motivation In order for observational learning to be successful, you have to be motivated to imitate the behaviour that has been modelled. A number of factors may come into play here. Motivation will be increased by the expectation of reward or if the person who provides the model is attractive or powerful.

A good example of observational learning in social work practice is pro-social modelling.

Pro-social modelling

Burns (1994, cited in Trotter 2006) in a qualitative study conducted in Australia found that probation officers often inadvertently reinforced anti-social behaviour in clients by their reactions, as much through their body language as by what they said or did. An example would be smiling while the client recounts criminal behaviour. Pro-social modelling as developed by Trotter (2006) provides an approach *in which the worker acts as a good motivating role model in order to bring out the best in people* (Cherry 2005, p2). Summarised in simple terms by Trotter (p 89) pro-social modelling requires workers to:

- *identify positive or pro-social comments or behaviours as they occur in their interaction with clients;*

- *reward those comments and behaviours where possible, most often with praise;*

- *model pro-social expressions and actions;*

- *challenge anti-social or pro-criminal comments or behaviours.*

Cherry (2005) suggests the following behaviour on the part of the worker to provide a positive role model for clients.

- Respect for the individual. The client can learn to respect others through the experience of being respected by the worker.

- Respect for the law and rules.

- Punctuality is one way of demonstrating consistency and trustworthiness.

- Consistency.

- Fairness.

- Putting things right. The worker is able to model that it is OK to make mistakes, but it is also important to acknowledge mistakes and to make amends to people who have been inconvenienced or hurt.

- Assertiveness. The worker demonstrates that they are in pursuit of an objective and they are clear about what they are feeling and thinking and wanting to happen; at the same time they communicate to the client that they also want to understand what they are thinking, feeling and want to happen.

In order to provide an effective (and attractive) role model, the worker needs to be respected by and credible to the client. This is achieved by being fair, transparent and consistent, by acting with confidence but also by being prepared to admit to being less than perfect, recognising mistakes and being forthright about how, at times, the worker has to struggle.

Cherry (2005) places pro-social modelling at the centre of a wider approach to which she refers as *pro-social practice*. Emphasis is placed on a clear and transparent use of authority, and clarity and openness about the worker's role. Otherwise, however, most of the additional elements which go to make up pro-social practice will be familiar to you by now. These include developing an honest and empathetic relationship in which you show genuine concern, work in partnership with the client and treat the client as an individual.

RESEARCH SUMMARY

Trotter (1996, cited in Trotter 2006) in a study of probation practice in Australia found that the use of pro-social modelling and reinforcement was strongly, consistently and significantly correlated with lower offender and imprisonment rates (p 29). In a later study, Trotter (2004, cited in Trotter 2006) found that better outcomes were achieved where social workers modelled courtesies such as being punctual, keeping appointments and following through on what they said they would do. Studies into the use of pro-social modelling in probation hostels found that it resulted in improved resident behaviour and better staff–resident relationships (Henry et al. 2000 and Loney et al. 2000, both cited in Cherry 2005). Dowden and Andrews (2004, cited in Cherry 2005), in a review of a number of research studies of work with offenders, found that the degree to which workers modelled pro-social behaviour was an important factor in reducing their future offending.

Cognitive learning

We turn now to the fourth and final type of learning. We have seen that Bandura's (1977) ideas added a social element to ideas about learning. This opened the way for other theorists to consider how behaviour is influenced by people's thoughts, memories, beliefs and the meaning which they bring to their experiences. For example, a person who believes that an area of town is very safe may venture there alone and at all times of day and night. Having been attacked there on one occasion they then develop a belief that nowhere is safe and rarely leave their home unless in company. Kelly (1955) demonstrated how people construct internal ideas of reality in order to make sense of the world around them. Ellis's (1962) rational emotive therapy was based on ideas that we upset ourselves and frustrate our goals by adopting irrational beliefs about the world, ourselves and others. Meichenbaum (1977) suggested that the stories we tell ourselves affect our behaviour, so that students sitting an examination who tell themselves that they are doing badly go on to perform below their actual ability.

Cognitive behavioural practice

You will be pleased to discover that Dryden and Scott (1988) suggest that *social work students on a three month placement can become confident cognitive therapy practitioners by the end of the placement* (p174). Cognitive behavioural practice is underpinned by knowledge about how we learn and can be divided into four main areas: increasing coping skills, problem-solving, cognitive restructuring and structural cognitive therapy (Scott and Dryden 2003). We will look now at each in turn.

Increasing coping skills

Scott and Dryden (2003) suggest that coping skills have two components. The first relates to cognition – what the person tells themselves – and the second concerns their behaviour. A person may believe, for example, that they shouldn't ever express their own needs and so when they attempt to they are incoherent and mumble. The best known intervention for the improvement of coping skills is the stress inoculation training developed by Meichenbaum (1985), which focuses on both the cognitive and behavioural levels. Stress is seen as resulting from the interaction of the individual and the environment. Consequently both need to be changed. There are three stages, described below.

The *initial conceptualisation* phase involves the worker in educating the client about the general nature of stress. An important idea to convey is that people sometimes make their stress worse by what they say to themselves and how they behave. The worker and client identify the nature of the stressors the client is facing. An important idea to communicate here is that stressors shouldn't be seen as obstacles but as puzzles to be solved and as opportunities to find new exciting ways of being.

The *skills acquisition and rehearsal* phase is when the client learns the skills that they individually and uniquely need in order to cope. This could take some time as the client learns skills from a long menu, perhaps of emotional control, relaxation, assertiveness, problem-solving, socialisation and/or communication skills. You will probably be aware of anger management programmes, where clients are taught breathing control, for example, so as to control angry feelings.

In the final phase, *application and follow through*, the worker provides the patient with opportunities to practise coping skills. This could be done by use of role play, watching videos, practising the skill in unthreatening situations or repetition of the desired skill until it becomes automatic. In relapse prevention work alcohol misusers might learn and rehearse skills in refusing a drink.

Problem-solving

The most commonly used problem-solving method has been developed by Nezu et al. (1989). Clients are encouraged to work through the following six stages of problem-solving.

1. Problem orientation – that is, recognising the existence of a problem.

2. Defining what the problem is.

3. Generating as many possible solutions to the problem as possible.

4. Choosing the solution most likely to be effective.

5. Planning how to implement the solution.

6. Reviewing progress. If the chosen solution has not worked, another is chosen, implemented and reviewed.

Payne (2005) comments on similarities in this approach with task-centred work (see Chapter 5).

Cognitive restructuring

Within social work practice cognitive restructuring is probably the best known form of CBT. Jehu, Klassen and Gazan (1986) suggest the following main components in the cognitive restructuring approach:

- identifying beliefs, for example around the topic of concern;

- recognising and identifying cognitive distortions, usually those that are contributing to the formation or continuing existence of the problem;

- finding and substituting cognitive distortions with more accurate and helpful beliefs.

The two best known forms of cognitive restructuring are Beck's (1989) cognitive therapy, where the aim is to identify and change dysfunctional thinking, behaviour and emotional responses, and Ellis's (1962) rational emotive behaviour therapy (REBT, formerly RET), which we will now consider in more detail.

Rational emotive behaviour therapy

A key concept in REBT is that people get upset not just by what happens to them but also by how they construct their views of reality; that is, through the meanings they attach to what happens and by their beliefs and philosophies of the world, themselves and other people. This is represented by the A-B-C model where A is an activating event, B is a belief that affects the response to the event and C is the consequence of the response.

A, an activating event may be external and real – a knock at the door – or unreal – 'there is a psycho-killer at the door.' It can also be internal and real – 'I am afraid' – or unreal – 'I am about to die.' The activating event may also be in the past, present or future.

B, a belief is, according to Ellis (1962), an evaluation which can be 'rational' or 'irrational'. An 'irrational' belief is one that prevents people from achieving their personal goals, or is illogical or inconsistent with reality. Rational beliefs are helpful and irrational beliefs are unhelpful. Geldard and Geldard (2004) make the point that labelling beliefs as irrational may provoke unnecessary arguments with clients about whether a belief is rational or not; they prefer to use the term 'self-destructive beliefs' and this is the term we will use here. These beliefs may not be self-destructive in themselves but are destructive in their consequences. It is not necessarily self-destructive to believe that your boss is an incompetent idiot, but when that belief affects how you behave, the consequences could be very destructive for you.

C, the consequence is likely to be self-defeating and destructive if a person's belief about the activating event is rigid, dogmatic, absolutist and dysfunctional. On the other hand, if a person's evaluative belief is logical, flexible, constructive and consistent with reality, the emotional and behavioural consequence is likely to be helping and constructive.

Ellis (1983, cited in Dryden 2007b) suggests four categories of self-destructive beliefs.

> **Demands** are expectations of oneself and other people that are unrealistic and expressed in absolute terms. They can usually be identified by the inclusion of words such as 'must', 'ought', 'should', 'have to'. For example, 'I have to have a drink', 'People should trust me', 'I must not cry'. Ellis refers to this as 'musturbation'.

> **Awfulising** takes the form of exaggerating the consequences of a situation to the point that it becomes a catastrophe. 'It will be a total disaster for me if I don't get this job.'

> **Low frustration tolerance** reflects an intolerance of any discomfort. A task is just too difficult to be undertaken. A situation is too painfully embarrassing or boring to be endured. In this way these undesirable qualities outweigh any possibility of being able to cope with them.

> **Depreciation beliefs** come in three forms: depreciation of self, where you depreciate yourself for not meeting the demands you have placed upon yourself; depreciation of others for not meeting your demands; and a depreciation of life conditions where you depreciate these when they don't meet your demands. Depreciation can result from the global rating of self and others – that is, rating oneself and other people in an over-generalised way so that some are considered to be worthless or much less valuable than others. People come to be defined by what they have supposedly done wrong: 'She never even came around to see me when I was ill, so she is no use to me as a friend'.

To these general categories Burns (1992, cited in Milner and O'Byrne 2002) adds:

> **all or nothing beliefs** if it isn't perfect it's a disaster;

> **overgeneralisation** one failure is regarded as evidence of a complete inability to succeed;

mental filter recognising and dwelling only on negatives, while filtering out all positives;

disqualifying positives failing to recognise positives or discounting them as being of no significance;

jumping to conclusions which are usually negative and based on slim evidence;

magnification/minimisation exaggerating own faults and others' strengths;

emotional reasoning believing that what one feels must be true;

labelling/mislabelling 'I am no good', 'I am stupid', I am a bad person', 'he is a scumbag';

personalisation assuming responsibility for negative events, regardless of the evidence.

Geldard and Geldard (2004) add:

always and never beliefs 'Everybody is always on my case', 'I always make the wrong decision';

blaming beliefs 'I wouldn't drink so much if my boss didn't bully me.'

CASE STUDY

Brenda has been using a star chart to try to get 16-year-old Sandra to change her behaviour and not stay out too late at night. This worked well for a short while but Aisha has been wondering about its suitability with a 16-year-old. Then Brenda rings Aisha first thing one Monday morning to say that she cannot cope with Sandra's behaviour any more and has asked her to leave. Sandra failed to return home on Saturday night and wandered in at two o'clock on Sunday afternoon. Today she has refused to go to school.

Aisha agrees to visit and when she arrives she finds a full-scale battle is in progress, with both parties highly emotional and Brenda still threatening to throw Sandra out of the house. Aisha suggests seeing Sandra alone.

Sandra's story is as follows.

I had to go to Tracey's house for a party because Tracey would never have forgiven me if I didn't go. Also, everyone was going and I would have been a total dork if I didn't go. I couldn't tell Mum I was going, because everyone was staying late and she always makes me come home for eleven. She just does that to make me look stupid. I wouldn't have been able to leave that early because they would all have laughed at me and I'd be too embarrassed ever to go out again. I did think about ringing her when the party was over to tell her where I was but she'd have gone totally mad and made a big scene at Tracey's and it would have been a total disaster. You can see what she's like – she is always totally losing it, so it's not my fault. I don't see why I should have to leave home just because she's a nutter.

Aisha thinks that it may be appropriate to work with Sandra using REBT.

Is Sandra showing any signs of having self-destructive beliefs? Go through her statement, listing the different things she says in terms of the list of self-destructive beliefs above.

COMMENT

We can see many examples of self-destructive beliefs in the statement. Sandra *had to go to the party.* Everyone *would think* badly *of her if she didn't.* Her mum *never* lets *her out after eleven.* She *wouldn't be able to cope* with *the embarrassment of leaving early.* It *would have been a* disaster *if her mum picked her up after the party.*

Intervening

Coulshed and Orme (2006) suggest the eight stages to be followed in CBT, which we will apply here to REBT.

- **Engagement** is common to most interventions and involves joining with the client, exploring expectations of the contact, being clear about roles, responsibilities, etc.

- **Problem focus** during which problems are identified and prioritised.

- **Problem assessment** One example is selected for attention. As the client and worker focus on the example, the worker breaks it down into its ABC components. It is usual for a client to think of the example in terms of only A and C. This happened (A) and the consequence (C) was this. When the client is describing A the worker tries to get the client to be as specific and precise as possible. The client will often want to go into a long-winded description of what happened; talking about it helps them to feel better. However, the worker is not interested so much in what happened but in the belief (B), since the consequence (C) came about not because of A but because of the belief (B). In the example in the case study, Sandra is interested only in the activating event – that she stayed out all night at a party – and the consequence – she is in big trouble with her mother who is now behaving unreasonably towards her. Aisha needs to help Sandra to identify and assess the beliefs that have brought the consequences about.

- **Teach cognitive principles** In order to move on, the client needs to understand how their problems arise largely out of their self-destructive beliefs and how they therefore need to identify what these beliefs are. This is not an easy matter. People's beliefs can be very complex, interlinked and contradictory. In the example Sandra is full of self-justification and anger now, but may well also be experiencing or suppressing feelings of guilt and shame. The client needs to recognise these beliefs as being self-destructive.

- **Dispute and challenge** The worker teaches the client how to dispute their self-destructive beliefs. Three basic disputing strategies are used.

  - *Empirical disputing* challenges the evidence upon which a belief is based. *I had to go to Tracey's house for a party because Tracey would never have forgiven me if I didn't go.* Where is the evidence that Tracey would be so unforgiving? If Tracey was going to be upset if Sandra didn't go to the party, did that mean that Sandra *had to* go? Does she *have to* do everything that Tracey wants? Where is the evidence for that?

– *Logical disputing* involves the worker in identifying logical inconsistencies in the client's thinking. *I couldn't tell Mum I was going, because everyone was staying late and she always makes me come home for eleven.* Sandra assumes that because this is a Saturday night and she has already had her late night on the Friday, that her mother will not let her go to a late party. Is this logical? Brenda has shown that she is prepared to negotiate around this issue with Sandra. Why would she not be prepared to negotiate again? She does not always make Sandra come home for eleven.

– *Pragmatic disputing* involves the worker focusing on the pragmatic disadvantages for the client of holding a particular belief. The belief that her mother insists that she doesn't stay out because she wants her to look stupid prevents Sandra from realising that it is because her mother doesn't want her to come to harm. Adhering to this belief prevents Sandra from negotiating a deal where she can be out late so long as she is safe.

• **Encourage client self-disputing** this can be done by the use of questions, the intention being to get the client to think for themselves. Does this make sense? Is there another way of looking at this? Workers using a CBT approach often use the Socratic Method, where clients are guided through a process of revealing distortions in their thinking, using techniques such as probing questions and reflective statements. One example is the downward arrow questioning technique, characterised by questions such as:

– What is your concern about … ?

– What would the implications be … ?

– What would be the consequences of …. ?

• *Set behavioural homework* Setting homework tasks agreed by the client and worker is a good way of ensuring that the lessons learned in face-to-face sessions are applied when they are not in contact; the client then perceives the whole week as time to focus on change rather than just the session. It also encourages the client to become responsible for their improvement rather than relying on the worker. Often the homework takes the form of a diary in which the client records events under ABC headings.

• *Ending* The ending stage is a time to review and evaluate progress and to look to the future. It may include coming up with ideas about what to do if things start to go wrong again in the future and teaching self-therapy techniques to maintain improvement, such as the use of flash cards on which the client has written helpful thoughts.

CASE STUDY

Aisha arranged to see Sandra at her office two days after the row. She decided to focus with Sandra on her relationship with her friends.

Aisha: *So you felt you didn't really have any choice but to go out that night because of your friends' attitude to you.*

Sandra: *Well, yes. If I hadn't gone to the party they'd think that I was a complete wally.*

Aisha: Why does that matter to you?

Sandra: Well, they wouldn't think I was cool and they wouldn't hang around with me.

Aisha: And the consequences of that would be?

Sandra: I wouldn't have any friends at school.

Aisha: And how would that affect you?

Sandra: Well, I'd probably just have to leave.

Aisha: What would that mean for you?

Sandra: I wouldn't be able to take my exams and I couldn't do A levels and get a decent job.

Aisha: So not going to the party on Saturday would have meant you having to work in a shop for the rest of your life?

Sandra: Well, no, of course not. Hey, can we go over that again?

COMMENT

Here we see Aisha making good use of the downward arrow technique to help Sandra recognise how her distorted thinking is adding to her problem.

Once a self-destructive belief has been identified and confronted the client is taught to replace it with a constructive belief. For example, Sandra might replace 'My friends will laugh at me if I leave the party early' with 'My friends also have parents who worry about them and will understand if I leave the party early. I will probably not be the only one to do so.'

Structural cognitive therapy

These first three approaches, coping skills, problem-solving and cognitive restructuring, have been criticised for focusing only on surface-structural issues, directed towards the identification and modification of problematic self-statements and behaviour. Structural cognitive therapy, on the other hand, is concerned with *deep structures* (Liotti 1986, cited in Scott and Dryden 2003). This is a specialised form of CBT rarely, if ever, found in social work but it is briefly included here for the sake of comprehensiveness. Liotti suggests that cognitive structures exist at three levels.

- **Core level** beliefs are those beliefs, usually formed during childhood, that we accept as 'givens', that is, immutable 'truths', about ourselves or the world: 'the world is a safe place', 'I am a person of value', but which are tacitly held.

- **Intermediate level** beliefs are those we have about the world and ourselves which are held explicitly and which we can and do verbalise.

- **Peripheral level** beliefs are those that determine our plans of action and the problem-solving strategies we develop individually and use on a daily basis.

The primary concern in structural cognitive therapy is to make the core level beliefs explicit. Consequently, although the intervention, for example, may initially have the aim of replacing self-defeating ideas with more constructive ones, longer-term work focuses on revealing the origins of the core belief from which the self-defeating idea originated.

While the first three categories of CBT lend themselves to brief intervention, making them very appropriate in terms of social work practice, structural cognitive therapy typically takes much longer and is not really a viable option within social work.

RESEARCH SUMMARY

Sheldon (2000) suggests that the research evidence for the effectiveness of cognitive behavioural methods is so vast (over 4,000 empirical studies) and so convincing that there is hardly any need for further studies. These results add up to the fact that, within this literature, in respect of a wide range of demanding problems, virtually no other approach ever does better (p70). There are a large number of studies, in respect of a large number of problems, that support Sheldon's assertion. However, Sheldon may be rather overstating the case. Holmes argues that:

> it is hard to escape the suspicion that cognitive therapy seems so far ahead of the field in part because of its research and marketing strategy rather than because it is intrinsically superior to other therapies.

(Holmes 2002, p289)

Barkham cites studies that support the concept of 'equivalence paradox'. This suggests that:

> technically different therapies result in broadly similar outcomes ... It is not disputed that there is often a reported advantage to one particular method of therapy (invariably cognitive-behavioural), but what is important is that the size of this advantage is relatively small.

(Barkham 2007, p461)

Having said this, there is a significant body of evidence of the comparative effectiveness of CBT in respect of a number of problems and conditions. CBT is the first-choice treatment in The Department of Health's (2001) research-based guidelines for post-traumatic stress disorder, depressive disorders, panic disorders, agoraphobia, generalised anxiety disorders, bulimia and chronic fatigue. It has been adopted as the most effective method in the reduction of offending behaviour (Farrall 2002, but see Kendall 2004 for a critique of correctional cognitive behaviouralism). It is also important to note that CBT has been demonstrated to have prophylactic effects. So, for example, clients who have been suffering from depression who have learned CBT techniques and coping strategies are less likely to have a recurrence of their symptoms (Evans et al. 1992, cited in Barkham 2007).

Application in social work practice

From time to time a particular approach becomes fashionable in social work practice. Within the space of the author's career, psychosocial, transactional analysis, therapeutic communities, systems theory, social skills training and various forms of family therapy have all had their day. Now it is the turn of cognitive behavioural approaches. However, while there is a certain amount of evidence that most methods work (see McLeod 2003; Department of Health 2001), cognitive behavioural approaches do seem to have been developing an edge on most others. For this and a number of other reasons it has won the confidence of government policy-makers: it seems easy to understand, it is usually delivered against standardised research-based and therefore consistent methods, evaluation is straightforward, it can be delivered over a relatively short period and is therefore cheap. Furthermore the method has the advantage of being collaborative and client centred. In CBT clients find their own resources, especially those within themselves, and develop self-helping methods and skills. Given all this and the fact that it has applicability across most of the wide range of social work practice, it is surprising that it is not as widespread within the profession as one might expect. There are a number of possible reasons:

- The literature in support of the universal efficacy of cognitive behaviour therapy is not unequivocal (see for example Beidel and Turner 1986; Kroese 1998; Holmes 2002) especially in relation to social work practice (see Gorman et al. 2006; Cowburn 2006; Mair 2004; Kendall 2004; Parton and O'Byrne 2000; Haines and Drakeford 1998).

- Another reason may be the cynical, if rather justifiable, suspicion with which many practitioners view anything that is not only evidence-based but favoured by policy-makers and also 'flavour of the month'. This is particularly so when the approach appears to be supported by a government whose ethical values often seem to run counter to those of the more politically motivated practitioner.

- Practitioners may regard CBT as providing wholesale mechanistic responses to individual human problems. Much behaviour may be perceived as being emotionally driven and irrational when it represents, in fact, a rational response to very upsetting and disturbing experiences.

- CBT, in common with other individualised approaches, starts from an assumption of deficit: that the client is lacking in something (the ability to behave or to think rationally) that can be corrected. It does not take account of socio-economic factors such as inequality of opportunity and oppression. Concerns in practitioners' minds about this potential to reinforce disadvantage can be magnified by disquiet about CBT language, terms such as cognitive distortion, dissonance, irrationality and dysfunctionality.

- CBT requires a high level of knowledge of the method and well-developed skill in applying it. This takes time and effort to acquire, the support of the employing agency and the existence and availability of such training.

> ### CHAPTER SUMMARY
>
> - Cognitive behavioural therapy is concerned with the thoughts, images, beliefs and attitudes that we have (our cognitive processes) and how these relate to our behaviour, particularly insofar as they may be linked to our emotional problems.
>
> - Cognitive behaviour therapy is based on a number of theories concerned with learning: classical or respondent conditioning, operant or instrumental conditioning, observational, modelling or vicarious learning and cognitive learning.
>
> - Reward schemes, such as star charts, are examples of operant conditioning.
>
> - Pro-social modelling, which is most commonly found in offender work, is an example of the application of observational learning theory to practice.
>
> - The most commonly used interventions by social workers are based on cognitive learning theory. There are four main approaches: increasing coping skills, problem-solving, cognitive restructuring and structural cognitive therapy. Only the first three are to be found in social work practice; many programmes have been developed in the area of cognitive restructuring.
>
> - Cognitive behavioural approaches are effective with clients with a wide range of issues.

FURTHER READING

Cherry, S (2005) *Transforming behaviour: Pro-social modelling in practice*. Cullompton: Willan Publishing.
This text provides an accessible guide to what pro-social modelling is and how to put it into practice.

Dryden, W and Mytton, J (1999) *Four approaches to counselling and psychotherapy*. London: Routledge.
This contains a practical guide to Rational Emotive Behaviour Therapy and includes some useful case studies showing the method in action.

Cigno, K and Bourn, D (eds) (1998) *Cognitive-behavioural social work in practice*. Aldershot: Ashgate.
This is an edited collection which covers a range of cognitive behavioural intervention methods with clients in a variety of social work settings.

Chapter 7
Groupwork

Trevor Lindsay

ACHIEVING A SOCIAL WORK DEGREE

This chapter will help you to develop the following capabilities from the **Professional Capabilities Framework**:

- **Professionalism**
  Identify and behave as a professional social worker committed to professional development.
- **Knowledge**
  Apply knowledge of social sciences, law and social work practice theory.
- **Intervention and skills**
  Use judgement and authority to intervene with individuals, families and communities to promote independence, provide support and prevent harm, neglect and abuse.

It will also introduce you to the following academic standards as set out in the social work subject benchmark statement.

5.1.1 Social work services and clients.
5.1.4 Social work theory.
5.1.5 The nature of social work practice.
5.5.1 Managing problem solving activities.
5.5.3 Analysis and synthesis.
5.5.4 Intervention and evaluation.

Introduction

This chapter aims to provide you with a basic understanding of the groupwork method, using the example of the Women's Aid *Power to Change* programme as a case example. This should help you to identify some of the advantages and disadvantages of working in groups with social work clients, to consider how a facilitator might plan a group intervention and deal with some of the challenges, including issues of power and oppression, that can present themselves during the life of a group. Having read this chapter it is unlikely that you will be in a position to facilitate a group yourself. To prepare for this task you will need to become more familiar with the detail of the method and it would be useful to consult the resources suggested at the end of the chapter.

Lindsay and Orton (2011, p7) define groupwork as:

> *a method of social work which aims, in an informed way, through purposeful group experiences, to help individuals and groups to meet individual and group need and to influence and change personal, group, organisational and community problems.*

Let us look at that definition a little more closely. Firstly, it is defined as a *method* of social work and therefore one of a range of approaches, many of which are discussed in this book. Secondly, it is *informed*, that is by a body of literature and research and also, as we develop as groupworkers, by our experience of what does and does not work for each of us as facilitators. Thirdly, it is *purposeful*: we and the group members have an idea of what a positive outcome might be and this is achieved through the *experiences* arising out of the involvement. Fourthly, it is intended to provide some means of meeting either and/or both *individual and group need*. Lastly, it is directed at resolving *problems* that people are experiencing as *individuals, an organisation, or community*.

CASE STUDY

Aisha gets the following letter in the post from the local Women's Aid group.

Dear Aisha

I am writing with regard to the self-help support group, 'Power to Change', that we facilitate. 'Power to Change' is run specifically for survivors of domestic abuse, and is based on the idea that women working together in a safe, friendly and non-judgmental environment can change their lives for the better. The formal programme is a psycho-educational group run in weekly 2-hour sessions over a period of 14 weeks.

The three main aims of the support group are:

- to change patterns of behaviour learned by women within abusive relationships;

- to raise awareness of women's basic rights;

- to build self-esteem, self-determination and empowerment.

Domestic abuse includes physical, sexual, psychological or financial violence that takes place within an intimate or family-type relationship and forms a pattern of coercive and controlling behaviour. One in four women, regardless of ethnicity, religion, class, age, sexuality, disability or lifestyle, will experience domestic abuse in their lifetimes. Survivors often draw strength and benefit from interaction with other survivors of abuse.

'Power to Change' increases survivors' understanding of the dynamics of abusive relationships by working through the weekly activities; and, by sharing their experiences with other women, survivors' feelings of shame, guilt and loneliness diminish. For the group to function effectively, however, participation must be an autonomous choice. We would like to take this opportunity to offer the group's services to any survivors of domestic abuse with whom your agency works. Women who are referred to the group are under no pressure whatsoever to join, and all women prior to attendance undergo a full risk assessment which helps to determine whether they are at the right stage in their lives to participate in the course, and to do so safely. Both self-referrals and agency referrals are accepted.

CASE STUDY continued

We are enclosing a leaflet on the 'Power to Change' programme, which can be used for your further information, or be given to women who might wish to contact the service. Thank you for your co-operation, and we hope to hear from you soon.

With best wishes,

Denise Wilson and Shakila Ali

(adapted from Martins et al. 2008, p186)

Aisha telephones Denise Wilson and discusses Brenda Cartwright's situation explaining that although it is her understanding that David has never been physically violent towards Brenda, he has certainly abused her financially and has been largely responsible, therefore, for Brenda's depression and low self-esteem. Aisha learns that in fact there are two programmes within Power to Change *– a self-esteem programme and a further programme which focuses on changing abusive relationship patterns. Brenda thinks the self-esteem programme would be best for Brenda at this stage and Brenda could choose later to join the other group if she wished. Denise confirms that, on the face of it, Brenda would be suitable for referral to the self-esteem group; the risk assessment mentioned in the letter and a face-to-face interview would need to take place before the facilitators could reach a final decision. Aisha and Denise agree that Aisha speaks to Brenda about the group and then makes a referral if Brenda is agreeable.*

Later that week Aisha sees Brenda, explains about the group and gives Brenda the referral leaflet. Brenda is enthusiastic and decides to self-refer.

ACTIVITY 7.1

In the letter Denise and Shakila suggest a couple of ways in which the group might be helpful to survivors of abuse. In what ways do you think it could be helpful to Brenda? List these on a piece of paper.

How might the group help Brenda?

People with similar life experiences, situations and problems can be a source of support to each other

People, like Brenda, who have had particular damaging and hurtful experiences or who are at present experiencing very difficult situations often either feel isolated and alone or are prevented by their situation from joining with others. Meeting up with other people who have similar experiences may therefore be a great source of help to Brenda as she comes to realise that her situation is not unique.

Groupwork can be empowering

Generally speaking, social workers and social care staff are in relatively more powerful positions than the people with whom they work. This can be because of the statutory power given to the agency, by the resources that it holds or simply because of the knowledge and information held by the worker. In a one-to-one situation, this puts Brenda very much at the weaker end of the power equation. However, in a group the worker's power can be balanced by the power which comes to the group members because of their greater numbers.

Groups offer opportunities for giving and receiving help

This advantage arises again out of the numerical facts. In a group, Brenda will have a number of other people available who can offer support, advice and suggestions. A vast range of experience can be brought to bear on problems and situations. It is also important to realise that it can be as beneficial to have opportunities to give help, as it is to receive it.

RESEARCH SUMMARY

Hopmeyer and Werk (1993) conducted a study of four family bereavement groups. They found that 40 per cent of the respondents felt that they had given and received help in equal measure in their group.

Groups offer opportunities for social comparison

People in groups are exposed to a range of different ways of behaving. Brenda may find herself exposed to new ideas and beliefs. She may find herself exposed to the expression of feelings that she may share but would never dare to express herself. Button (1997) suggests that groups have the capacity to hold 'big feelings' such as shame, terror and rage. He suggests that a common factor in thwarted expression of big feelings is the sense of being unmet, unheard or unseen. Many survivors have that experience. An important function of a group can be for these feelings to be met, heard and seen by a number of people in a safe and valued way.

Groups offer learning opportunities

Some groups are established with the main aim of providing information. In this case, it is clear from the letter that one aim of the group is to increase the members' understanding of the dynamics of abuse. Jaques (2006) provides a comprehensive discussion of the benefits of a group membership for learning.

- **Group members have the opportunity to learn from each other** This can happen in a number of ways. Firstly, people who share problems can learn from others about effective ways of dealing with the situations that arise. There is also the possibility of learning from each other through a process of discovery. Being able to arrive at solutions through discovery with others can promote deeper learning in Brenda than being presented with a 'ready-made' solution. Opportunities for personal growth are offered also by the opportunities to observe the behaviour of others and to learn from it. Additionally Brenda may be able to see what the outcomes are of the behaviour of the other group members, for example, what happens if someone challenges the facilitator or another group member.

- **A group provides opportunities for acquiring information about how one's behaviour is experienced and responded to by others** In groups feedback can be more powerful since it comes from a number of people who are in similar situations or perhaps of a similar age, ethnicity, class and so on. All social situations provide individuals with feedback, in the sense that all behaviour has consequences that occur in the form of a response to that behaviour. In groups the amount of feedback is increased. Particular activities can be provided that will encourage the members of the group to provide feedback.

- **A group offers opportunities for trying out new behaviours** A group can provide a safe environment in which Brenda can experiment with behaviour that is new to her or try out solutions that had not previously occurred to her.

Possible limitations of groupwork

It would be disingenuous not to make it quite clear that there are some potential disadvantages to groupwork and for some people it is not a good way of working. There are also social workers and care workers for whom groupwork may not be a comfortable way of working. Davies (1975) and Brown (1992) suggest a number of limitations.

Groups can become self-obsessed
As individuals in the group find common concerns, goals and a sense of identity, they can come to value this over all else. For some people the main concern becomes the group itself, its survival, its reputation, its cohesiveness and its control over its members. Groupworkers need to work hard to keep a sense of reality by linking the group experience to what is happening outside.

The individual is likely to get less undivided attention
It follows that it is difficult for a group to cater for all the needs of all the group members at the same time as providing the same attention as each might expect out of individual contact. It is important, therefore, that the facilitator has a continuing awareness of the needs of each individual as well as of the whole group.

No guarantees of confidentiality can be given
Confidentiality can be even more of an issue when working with groups than in one-to-one work, simply because there are more people involved and listening to what is being said. People can rarely be given absolute guarantees of confidentiality by their social workers, who have responsibilities to protect other members of society as well as their clients, but at least they can spell out the limits of their confidentiality. Members of groups have to rely on the discretion of all the other members as well as the facilitators and have to be informed that the risk of their confidentiality being breached, while undesirable, is always present.

Groups can be complex and expensive to plan and implement
A substantial amount of work needs to be undertaken in planning and facilitating a group. To this needs to be added the work that needs to be done with employing agencies and one's colleagues to ensure that the project is properly supported. Most groups

require the allocation of resources in addition to staff time, whether this should be a space to meet (which can often present a major hurdle) or something as simple as the provision of tea and coffee.

Groups can be harmful for some

There are a number of ways in which membership of a group can prove harmful to an individual. Belonging to a small helping group can add to stigmatisation. The users of social work services are often already stigmatised and labelled as a consequence of their problem. Membership of a group aimed specifically at addressing these problems can add to the stigma.

Whitaker (2001) includes a chapter on group situations where there is no gain or there is actual harm. These include situations where:

- one person is more vulnerable than the others and is threatened or attacked;
- one person is conspicuously different from the others and is stereotyped or oppressed;
- the group adopts a collusive defence that requires one member to occupy a role that is harmful to them;
- an individual is excluded or ignored;
- a group member is drawn into experiencing unbearable feelings with which they do not have the resources to cope.

As Brown (1992) points out, many of these scenarios may not be illustrations of the limitations of groupwork, but provide indicators for protecting some people from unsuitable groups or are pointers about issues of which we need as facilitators to be aware, plan for and deal with. The risk assessment which takes place as part of the referral process for the *Power to Change* programme, seeks to prevent women joining the group who are not yet sufficiently robust emotionally to cope with some of the content.

The tasks of facilitation

The term 'facilitator' describes the person who initiates and plans the group, leads the group while it is 'meeting' and manages its finishing. They need to make some plans and consider how they can fulfil the role before setting up the group in question. Sharry (2001 p5) suggests that *the aim of the facilitator is to establish the conditions and trust in the group whereby clients can help one another and then to 'get out of the way' to allow them to do it.*

We can perceive the principal tasks to be fourfold, which are:

- planning the group;
- intervening in the group;
- monitoring the group;
- maintaining the group.

Let us turn to Denise and Shakila to discover how they undertook each of these tasks.

Planning

Planning is the most important part of the groupwork task. Although the *Power to Change* programme is an 'off-the-shelf-programme' with a manual that takes the facilitators through all the stages of planning, Denise and Shakila still had to spend as much time and effort in the planning of the group as actually working with it. Good planning makes a successful outcome much more likely and reduces worry and stress as many problems will be anticipated and avoided.

ACTIVITY **7.2**

A number of the practical problems identified by Aisha and Brenda have been to some extent resolved and Aisha has offered Brenda a range of helping interventions but Brenda continues to be unhappy and often cries during visits. She complains of feeling very lonely and while she appreciates Aisha's support, it is not enough for her on a day-to-day basis. The first task of the group facilitators is to identify the needs that Brenda has and which she might share with others.

What do you think are Brenda's unmet needs at this time? Make a list and then consider which of these may be met through the medium of groupwork.

COMMENT

Identifying unmet need that may be met by a group is the first and most fundamental task of the groupworker. One of the problems about an 'off-the-shelf' programme, such as Power to Change, *is that the facilitators have to start with a programme that is already written rather than plan the group from scratch to meet a range of identified needs. Brenda has a number of needs. Think of Maslow's (1954) hierarchy of needs. At this time Brenda's main biological and physiological needs are being met. Brenda has certain safety needs, in particular she has justifiable anxiety about her financial safety, which in turn may threaten her physiological stability, for example should she lose the family home. The group may help her with ideas about increasing her financial security. She has very clear unmet needs in the area of love and belonging. She is parted from her husband and socially isolated. Again she has unmet need in self-esteem. Her lower-esteem needs (status, recognition, fame, prestige and attention) are badly affected by the abuse she has experienced and stigmatisation and she has obvious unmet need in the higher area esteem needs (strength, competence, mastery, self-confidence, independence and freedom). Until these needs are met she has little prospect of self-actualisation. These are needs which she has in common with other women who are survivors of domestic violence and this allows the construction of the aims of the group which are stated in the letter.*

- to change patterns of behaviour learned by women within abusive relationships;

- to raise awareness of women's basic rights;

- to build self-esteem, self-determination and empowerment.

How are the group aims and objectives to be met?

Having decided what needs the women have that may be met through groupwork and having formulated the aims of the group, the programme sets out what the group will do in order to achieve these and so what sort of group it will be. What follows are some of the types of groups that commonly take place.

- support and discussion groups;

- skill-development groups – social skills, parenting skills, literacy;

- therapeutic groups – bereavement, trauma, psychodynamic, gestalt, cognitive, behavioural;

- action groups, where the group is set up to achieve some desired change outside the group, for example age concern, child poverty, improved housing, community issues;

- activity groups – walking, cookery, reading;

- self-help groups – community, women's groups.

Power to Change combines support and discussion with skills development and the provision of information relevant to abusive relationships.

What will be the content of the group?

For Denise and Shakila this is comparatively easy. A programme of activities has been devised by the authors of the programme that they can follow and is summarised below.

Power to Change programme

Session 1: Defining self-esteem

This session aims, among other things, to create a warm, safe and welcoming environment for everyone attending, and ensure that everyone has a good understanding of what self-esteem means.

Session 2: Understanding self-esteem

This session aims to create a group definition and gain a deeper understanding of the concept of self-esteem.

Session 3: Rights

This session aims to ensure participants have a basic understanding of fundamental human rights, and to encourage healthy and positive debate.

Session 4: Needs

Participants will be helped to identify and prioritise needs, and learn how to differentiate between different types of needs ...

Session 5: Self-evaluation of personal needs

Following on from the last session, participants will continue to identify and prioritise needs, learn practical steps for fulfilling them, and identify obstacles to their fulfillment ...

Session 6: Education and socialisation of girls and young women

In this session, participants will become better able to understand how upbringing can affect children, and, in particular, how girls and young women are socialised into behaving and expressing themselves ...

Session 7: Gender stereotyping and social norms

This session aims to enable participants to think about women's roles in society, their effects, and how they can potentially affect self-esteem. The participants will also be encouraged to identify positive female role models ...

Session 8: Needs within a relationship

Participants will be helped to identify their needs within a relationship, and communicate these to their partners. They will also be encouraged to identify the positive aspects about being single.

Sessions 9 and 10: Boundaries

The aims of these sessions include: defining boundaries, identifying potential situations in which boundaries could be challenged, looking at positive ways of asserting boundaries (and the potential dangers in this), and understanding the link between the lack of clear, healthy boundaries and domestic abuse ...

Sessions 11 and 12: Emotions: Anger, guilt, grief and fear

The aim of these sessions is to acknowledge and start to understand feelings of anger, grief, fear and guilt, and learn to manage these emotions constructively ...

Session 13: Assertiveness

In this session, participants will gain a better understanding of assertiveness (including the difference between assertiveness and aggression) and learn practical ways of being assertive.

Session 14: Endings and new beginnings

The final session will recap what has been learnt in the course, celebrate how far the women have come, help women to recognise individual strengths, and accept the ending of the course, while anticipating new beginnings.

Martins et al. (2008, pp53–55)

ACTIVITY **7.3**

Read through the 14 sessions and then compare the sessions with the stated aims of the group as stated in the case study. Which of the sessions fulfil which of the aims?

You should have found that all the sessions relate either directly or indirectly to one or more of the stated aims or else contribute to the successful conduct of the group.

How is the group to be structured?

The structure of the group is very important as it has an impact on how the group will run and on the outcomes. At this stage in their planning, the faciliators are able to get into more detail about the structure of the group. This includes deciding on the composition of the group, its size, its frequency and length and other practical issues like where and when it will meet. Different types of groups call for different decisions at this stage. In many cases the decision we arrive at will have both advantages and disadvantages. Douglas (1995) argues that these factors are interrelated, so that changes in one characteristic will inevitably affect another. For example, the size of the group will determine where it can take place; the location of the venue will have an impact on the balance of the people able to attend. Douglas (1995) lists 11 factors, while Doel and Sawdon (1999) list 12 variables, giving a total of 17 different aspects to be taken into account. Each of these presents us with a continuum with opposites at either end. For example, in terms of length, a group can run for either a long or a short period; each has advantages and disadvantages.

- **Size** The size of the group will have an impact on how it is experienced, both by the members and by the leaders, so the optimum size will depend on the type of group being planned. A group that has the aim of facilitating members in expressing their feelings needs to be sufficiently small for the members to feel safe enough, but a larger group, set up to tackle a shared problem, may come up with a greater number of solutions. *Power to Change* suggests an ideal of 8 to 12.

- **Frequency** The frequency of meetings will be determined by the benefits you hope for the group and the character of the people in the group. The more frequently a group meets the more intense the experience is likely to be and the more importance it has for the members' lives. Frequency is important for a sense of continuity.

- **Duration** How long will the group exist? Once more, this will depend on the purpose of the group. Short-term groups of five or six sessions are useful for certain specific purposes, for example providing information, while groups aimed at therapeutic experiences, need time for necessary trust-building to take place.

- **Constancy of membership** Closed or open? Closed groups start and finish with the same members, whereas the membership of an open group changes as people join and leave. There are pros and cons with both. Very rapid turnover of membership, with members dropping out and being replaced, affects the level of intimacy that can be achieved.

Power to Change is a closed programme with a suggested frequency of 2 hours weekly for 14 weeks.

Facilitation

Denise was the originator of the idea for the group but decided that it would be helpful to have a co-facilitator. This has a number of advantages.

Table 7.1 *Co-working: Potential gains*

Benefits for the group	Benefits for the facilitators
Facilitation resources available to the group are enriched – styles, personalities, experiences, knowledge.	More than one view is available about what is happening in the group.
Group members experience the concern or interest of at least two people in authority.	Co-workers can support and counsel each other and can provide feedback to each other on their performance
Group members have more than one facilitator to test themselves against or with whom they can identify.	The impact of the dependent behaviour of group members can be shared.
The facilitators can model specific social and interactional interpersonal skills and the working relationships.	If one groupworker loses touch or control or becomes overly tired, the other can take over.
Co-facilitators can provide an improved balance for the group in terms of ethnicity, gender and other characteristics and can model positive working relationships between these groups.	Facilitation tasks can be shared e.g. one monitors/one records, one leads 'up front'/one looks after emotional needs etc.
If one groupworker is ill or unavailable, the group meeting can still take place.	Co-working provides training opportunities for less experienced groupworkers.

However, a difficulty is that co-working adds a further level of complexity to the task of facilitation. Now the facilitator has to be aware and take account of the co-facilitator in addition to the group and the individual members. Hodge points to the pitfalls (1985):

Co-working: Potential pitfalls

- Inadequate preparation by the co-facilitators leads to mismatching perceptions of task and role.

- The co-workers have irreconcilable differences in theoretical orientation.

- They have differences of opinion about techniques skills or styles required.

- They are in competition.

- There are agency related tensions where facilitators are from different agencies.

- They fail to build in planning and review sessions and this leads to discrepancies in perceptions of task, role, and group development.

- The co-workers are split off by group members.

Good preparation for the task of co-working is also very important and clear and honest communication between the co-facilitators will go a long way towards preventing problems before they occur. Hodge (1985) provides a long list of questions that intending co-workers can work through in preparation for facilitating a group together. These cover most of the issues identified above.

Another safeguard is to employ the service of a consultant or mentor. Facilitating a group either on your own or with a co-worker is a difficult and demanding task. Groupwork is almost by definition more complex than one-to-one work as there are so many more variables and you are engaged with so many more people. Facilitators come under pressure from the group. The feelings aroused in the group and the workers can be very powerful.

Being aware and coping with your own feelings, recognising and responding to emotion in the group, while conducting the group programme and following through the group aims all at once, is far from easy. Having one or more co-facilitators is often a great help, for the reasons given earlier, but the co-working relationship itself introduces another variable in the group equation. It is very difficult for co-facilitators to sort out difficulties in their relationship on their own. Often they will conspire together not to discuss them. For all these reasons it is very useful for groupworkers to have someone, a consultant or mentor, with whom they can discuss what is happening in the group and to help them think of ways of sorting out issues. During mentoring sessions, the workers can explore the power relationships between them. Issues such as sectarianism, sexuality, race and gender need to be addressed by co-workers in terms of how they work together, what role models they provide, how they deal with conscious or unconscious racism, sexism etc. directed towards one or more of them. We think that for the new groupworker mentoring is essential.

Intervening

Denise and Shakila need to take responsibility for creating a supportive environment and to state and or negotiate boundaries. There are personal and interpersonal issues in every group, whether articulated or not. They include the elements which make up who we are and how we function, including our gender, age, faith, ethnicity, sexual and cultural identity as well as communication styles, personality, and learning preferences. Other process issues concern the cultural norms of participants, the group's stage of development, relationships and agreements, both stated and un-stated, inside and outside the group. For best practice the workers need to take responsibility for managing all of these elements and to be equipped with the skills to do so.

Heron (1989) identifies six categories of intervention.

- Supportive (affirming the worth and value of all the individuals in the group, including their qualities, attitudes or actions).

- Catalytic (encouraging self-awareness, self-directed learning and living).

- Cathartic (enabling group members to discharge, to relive painful emotion, primarily grief, fear or anger by being supportive and not pushing, but by giving value to an emotional response).

- Informing (providing information, knowledge or meaning at the level it is required, by checking out with the group what they need or require).

- Confronting (helping the group or an individual to raise their consciousness of some limiting attitude or behaviour of which they are relatively unaware, and to do this in a supportive way).

- Prescribing (drawing attention to the consequences of certain behaviour and suggesting an alternative or alternatives).

ACTIVITY 7.4

Thinking about the categories of intervention listed above; make a list of the skills that you now think Denise and Shakila need in order to facilitate the group.

The *Power to Change* manual (Martins et al. 2008, p18) lists the following skills required for facilitation of the programme, or, for that matter, any other groupwork programme.

- Excellent group management skills, including the ability to plan and facilitate group sessions effectively.

- Excellent communication skills, including clear verbal delivery and positive body language.

- Active listening skills, and the ability to respond empathetically to the group members.

- The ability to challenge participants, where relevant and necessary, in a non-confrontational but assertive manner.

- The ability to handle issues, such as anger, in the group.

- An understanding of professional boundaries and the facilitator's limitations within the group, e.g. not getting personally involved with the women's lives.

- The ability to work on their own initiative and plan their workload effectively.

- The ability to apply anti-discriminatory practice and equal opportunities into all aspects of the support group.

- The ability to evaluate the effectiveness of the support group and report on the outcomes.

Having planned out the groupwork programme, Denise and Shakila's first task is to meet with each individual potential member. This does not happen in every groupwork programme but is good practice for the following reasons.

- **Introductions** It will be beneficial for the prospective members to meet Denise and/or Shakila – to put a face to the name and make some assessment of the facilitator, for example in terms of warmth, openness etc. It will help them to get an initial impression of the group member and any special individual characteristics that they may have to take into account.

- **Provision of information about the group** People will want to know what benefits the group will have for them individually, what the activities will be and what demands membership will make of them. They will want to know who else is going to be in the group. Confidentiality and safety will certainly be issues.

- **Promoting motivation** It is important for Denise and Shakila not to set out to *sell* the group. However, if the group members are not well motivated towards the group, especially at this stage, the group will fail. In this initial contact, the clients' attitudes will be greatly influenced by their perception of the facilitators. It is important to listen carefully to concerns expressed because they will help shape and improve the planning.

- **Ensuring an actual match between the needs of the members and the services the group will provide** A meeting is an opportunity to explore the potential members' motivations and to make sure that the group is relevant to their needs. In this case considerable importance is placed on whether the individual can safely participate and for this reason a risk assessment is conducted.

- **Individualisation** Having individual contact with prospective group members will be affirming and validating for them. The client will be assured that the purpose of the group is to meet their needs and that they are valued as an individual person.

- **Giving people choice** It is important that people know that they have choices and that their right to choose is a central issue for the group facilitators. Allowing and negotiating around choice is central to the philosophy of groupwork as an empowering and democratic method.

Monitoring

Monitoring includes all of the tasks that help facilitators understand how the group is working and developing so that they are gathering information and making changes as and if needed. Listening, reflecting, talking through and note taking may all be involved, both alone and with co-facilitators, with group members, colleagues and other profession-als as appropriate. Facilitators monitor and give attention to each zone of their awareness at a personal, individual, interpersonal and a group level. How am I reacting and what am I feeling? What is going on with each individual? What is going on between individuals? Is there anything happening at the level of the whole group, perhaps an atmosphere of hostility, of sadness, of happiness, of success?

Maintaining

Maintenance is all the tasks around the edge of the group meeting time. It can be helpful to look at three general (but overlapping) groups of maintenance tasks: practical, profes-sional and membership.

Practical tasks

These are all the things Denise and Shakila need to do to make sure the venue they have chosen and room they will use are appropriate and supportive for the group. Their inten-tion is to create a comfortable and welcoming space for the group. Doel (2006) has identified that the success of any one group often depends on very time-consuming prac-ticalities including:

- securing sufficient funding;

- allocating time to prepare and run a group and more importantly getting the timing of a group right for sufficient people to be able attend;

- choice of venue and access;

- transport, for individuals to and from a venue;

- health and safety including the provision of first aid, the consideration of fire hazards and access for people with disabilities or wheelchair users;

- a list of all the people attending the group, with contact details so the facilitators know when everyone has arrived.

Professional tasks

Included here are all the practical things that Denise and Shakila might need to do to pre-pare for facilitating the group – rehearsing exercises to be used, reviewing the last session, revising plans for the rest of the group and so on.

Membership tasks

This includes all those tasks that are required to keep the memebrship of the group full and actively engaged. It may be necessary for Denise and Shakila to 'chase-up' people who have missed sessions, partly in the interests of safety but also to ascertain whether an absence results from a problem the individual is having with the content or the group experience.

Coping with unexpected or unhelpful responses

RESEARCH SUMMARY

Williams (1966) identified a number of common anxieties amongst trainee group facilitators. These were:

- *encountering unmanageable resistance;*

- *losing control of the group;*

- *excessive hostility breaking out;*

- *acting out by group members;*

- *overwhelming dependency demands;*

- *group disintegration.*

Williams's research is interesting in a number of ways, not least in that it highlights how little imagination trainees have in thinking about what might go wrong. Whitaker (2001 p143) states I have a sizeable list of such descriptions. The situations referred to include: *(my emphasis) and then goes on to list thirty different difficult scenarios.*

Unfortunately it is neither possible nor wise to set out a long list of problems and matched solutions. More useful is the provision of general guidance. When things go wrong, there can be a tendency to see the difficulty as lying with the group members. Frequently, 'unhelpful' or 'difficult' behaviour by individuals or the group as a whole is more usefully understood as a symptom of some other problem related to the group process, the planning or resources of the group or the conduct of the groupworker/s.

Douglas (1991) identifies five potentially problematic areas for group facilitators.

- How the facilitator/s perform the role – what they know and how well they know it, their style of facilitation, their level of skill and the roles they adopt in the group, their aims and objectives and the extent to which all of these are congruent with any other facilitators involved.

- Supervision, training and development of groupworkers. This area is closely related to the first.

- Group members – their individual characteristics and behaviour.

- The group as a unit or system (whole-group problems) – problems which arise out of the way the group is structured and those which are to do with the nature and quality of the group's performance and processes.

- The conditions under which the group operated – external factors such as how it is organised, the venue and time and resources allocated to it, issues to do with colleagues, managers and the community; internal factors – the numbers, the construction of the group and how it is designed.

Difficulties arising from the group itself and its members

Reconceptualising 'Problems'

When faced with a difficult or unexpected situation in the group itself, we need to be able to analyse what is going on, so that we can make an appropriate response.

- **Problem or opportunity?** It is useful, as Whitaker (2001) suggests, to understand what is happening as an opportunity, rather than a problem. If a group member launches a verbal attack on another, for example, it may be an opportunity to have a useful discussion about issues such as the relationships in the group as a whole, acceptable ways of confronting, the group rules, or to provide feedback.

- **Problem for whom?** What may be seen as a big problem by the groupworker may not necessarily be a problem for anyone else. A useful question for facilitators to ask is 'For whom is this a problem?' If the answer is for 'the facilitator', then they know it is something which they are going to have to think about in terms of themselves and either adjust to or live with. If the answer is an individual in the group, they need to decide what action to take to protect them from harm. If it is a whole group problem, then they need to think in terms of a whole group response. If it is a problem for people outside of the group, they will probably need to do some work with the neighbours, colleagues or whomever it concerns.

- **Who benefits?** Many situations which you perceive as problems are actually functional in some way, either for the group as a whole or for individuals. Perhaps a group silence is a response to some difficult issue that has been raised and people need time to think things through or to protect themselves.

Responding to individual and whole group situations

Brown (1992) provides a useful framework of possible responses to difficult situations that may arise out of individual and whole group scenarios.

Do 'nothing' It is a good idea to wait a little while before making any intervention; providing no one is being hurt. Let the mud settle. Learn to wait, watch and listen. This way you are more likely to attend to the needs of the group rather than your own. Perhaps the group will solve the problem if given time and, if not, it is useful to have time to think.

Indirect approaches The worker does not confront the situation directly, or indeed even mention that there is a difficulty but finds an indirect way of dealing with the problem. For example, the simple tactic of sitting next to someone can be very effective in providing non-verbal support, without drawing unwanted attention to the individual or can make it easier to control undesirable behaviour.

Direct approaches Direct approaches involve making explicit reference to the problem. Brown (1992) gives three categories of direct approaches.

- **Speak directly to the individual at the centre of the problem** For example, where someone is monopolising the conversation in the group, the facilitator can point out to them that they are doing all the work in the group and it is time to have a rest and let the others have a turn.

- **Speak directly to the rest of the group** 'You seem to be allowing Moira to do all the talking tonight' – sometimes saying 'what is', naming the issue, is a sufficient strategy to resolve a difficulty.

- **Speak to the group as a whole** 'I am thinking that we don't seem to be very together tonight. There seems to be a lot of tension around. Has anyone else noticed that? What do you think is going on just now? Maybe we can talk about this for a while and see if we can find a better way forward.'

Of these three strategies, Brown suggests the last is to be preferred, as it does not reinforce possible splits in the group, nor does it locate the difficulty in a particular person or persons.

- *Make contact outside the group* Before deciding to make contact with a member outside the group, facilitators need to consider the following points. In seeing this person alone, are we missing an opportunity to facilitate a problem that lies in the group but is manifesting itself through this individual? Even if we are satisfied that this is a difficulty concerning this individual, would it be beneficial to try to resolve it in the group, so that all the members can benefit from the intervention? In seeing this person outside the group, are we perhaps making things worse for the person by pathologising them, or worse for the group by entering into a special relationship with this one individual?

CHAPTER SUMMARY

- Groupwork is a social work method that contains a strong element of clients helping themselves and others.

- It has certain advantages and also disadvantages of which facilitators need to be aware.

- The main facilitator tasks are planning, intervening, maintaining and monitoring. All of these require considerable attention on the part of the facilitators and while the success of the group depends on each equally the task of planning is probably the most time consuming.

- Difficulties inevitably present themselves for the facilitators during the course of the group. Success in resolving them depends on understanding that this is a normal part of the groupwork process and that they require some thought, analysis and confidence in handling them.

FURTHER READING

Brown, A (1992) *Groupwork*. 3rd edition. Aldershot: Ashgate Publishing.

Although published twenty years ago, this remains one of the most straightforward and clearly written guides to groupwork planning and facilitation.

Lindsay, T and Orton, S (2011) *Groupwork Practice in Social Work*. 2nd edition. Exeter: Learning Matters.

A text in this *Transforming Social Work Practice* series and therefore written specifically to address the learning needs of social work students, this book provides a hands-on guide to the practicalities of planning, establishing, facilitating and evaluating social work group projects. Much of what appears in this chapter is derived from this text.

Chapter 8

Motivational interviewing

James Marshall

Introduction

The use of motivational interviewing in social work practice has, compared to other methods, a relatively short existence. Although it had been developing since the 1980s, propagated by theorists such as Miller (1983) and was considered an alternative model to direct persuasion for facilitating behavioural change in clients, it has been used mainly by clinicians and therapists from the psychology discipline. Relatively recently, motivational interviewing has become part of the social work 'toolkit', with its main protagonists being social workers and probation officers working in the areas of mental health and criminal justice, where it is often used to change behaviour in the area of substance abuse and addiction. However, as this chapter will demonstrate, the potential use of motivational interviewing in many areas of social work practice to bring about change in clients' lives is expanding. We know from evidence-based research (Munro 2011) that simply telling clients what to do, informed by agency-led assessments and social work plans that plot how they need to change an undesirable behaviour, is rarely effective in practice. In all areas of social work, recurring clients' problems come around again, in the continual assessment and reassessment roundabout.

Motivational interviewing has been described succinctly by Miller and Rollnick as a *client-centered, directive method for enhancing intrinsic motivation to change by exploring and resolving ambivalence* (2002, p25). Ambivalence is a key concept in motivational interviewing as it prevents people from making the changes they desire. Motivational interviewing is a method and style of practice, initially developed for working with addictions and substance abuse, but has since been found to be effective in work with a variety of clients' situations, from parenting issues to work with sex offenders.

ACTIVITY *8.1*

Before we examine the approach in more detail in this chapter, examining the literature and research, reread the previous paragraph containing the quotation from Miller and Rollnick (2002).

Part A

Consider the other types of social work practice situations in which motivational interviewing may be applicable.

Part B

Make a list of the types of client problems you have encountered or read about, and list beside it the desired change outcome.

Presenting problem	Desired change outcome
Example Children are not attending school, hygiene poor, etc.	Father and mother complete a parenting course and their skills and motivation to care for their children increase, evidenced by better school attendance and hygiene over a three-month period

COMMENT

You could consider some of the following types of situation.

- *Other methods of intervention with clients have 'failed'.*

- *Practice issues require change to improve a client's situation but are currently 'stuck'.*

- *Clients and families have been re-referred with similar social problems and costly resources and intervention methods have been used before with little or no effect.*

- *Other methods of assessing a client's ability to change have proven to be inaccurate.*

RESEARCH SUMMARY

In the 1980s research began to show that confrontational approaches to dealing with addictions were simply not effective and relapse was common. In the criminal justice system re-offending rates were high and the costs of repeat offender incarceration and punishment strategies were expensive and deemed not effective for society (McMurran 2002).

Andrews and Bonta (2003) state that, *in our own field of criminal justice, evidence-based practice as outlined by criminologists has recommended that justice staff be responsive to motivational issues with offenders* (quoted in Clark 2005, p1). A range of professionals, including psychologists, social workers and probation staff, involved mainly in criminal justice and addiction work, began to explore and implement strategies that recognised and encouraged client autonomy, self-determination and the use of positive reinforcement.

Motivational interviewing emphasises the creation of a constructive and empathic relationship that helps the client to evaluate problem behaviours, such as addictions, alcohol misuse, gambling, for themselves, within the context of their own life goals and values. It particularly seeks to explore and resolve *ambivalence* about personal behaviour and seeks to encourage thinking about and achieving change. Prominent in the literature on motivational interviewing is the conceptualisation of *resistance* as a product of client–social worker interaction that can be influenced adversely by inappropriate practitioner behaviour.

Compared to non-directive counselling, for instance (see Chapter 2), motivational interviewing is more goal-directed and focused. The practitioner is intentionally directive, with the aim of getting the client to recognise and address ambivalence issues and create a dynamic for change in their lives. From the beginning, motivational interviewing has been practical in its focus, probably because it emerged from the practical challenges faced by practitioners and clinicians (Miller and Rollnick 2002). The challenge associated with working with clients who had alcohol problems, such as denial, resistance, avoidance and what was termed 'hiding behind the label', led to a new field of research that sought ways of overcoming these factors in bringing about change (Brown and Miller 1993; Holder et al. 1991).

Key components of motivational interviewing
The five central principles of motivational interviewing

- **Express empathy** by using reflective listening to convey understanding of the client's point of view and underlying drives.

Key learning points
- Acceptance facilitates change.

- Skilful reflective listening is fundamental.

- Ambivalence is normal.

- Develop the discrepancy between the client's most deeply held values and their current behaviour.

Key learning points
- An awareness of consequences is important.
- A discrepancy between present behaviour and important goals will motivate change.
- The client should present the arguments for change.

- **Avoid argumentation** that can lead to defensiveness in clients.

Key learning points
- Arguments are counterproductive.
- Defending breeds defensiveness.
- Resistance is a signal to change strategies.
- Labelling is unnecessary.

- **Sidestep resistance** by responding with empathy and understanding.

Key learning points
- Momentum can be used to good advantage.
- Perceptions can be shifted.
- New perceptions are invited but not imposed.
- The client is a valuable resource in finding solutions to problems.

- **Support self-efficacy** by building the client's confidence that change is possible.

Key learning points
- Belief in the possibility of change is an important motivator.
- The client is responsible for the change.
- The approach can increase confidence in other therapeutic techniques.

Source: Adapted from Miller and Rollnick (2002)

Summary

Motivational interviewing is an effective way of helping people to address current or potential problems, particularly clients who are reluctant to change. It is intended to resolve ambivalence, create a dynamic for change; it can be brief and can also be a pre-requisite for longer-term therapeutic work. In relation to the working principles, it is worth emphasising that change remains the responsibility of the client (Miller and Rollnick 2002). The aim is to increase the client's internal motivation, with them in most cases being facilitated to present the need and reasons for change in their life.

The 'cycle of change' model in practice

Related to the development of motivational interviewing has been the 'transtheoretical' model of change developed by DiClemente and Prochaska (1998). It suggested six stages that people go through when undertaking a change. As part of this chapter, you can quickly test these stages by matching them to any life change you have gone through yourself, or a change you are thinking about making.

Figure 8.1 The cycle of change

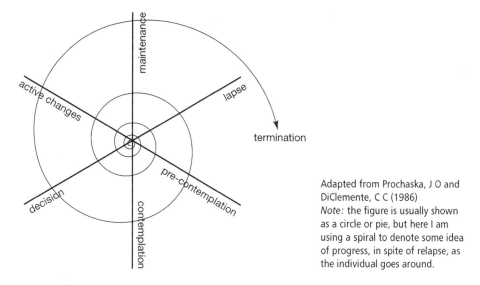

Adapted from Prochaska, J O and
DiClemente, C C (1986)
Note: the figure is usually shown
as a circle or pie, but here I am
using a spiral to denote some idea
of progress, in spite of relapse, as
the individual goes around.

The six 'cycle of change' stages can be briefly summarised as follows (see Figure 8.1).

Stage 1 Pre-contemplation

At this stage you have not even thought about changing and may be happy where you are, or have simply not considered that the change is possible.

Stage 2 Contemplation

You are thinking about change and part of you wants to change but another part of you wants to stay as you are. You are ambivalent; this concept will be examined in more detail later in the chapter.

Stage 3 Decision

You have decided to change and are going to do something about it. You may still have some ambivalence but you are going to make an effort to change.

Stage 4 Action to change

You undertake work to bring about the change you want. This might be a programme of action, getting information, making choices, or doing things differently.

Stage 5 Maintenance

At this stage you are maintaining your new behaviour. Often at first through a conscious effort, later it becomes your unconscious habitual behaviour.

Stage 6 Lapse

Sometimes called relapse, but this feels too much like failure. Everyone can have lapses from time to time. For some people this simply reminds them why they wanted to change and motivates them to continue with their new habit. For others it takes them back to the contemplation stage with high levels of ambivalence that need to be worked through again. However, lapse is not always failure, only a stage in the learning process.

Comment

We all attempt to change our behaviour from time to time – and we often fail. DiClemente and Prochaska (1988) developed their model in work with smokers and found that six or seven attempts were often required before termination.

The 'spirit' of motivational interviewing

What is referred to as the motivational spirit is the style of practice with the client and your disposition towards them. It is different from the techniques employed and comes from within the practitioner. The spirit is in essence a counselling style and part of the therapeutic relationship. Wahab (2005) termed it as *an availability and willingness to be present enough with a client, to glimpse their inner world* (p48).

ACTIVITY 8.2

Consider a habit or behaviour that you have attempted to change or have actually changed in your life – losing weight, giving up chocolate, drinking less, stopping smoking, watching less TV, taking more exercise, for example. Apply the six-stage model proposed by DiClemente and Prochaska (1998) to your identified situation. Please try to answer the following questions.

- *How long was the pre-contemplative stage for you?*

- *What factors influenced your decision to change (consider the impact of others)?*

- *How was the change in behaviour actioned and maintained?*

- *If you have lapsed since, how did you view this?*

The concept of unconditional positive regard, according to Rogers (1957), presupposes a non-judgemental, empathic relationship, in which the practitioner creates the circumstances that facilitate change in clients (see Chapter 2). The practitioner using motivational interviewing does not engage in a punitive or coercive fashion to argue with clients that they have a problem. Instead, the qualities required of the motivational interviewer, such as empathy, self-determination, dignity, and respect appear to have particular significance in producing behavioural change and sustainable outcomes (Miller et al. 1980). These values, essential for the motivational interviewer, fit very well the Social Care Council's 'codes of practice', under which social workers now work.

CASE STUDY

The Cartwright family

David is released from prison and returns home. He has been seeing a probation officer about his gambling while inside but is very worried that he will return to gambling now that he is released. In fact, Brenda is suspicious that he has started again already as she found a betting slip in his coat pocket, but she could not quite make out the date. The multidisciplinary team agree that Aisha should work with David using motivational interviewing.

COMMENT

- Given the previous problems associated with David's gambling, this could be a major crisis/problem for the family.

- David has already served a custodial sentence and if he has been gambling excessively again, this could affect his relationship with the criminal justice system. The probation officer may need to be informed.

- David and Brenda's relationship may deteriorate further if there is no trust between them.

- If David is being wrongly accused and it was an old betting slip this may also pose problems. Aisha may need permission from Brenda to address the issue with David. (This may taint her initial role as a practitioner hoping to use the motivational interviewing approach.)

- Aisha may have to work out her role in relation to any ongoing work by the probation officer.

ACTIVITY 8.3

In relation to the literature and research on motivational interviewing, consider the following questions.

- What stage is David at in relation to the 'cycle of change' model?

- As a practitioner, how appropriate do you think a motivational interview approach would be in addressing David's potential, re-emerging gambling problem?

- In working with David and Brenda, how would you introduce the idea of using this approach and how would you create a positive belief from David that he can change his addictive type behaviour?

COMMENT

- *Remember, labelling David as someone who is a 'gambler' may not be conducive to engaging him or producing change.*

- *The confrontational approach to denial is not advisable in motivational interviewing.*

- *David's own views on his gambling and his motivation to change must be assessed.*

- *Resistance can be met with reflection.*

- *Goals and change strategies must be negotiated and agreed between client and practitioner.*

- *Lapse is part of the learning process.*

Motivation interviewing in practice: A phased approach

Building motivation for change

The first session with David will be crucial in setting the scene and approach to the work. Practitioners should avoid the *question–answer trap* (Miller and Rollnick, 2002). Such a session can be unproductive and produce the stereotypical interaction between an active *expert* and a passive *client*. Miller and Rollnick (2002) suggest using a pre-session questionnaire, using open-ended questions, to establish baseline information from the client. In the first meeting, the approach will reduce the need for less immediate responses from the practitioner to any answers given; instead he or she can use more reflective listening. The client needs the space to become more pro-active and empowered, especially at the early stage.

The second practice to avoid is the *confrontational–denial trap* (Miller and Rollnick 2002). In this instance, the practitioner begins to tell the client they have – or may have – a gambling problem, for example. The client can then predictably respond by denying they have a problem or else minimising it – assuming, as we know, that they may be in a state of ambivalence. If the motivational interviewing practitioner confronts the perceived denial then the client can feel trapped. Clients may come to a session with many preconceived ideas of how you will react, and they may have a range of fears, hopes or concerns about the process. The aim of the motivational interviewer is to create an atmosphere of acceptance and trust, make the client do most of the talking and use only open-ended questions when necessary. Here are some examples.

- 'I assume the fact that you are here means you have some things you wish to talk over with me.'

- 'What would you like to discuss?'

- 'I would like to understand how you see things.'

The questions can become more focused, based on information provided; and, in the early contemplation stage, both sides of the issue can be explored. An example is given below.

- 'I understand that you are here to talk about your gambling; so help me get a picture of what it is like. What do you enjoy about gambling and what part of it is not so enjoyable?'

Listening reflectively is a key skill in motivational interviewing. The practitioner is not passive but decides what to reflect back and what to emphasise in order to reinforce certain key issues that the client has raised. Clients respond well to affirmation and support during this process. An example would be the following.

- 'I appreciate it must have been difficult for you to come here to discuss these issues, and I think it's great you want to do something or change something about this.'

The practitioner adopts a problem-change approach and it is important that the client be facilitated to elicit self-motivational statements. Below are some examples of problem recognition or self-motivational statements from a client.

- 'I never really realised I was gambling so much.'

- 'This may be more serious than I thought.'

- 'I feel so stupid starting to gamble again.'

Another stage in the process is then to get the client to look forward and describe what their change goal might be (in an ideal world perhaps). Here the *miracle question* described in Chapter 10 is useful. It may take a number of motivational interview sessions to reach this point but the practitioner must support the client and move at their pace. The client, hearing themselves use these self-motivational statements, can become more aware of the discrepancy between their overall goals and their present actions and lifestyle. These self-motivational statements can be encouraged and resistance to change may diminish as a result. The client can be supported in designing a change strategy in relation to their current issues and this should include a lapse strategy, for encouraging ongoing contact with the motivational interviewer.

The practitioner has a role in encouraging and strengthening the commitment to change. At this point, the client is ready to change, the window of opportunity may be limited, and the client may ask you for advice on what you think they should now do. At this stage, it is quite appropriate to offer your best advice but you should have explored fully the client's ideas for a change plan. The practitioner can assist the client to set clear goals using questions such as:

- 'What is it that you would like to change?'

- 'What do you think is the first step?'

The client's goals may not correspond exactly with yours. For example, there may be a reduction in the activity rather than total abstinence, or vice versa. Nevertheless, methods of achieving the goals must be chosen, with a variety of options explored. A written plan in the client's language is advisable as this will elicit commitment and it then has a better chance of translation into action. It is worth remembering that at any stage 'lapse', as opposed to relapse, is part of the learning process and the cycle of change, and for Prochaska and Di Clemente (1986) it is as much a positive motivator as a negative inhibitor for further change.

Comment

In the case study David may well be in the lapse phase of the cycle of change in relation to his gambling, and the practitioner must explore his views on this. A supportive, empathic response is essential at this stage to prevent permanent lapse and disengagement from the change cycle.

RESEARCH SUMMARY

The aim of the research by Harper and Hardy (2000) was to evaluate motivational interviewing as a method of improving probation officers' practice with offenders who had drug and alcohol dependency problems. The research, based on quantitative data, was looking at two key areas:

- *whether motivational interviewing had any effect on offender attitudes towards drug and alcohol misuse and their offending behaviour;*

- *the views of probation officers on the use and impact of motivational interviewing in their practice.*

The design was quasi-experimental, using a non-random sample of probation officers from four probation teams. A control group of probation officers was also selected who used another preferred method of working with offenders, a cognitive behaviour approach. Each officer in each group was asked to recruit the first six offenders who had recognised drug and/or alcohol problems. CRIME-PICS II scales (Frude et al. 1994) were used to score 'deviant' or 'criminal' attitudes for offenders before and after the use of motivational interviewing methods and the alternative method of intervention. The sample probation officers received motivational interviewing training prior to the research period.

Although the sample sizes were relatively small, Harper and Hardy (2000) concluded that the CRIME-PICS II scores indicated a significant improvement in the groups using motivational interviewing. Offenders in this group scored better, compared to the control group, on four of the five questionnaire scales used by the probation service: evaluation of crime as worthwhile; perceptions of current life problems; anticipation of reoffending and general attitude to offending.

Harper and Hardy (2000) found that motivational techniques had a beneficial effect on the attitudes of offenders with substance misuse problems, over and above the effect of non-MI intervention (p399). The analysis of probation officers' attitudes towards motivational interviewing indicated that the training had raised their expectations of using this method in their practice and they noted several advantages in using the technique, despite the time factor involved. The researchers concluded:

RESEARCH SUMMARY *continued*

In our research we found all offenders, irrespective of mode of intervention, improved their questionnaire scores when in contact with the probation service, irrespective of mode of intervention. MI however was more effective that non-MI work in bringing about change in offenders who had drug and alcohol problems (p399).

COMMENT

In the current climate of evidence-based practice developments, and a call by regulatory and funding bodies to demonstrate effectiveness in social work practice, the case for using motivational interviewing when dealing with certain addictive and other behavioural problems appears to be growing. The current alternative of using traditional practitioner-led assessments and change plans for clients is not sustainable, given the obvious failure and re-referral rates. The use of motivational interviewing is time consuming and the contemplation stage can be lengthy, but if it reduces any of the usual 'no change' outcomes, then it might pay dividends for practitioners, faced with often intractable problems and social issues.

CHAPTER SUMMARY

- Motivational interviewing grew out of the substance misuse and addiction treatment fields in the 1980s.

- Research showed that confrontational approaches were simply not successful.

- Motivational interviewing has been adapted by social work and other professionals and has proven to be a significant tool for facilitating positive behaviour change in clients' lives.

- Motivational interviewing encourages autonomy, self-determination and positive reinforcement.

- Motivational interviewing is a client centred directive for enhancing intrinsic motivation to change by exploring and resolving ambivalence.

- The spirit of motivational interviewing is the counselling style and a type of therapeutic relationship.

- Motivational interviewing is linked to the six-stage cycle of change, but they are not the same.

- Motivational interviewing in practice has measureable benefits for some clients.

- The method uses specific techniques such as avoiding confrontation and labelling, encouraging a positive change mode, reflective listening, and self-motivational change recognition.

- Motivational interviewing has a growing research base that demonstrates its effectiveness in all areas of practice, not just addictions.

FURTHER READING

DiClemente, C C and Prochaska, J O (1998) Toward a comprehensive, transtheoretical model of change: Stages of change and addictive behaviors. In Miller, W R and Heather, N (eds) *Treating addictive behaviors*. 2nd edition. New York: Plenum.

This is the second edition of the earliest descriptions of the model of change, now universally used in relation to motivational interviewing techniques.

Miller, W R and Rollnick, S (eds) (2002) *Motivational interviewing: Preparing people for change*. 2nd edition. New York: The Guilford Press.

This is one of the definitive texts on motivational interviewing, edited by two of its earliest exponents. It has some excellent practice examples of questions and answers used in work with clients.

Chapter 9
Family therapy and systemic approaches

Cathy Jayat

ACHIEVING A SOCIAL WORK DEGREE

This chapter will help you to develop the following capabilities from the **Professional Capabilities Framework**:

- **Professionalism**
  Identify and behave as a professional social worker committed to professional development.
- **Knowledge**
  Apply knowledge of social sciences, law and social work practice theory.
- **Intervention and skills**
  Use judgement and authority to intervene with individuals, families and communities to promote independence, provide support and prevent harm, neglect and abuse.

It will also introduce you to the following standards as set out in the 2008 social work subject benchmark statement.
5.1.1 Social work services and clients.
5.1.4 Social work theory.
5.1.5 The nature of social work practice.
5.5.1 Managing problem solving activities.
5.5.3 Analysis and synthesis.
5.5.4 Intervention and evaluation.

Introduction

This chapter will help you to make sense of and begin to develop an understanding of the main ideas inherent in working systemically with families. We will consider the historical context which gave rise to the development of systemic family therapy, and take a brief look at each of the three main schools of influence: strategic family therapy, structural family therapy and Milan systemic family therapy.

Historical context

With most models used in social work practice, attention to context is important and this is especially true of Systemic Family Therapy. Let us first look at the context and then map the territory for you from the beginnings of family therapy in the mid-1950s.

Our work with children and families is influenced by changes in practice ideas, in family networks, attitudes to child-rearing, and positions taken by the state. Social policy continually re-evaluates the roles of parents and carers, the function of family and the position of children in society as a whole.

Millar (2008) reminds us that the roles of men and women in the family, and the state's views about family have been changing and fluctuating since the post-war British welfare state, with the twentieth century seeing a dramatic increase in the caring professions as the state has vacillated between direct and indirect intervention in the lives of its citizens. Early state welfare provisions were premised on the continuing stability of traditional family roles: the man works to provide financial stability for the family and the woman remains at home to maintain and nurture the family. Women, effectively, became the main point of contact between the family and state services such as health care, education and social care services. The state struggles to accept and validate the changing pattern in family life in recent decades. As yet we have no clearly linked-up family policy, no Department of the Family – and no consistent strategies for children. This continues to be painfully apparent in the repeated shortcomings highlighted by a variety of inquiry reports into child abuse which continue to emphasise the need for better communication between professionals and systems engaged in work with children and families. Policies can be well intentioned, yet are often poorly co-ordinated, and in practice under-resourced. The social care field is governed by market ideas inherent in mixed economies of care and in many settings this often spells constant argument and battle to obtain sufficient funding just to keep staffing levels at an absolute minimum. Referrals which receive most concentrated input are often those at the higher end of the 'safeguarding' end of the spectrum. All this is at a time when meaningful family support and prevention of family breakdown need also to be priorities. Ongoing changes and restructuring in health and social services throughout the UK have presented social work with many challenges. Legislative and policy changes have affected our practices, our lifestyles and our world views.

Pinkerton and Campbell (2002) invite social workers in Northern Ireland to consider the impact of their experience of having lived through the 'troubles' upon themselves as professionals and on their clients. Similarly we need to consider this in wider contexts – how can we possibly hold open and meaningful dialogue with families and children, if the contexts of discrimination, fear, poverty, violence and oppression in our society are not given appropriate voice in our talks with each other? This fits well with the systemic principle that when we work with people we work with the whole person within the whole system and not just parts of it. Cecchin et al. (1994) emphasise the importance of developing awareness of our own prejudices. They stress that the very heart of therapy is to examine the interplay between those prejudices in a way which is experienced as non-threatening to our clients. Therapeutic encounters become polarised when the prejudices of both client and worker become locked. This in turn can lead to workers pathologising families and developing the notion of them as being 'resistant'.

The emphasis on challenging oppressive practices encourages us to examine ourselves in relation to our colleagues and our clients and fits well with the post-modernist world view of family therapy and systemic practices. We are reminded that social work is about the family and the individual in the social context and failing to address that undermines the effectiveness of our practice.

There are consequentially many challenges for us as social workers in carrying forward the changes in ideas which influence our practice: how to work in truly respectful and empowering fashion; how to engage in meaningful partnership practices with our clients; how to address power differentials; how to notice the impact on self and on those with whom we come into contact of dominant discourses (White and Epston 1990) in our lives and find different means and ways of viewing which will facilitate and permit change; the challenge of moving on from deficit models and descriptions of clients towards more collaborative and strengths-based models of practice.

The three main schools of family therapy and systemic practice

Drawing on the conception of systems theory by the biologist Ludwig Von Bertalanffy, therapists in the 1940s began to see families as open systems – engaged in transactional processes. They became interested in noticing interactional patterns and the relationships between parts of the system. General systems theory states that a system is a whole and that its component parts can only be understood as functions of the whole system (Bertalanffy 1968). Bertalanaffy built on the idea of circularity to provide a theoretical base for biological systems and recognised that patterns develop when elements of a system interact.

Walrond-Skinner (1976) uses the analogy of the game of chess.

> *It would not be possible to gain much understanding of chess, simply by looking at individual pieces; one would need to examine the game as a whole, and to take note of how the movement of one piece affects the position and meaning of every other piece on the board.*
>
> Walrond-Skinner (1976, pp11–12)

CASE STUDY

Aisha continues to work with David who is maintaining control of his gambling. The relationship between Sandra and her mother has improved but there are still many rows and Sandra's eczema has worsened. The school has complained about Philip's behaviour. He has been sent home from school on occasions for cheeking teachers and was suspended for three days for fighting with another pupil. Brian is still unemployed and divides his time between being in bed, watching TV and surfing the net. It seems to Aisha that, as soon as there is an improvement in one area of the family's life, another area gets worse.

ACTIVITY 9.1

Consider the case of the Cartwright family as presented so far. What indications are there that what Aisha may be dealing with is not just a collection of individual difficulties but a family system that is not functioning to its capacity? List the reasons that this might be the case.

COMMENT

On the face of it, there is nothing to suggest that the problems are anything other than individual difficulties. However, on closer examination, there are some indications to suggest otherwise. Brenda reacts badly to traumatic events in the family, resulting in her depression and anxiety and perhaps adding to the children's distress. All is not well in the marriage relationship, which is characterised by a lack of openness and honesty. All the members of the family are showing signs of being under stress and not coping. A key indicator is that Aisha feels that when one area improves another gets worse. This is a typical indication of a systemic problem. You may have picked up some other indicators.

Gregory Bateson (1972), an anthropologist, provided much of the intellectual foundation of the emerging field of family therapy because of his ideas and studies of pattern and communication, influenced by the study of cybernetics in engineering and mechanical systems. The word *cybernetics* was coined by Norbert Weiner (1894–1964) to mean the science of communication and control in man and machine. The study of cybernetics proposed that causation was a continuous circular process, occurring over time. Cybernetics and systems theory presented a significant challenge to the existing psychiatric orthodoxy whose roots at that time were firmly in the psychodynamic realm. (For fuller discussion see Bateson, 1972, 1979; Watzlawick et al. 1967). Bateson brought to the field the idea that, if you were to intervene in a human system, you needed to become very aware of your influence and impact upon it. In fact, you then became a part of the system and had to attend to your part in it. He believed that the emphasis of our work with families should be on what happens between people, rather than on people's individual and innate characteristics. Still current and relevant to the practice of family therapy and systemic psychotherapy today are his ideas about patterns of information, feedback, circularity and recursiveness. Recursiveness refers to the repeating circular connectedness of an interactional process. For example, information provided by the client informs the social worker's next interaction, which in turn informs the client's response, and so on. Thus individuals both respond to and elicit feedback in relation to those with whom they interact. This recursive feedback is the basis of active listening skills and reflective statements in social work practice, in which meaning is made in conversation with clients, and social workers are encouraged to engage in a less deterministic and directive fashion.

Schools of family therapy began to emerge and evolve – among them Haley's *strategic approach*, Minuchin's *structural therapy* and later the *Milan systemic approach*. We will now look at each of these in turn.

Strategic family therapy

The main ideas emanating from this school are that change can be brought about by altering the family's attempted solution to a problem, the focus being on changing the presenting symptom. The belief here is that if the symptom can be removed (first order change) then the family will reorganise itself differently and more lasting change may follow (second order change). Strategic therapists hold the view that families generally manage to negotiate their own life transitions but can get stuck at transitional points on the life cycle. For example, when previously tried solutions do not appear to work the difficulty may become intensified by the family's efforts to control it and thus the solution actually becomes the problem.

CASE STUDY

In the past when Sandra was younger, Brenda was able to control Sandra's behaviour by 'laying down the law'. However, now that she is 16, not only does this strategy not work, but it also leads to heated arguments that have a very negative effect on the mother–daughter relationship. Sandra has responded to this by trying to recruit other members of the family, particularly her father, with some success. This in turn has then caused problems between Brenda and David. Brian, aged 20, has sided with his mother, resulting in a deteriorating relationship between Sandra and him. At times David has become angry with Brian, telling him to 'butt out' of things that don't concern him.

COMMENT

We can see here how a problem in the family arises out of difficulties it has encountered in responding to the development of the children. In this example, Brenda continues to respond to Sandra's behaviour as she did when she was younger and this snowballs into other relationship problems in the family. Similarly, David reacts to Brian's moving into a more adult role in the family, perhaps resenting what he sees as Brian's usurping his position as 'alpha male'.

The strategic therapist is interested in how the family organises itself around the symptom. The therapist adopting a position of neutrality or emotional distance is seen as important here and the therapist is the 'expert'. Strategic therapists often take the view that there is natural resistance to change where homeostasis (stability of the system) is threatened (Haley 1973). Working as a strategic therapist you are not interested in the past but in understanding here and now. Your stance is defined by action, not feeling. You seek to join with each family member, hear their view of the presenting problem, determine which solutions have already been attempted, which haven't worked, and what if anything has been tried and worked previously. Your interest is to build on what works and develop new strategies for coping. You offer a diagnosis and a prescription for cure, often in the form of tasks and directives and you use techniques such as reframing, directive and paradoxical tasks.

Techniques

- **Reframing** is when the therapist provides a plausible alternative explanation for the symptomatic behaviour presented. This offers new meaning to a situation, thus introducing a difference in the communication patterns, which allows for the possibility of change and more choice for clients. For example, a teenage girl's struggle with anorexia may be seen not as a sickness but as an effort to draw attention to difficulties within the family. Brenda is seen not as being authoritorian with Sandra but as showing caring. Sandra is seen not as disobedient but as demonstrating the natural behaviour of young people as they move towards independence.

- **Directive tasks** These are usually in the form of homework tasks to be undertaken between sessions. Most often a task will involve the whole family in carrying it out. For example, in a family such as the Cartwrights, where communication patterns are negative, family members may be encouraged to do or say something during the week which is aimed to be pleasant for other family members and all are asked to notice at least one behaviour from each family member during the week which pleased them. Often, when focused on positive behaviours, family members will notice more than one. These tasks have the effect of disrupting negative patterns of behaviour and increasing more desired patterns of communication and behaviour.

- **Paradoxical tasks** include encouragement to the family to do more of the undesired behaviour in the hope that their natural resistance to change will have the opposite effect. For example, a patient who complains of not being able to sleep may be asked for the coming week, usually for a prescribed period, to try to increase the symptomatic behaviour – and stay awake! The patient would usually be given the explanation that if they can succeed in making the symptom worse then this shows they are able to exert some control over it. Usually the symptomatic behaviour decreases (Dallos and Draper 2000).

ACTIVITY **9.2**

Thinking about our discussion of the strategic approach, what do you consider to be the advantages and disadvantages? List these on a piece of paper.

COMMENT

Advantages and disadvantages

While strategic therapists are concerned to work from a sensitive and respectful position, some criticisms of the approach see it as manipulative and distant from the family. It tends to see families more from a 'deficit' and 'dysfunctional' perspective, rather than from a collaborative strengths-based frame. This approach is sometimes seen as not client centred, and has much to do with conducting a tactical campaign to gain advantage. The power and influence of the therapist position, beliefs about resistance, and the therapist's designing of 'strategies' to overcome the 'resistance' make it an approach that does not share the view that families are their own best experts and that, with support, they are very capable of finding their own best solutions. The therapist's

COMMENT *continued*

use of 'paradoxical' tasks and their concept of 'resistance' have been heavily criticised by Dell (1982, cited in Dallos and Draper 2000) as overtly implying a positivist and mechanistic view of families. Instead, a family's inability to comply with and carry out tasks could be seen in terms of their absolute exasperation and sense of failure, which makes it even harder for them to trust. Dallos and Draper (2000) point out that this approach also seems to fail to view the family within gender inequality constraints constructed in society and may therefore unconsciously collude in disempowerment of women.

On the other hand, some of the ideas and techniques in the strategic approach are useful for encouraging and assisting change in family work sessions, such as taking transitional points on the family life cycle into consideration (while acknowledging the normative assumptions made about family in the family life cycle model) and reframing – which seems to have the effect in practice of freeing families to view a situation from another, more positive perspective.

Structural family therapy

Salvador Minuchin (1974) led the way in the development of structural therapy which highlighted the importance of structural organisation within the context of both the family and wider society. Within this approach clear boundaries regarding family roles and subsystems are seen as important; blurring of boundaries is seen to raise power imbalances, unhealthy cross-generational coalitions, and unhelpfully facilitate the development of enmeshed or detached relationships.

An idea is that the parents/carers need to be able to work collaboratively on the task of rearing their children.

In common with strategic approaches is the belief that problems occur at transitional points in the life cycle and the focus is also in the present. The Structural school believed that families develop structures and rules to organise family roles and functions. For example, families construct hierarchies (the parental subsystem having executive function), alliances between members and boundaries which constitute the rules which govern the functioning of the family and which are understood and accepted by family members.

ACTIVITY 9.3

Look over the case studies of the Cartwright family, presented in this and earlier chapters. What hierarchies might exist in the family? What subsystems might there be and what alliances? What might be the unspoken rules which govern the functioning of the family and its patterns of interaction and communication? Write your answers on a piece of paper or draw a diagram to illustrate this.

COMMENT

It seems clear from the earlier part of the story in this chapter, that there may be some alliances in the family. Sandra looks to her father for support in arguments with Brenda. Brian comes to Brenda's support. Brian sees himself as part of the parental hierarchy, feeling that he has the right to takes sides in how Sandra's behaviour is managed. Are there perhaps unspoken rules about David's gambling? Has it been an open secret which is not discussed?

Minuchin (1974) believed that when boundaries are diffuse, enmeshment will occur, or when they are rigid, disengagement between family members will occur. While structural therapists view enmeshment in a negative sense, feminist thinkers (for example, Walters et al., 1988) point out that women approach relationships differently to men, seeking a greater degree of genuine intimacy; so enmeshment can actually be a valued experience in connecting closely to another person. The structural therapist's goal is to restructure the family and create conditions which give rise to greater flexibility (Hayes 1991). The therapist must here also be highly directive. Minuchin (1974) claimed that therapeutic change occurs when the family's perception of reality is challenged; the family is given alternative possibilities that make sense to them and when new patterns and relationship structures emerge this then reinforces the possibility of real and meaningful change. Central to this view was Minuchin's belief that clear decision-making in families is vital and that children thrive best when the adults in charge of them can collaborate in looking after them.

Structural therapists, like brief/strategic therapists, believe that change actually occurs in the therapy sessions in a continuous, step-wise fashion, and they tend to focus mainly on the nuclear and at times on the extended family; they do not often integrate their interventions into the wider system, nor do they attach a great deal of importance to past history (Israelstam 1998), preferring to work in the here and now.

ACTIVITY 9.4

Suppose you are adopting a structural family therapy approach with the Cartwrights. What strategies might you adopt in your work with the family? Write these down and discuss with a friend or colleague.

COMMENT

You may have come up with a number of possibilities. David and Brenda could be asked to agree a common line to take. Perhaps you could ask Brian and Sandra to go out together. This might help create a shift in family dynamics, at the same time assuaging some of Brenda's concerns about Sandra being out at night.

Techniques

Some familiar Structural practices which continue alive and well today include the importance of joining with each family member, seeking to understand and unbalance the system before restructuring it. Techniques used may include sculpting, assigning enactment tasks, focusing also on patterns of communication, hierarchical structures and imbalances, alliances and coalitions between members.

Criticism of this approach is that it is directive and patriarchal and that it stigmatises non-standard family norms, such as single-parent and reconstituted families. However, as Dallos and Draper (2000) point out, *the important point is that the child experiences support, a sense of co-operation and clarity from the adults placed in charge of him or her* (Dallos and Draper 2000, p41). Reimers and Treacher (1995) also held the view that Structural therapy fails to address feminist issues in its thinking and in its practices.

Milan systemic family therapy

The Milan Associates (Palazzolli, Prata, Cecchin and Boscolo) in 1967 became interested in the strategic approach because of the success they were having in work with family members suffering from anorectic and schizophrenic conditions. Their paper *Paradox and Counter Paradox* (Palazzolli et al. 1978) outlined their view that families coming to therapy present with the paradoxical message 'help us, but don't change us' and they argued that therapists must be change agents who argue against change and break the family's resistance to therapy! They also, initially at least, embraced ideas about families' 'resistance to change' which stemmed from the Strategic view that family and therapist must remain separate and distant and that it is the therapist's responsibility to effect change in the family's organisation around the symptom.

However, in the 1970s, the Milan Group became disenchanted with the Strategic way of thinking and the implication of the idea of 'war' in the relationship between family member and therapist. Consistent with Bateson's (1979) ideas they began to see change as evolutionary and became more interested in the idea of observing systems which emphasise *the observer's inclusion and participation in the system and includes such concepts as therapist attention to self, recursivity and the social construction of reality* (MacKinnon and James 1987b, p90).

At last we were being freed from views about families as being 'dysfunctional' and family systems as 'resistant' to change. The therapist's stance moved from one of pathologising family behaviour to collaboration with families in finding ways to improve their experience of family life.

Milan Associates reminded us that we cannot make people change, but we may create little perturbations in thinking and introduce ideas of 'difference' that may encourage the stimulation of change within the system. The therapist does not assume an 'expert' position, as in the previous approaches, but rather one which facilitates constructive dialogue and exploration of issues which present as problems for the family. The therapist does not presume to know best or to make normative comparisons with how families 'should be' (MacKinnon and James 1987a, p90).

Key concepts in Milan systemic therapy

The key concepts of hypothesising, circularity and neutrality were developed by the Milan team and all three concepts are inextricably linked. As systemic therapy has developed and moved towards a second order stance – that is, understanding of the influence and impact of the therapist as part of the system – the concept of neutrality has been heavily criticised as implying aloofness or detachedness from the family. Cecchin (1987) redefined 'neutrality' as 'curiosity', whereby multiple ideas and hypotheses could be entertained by the worker, undertaking a more collaborative and less 'expert' role in the work with the family.

- **Hypothesising** is generally the organisation of thinking which is done prior to and post session in relation to the presentation of the patterns of behaviour and interactions. It is the activity of speculating in relation to the available information in order to rule out and rule in useful understandings, so as to progress the work in a meaningful way with the family. The speculations and ideas must be linked to the available information about the family and to each member of the family, in order to understand how the presenting issues are experienced by each family member and how this in turn impacts on others in the family group. Hypotheses generally consider individual and family beliefs and premises about the family situation and ways of experiencing the world, family life cycle and transitions, as well as about patterns of communication and alliances within the family (Jones 1993).

ACTIVITY 9.5

In relation to the Cartwrights list three hunches you have about the reason for the family problem/presenting symptoms. Now take each hypothesis in turn and write about what you now wish to find out more about and the lines of inquiry you might follow.

COMMENT

It is important to realise that hypotheses are only guesses. Some will be correct and some will be proven to be wrong. In the case of the Cartwrights here are some plausible explanations. You may have come up with others.

- Brenda has difficulty in coping with crises, leading to her becoming anxious and/or depressed. Perhaps this leads to her being unable to fulfil her usual roles in the family, resulting in other members of the family becoming confused and uncertain. The family tries to readjust but family members themselves find unhelpful coping strategies – gambling, drinking, etc.

- Alternatively, David's gambling addiction has resulted in great pressure and stress for the family, causing the other problems in the first hypothesis. But what is the reason for his addiction?

- Brenda and David's marriage is on the rocks and has been for some time. They certainly have secrets from each other and presumably do not communicate well. This leads to inconsistent parenting which unsettles the other members of the family and which individuals exploit to their advantage.

- David has an unhealthy relationship with Sandra. If not actually sexual the two of them are unnaturally close. Consequently Brenda has increasingly relied on Brian and placed him in the position of pseudo-father to the family.

- *Genograms* Genograms (McGoldrick and Gersen 1985) are useful when trying to understand the transgenerational patterns of behaviour and beliefs that may exist within families (for example, beliefs about gender roles, parenting) and can inform your hypotheses. These are normally three-generational maps, or family trees (see Parker and Bradley, 2010 for explanation and examples).

- *Circularity* The Milan therapists (Palazzoli et al. 1980) defined circularity as the circular pattern of interactions between family members, where an individual's behaviour is part of a sequence of behaviour patterns and understandings in a family: A causes B, B causes C,C Causes D and D causes A. Brenda gets into heated arguments with Sandra (because she is worried that she puts herself at risk). Sandra seeks and gets the support of her father. This annoys Brian who complains to Brenda that Sandra gets away with too much. Brenda, feeling supported by Brian and unsupported by David, has another go at Sandra. The interactions between the worker and the family are also important as these provide further information in relation to the hypotheses being developed by the worker and colleagues. For workers operating on their own it is essential that they attend to their interactions with family members and reflect on their influence within the system and how they may be drawn in to the family pattern.

- *Neutrality* This concept has been open to much debate and criticism in the family therapy field and beyond. As originally defined by Palazzoli et al. (1980) it means that the worker should work to create a link with each person present so that no one at the end of a session has the impression that the worker is allied to one person's views over any other's. In early Milan practice this also meant keeping a certain distance from the family and maintaining a detached overview. While elements of this concept continue to prove useful in practice, especially where there is an invitation or an inclination to 'join' more with one person than another, it has been criticised as encouraging the belief that no one holds accountability or responsibility for the problem, as all family members can be seen as having a role to play in the problem and its maintenance. This is particularly problematic in situations where there is an abuse of power, as in domestic abuse and child abuse, where there are clear lines of responsibility.

For a fuller description of these three key elements and other techniques relevant to Milan systemic therapy refer to Dallos and Draper (2000).

Some of the challenges the Milan approach presents to us in terms of practice have been documented in feminist literature (MacKinnon and Miller 1987).

The feminist critique has much influenced Systemic practice as it currently stands. It has contributed much to encouraging a definition of therapy that attends to misuse of power, bringing attention explicitly to power differentials and to Systemic therapy's commitment to equality within therapy and to *political, economic, and social equality between the sexes* (Dallos and Draper 2000, p111).

The work of White and Epston (1990) also emphasises the need to take account of 'dominant discourses' in society – those cultural beliefs that can encourage and maintain inequality and remind us that when we work with families to challenge power differentials we are:

inevitably engaging in political activity ... not a political activity that involves the proposals of an alternative ideology, but one that challenges the techniques that subjugate persons to dominant ideology.

(White and Epston 1990, p29)

Family therapy and social work

Systems theory proposes that systems such as families have an in-built mechanism (homeostasis) which protects them from change. The concept of homeostasis means that the family system seeks to maintain its customary organisation and functioning over time. It tends to resist change. Working with an individual member of the family may provoke change in that individual but the family reacts in a way to accommodate that change which leaves the family system as it was. This may be why Aisha thought that as soon as one problem improved another arose to take its place. Consequently, in order to facilitate lasting change, it may be necessary for social workers to work with the whole or parts of the family concerned.

As a student or beginning social worker, it is unlikely that you will be called upon to adopt a family work approach. Nevertheless, family therapy theory and practice will provide you with a number of useful insights and techniques in your work. We have encountered a number of these in this chapter: how to help families communicate better; how to help families understand the dynamics taking place; how to avoid being thrown off course; how to mobilise strengths in the family and free up stuck situations.

While family therapy has been criticised from a feminist perspective for its failure to address the family as the primary site of oppression of women, Coulshed and Orme (2006) argue that social workers in family situations:

might address the issue of power, using their advocacy, negotiation and education skills ... techniques such as circular questioning which allows different perceptions of the relationship to be articulated, can contribute to the restructuring of oppressive power relationships within families.

(Coulshed and Orme 2006, p211)

Coulshed and Orme (2006) suggest that feminist thought not only provides a critique of family work but a framework for working with women and significant others in their lives including men.

The field of family therapy practice continues to grow, develop and contribute much to effective practice with a wide range of clients across many settings – not least of which are children and families. It offers much to the development of good practice in every field of social work and reminds us that we take our 'knowing' from the past into the present: with insight and assistance we shed that which holds us back and seems no longer relevant, and move forward, hopefully equipped with new ideas, the formation of new patterns, difference in our thinking – and so on – in a circular fashion.

RESEARCH SUMMARY

How often do we hear requests for 'Evidence-based' approaches? It seems we live in a world where 'evidence' is the only barometer by which we measure whether something exists or provides successful outcomes. Jay Haley (1971), one of family therapy's most prolific researchers, presented a familiar argument that research and therapy have two very different purposes and that change could occur in a system without our being always able to pinpoint the reason for it. However, as pointed out by Dallos and Draper (2000 p152), the fundamental systemic notion of revising interventions on the basis of feedback is a microcosm of the research process. For further reading relating to the types and categories of research methods relevant to evidencing family therapy intervention refer to Dallos and Draper (2000), Chapter 5, 'Does family therapy work? – The answer is yes'.

Family therapy works for a wide range of family and child-focused problems and the research supports the effectiveness of systemic interventions for sleep, feeding and attachment problems in infancy; child abuse and neglect; conduct problems (including ADHD, delinquency and drug abuse); emotional problems (including anxiety, depression, grief, bipolar disorder and suicidality; eating disorders and somatic problems (Carr 2000b).

It works and its cost-effectiveness is beginning to show in some recent studies. For example, Pinsof and Wynne (1995) indicate high effectiveness for family therapy interventions in work with substance misuse and alcohol problems and state that it is more cost-effective than alternative interventions.

CHAPTER SUMMARY

- The purpose of family therapy is to work with family members to improve communication between family members, solve family problems and facilitate the family to find more satisfactory ways of functioning.

- Family therapy is based on family systems theory, in which the family is viewed as a system of people rather than just a collection of individuals. It treats problems by changing the way the system works rather than trying to fix a specific family member. Family systems theory is based on several major concepts.

- There have been three main schools of thought in the development of systemic practice: strategic family therapy; structural family therapy and Milan systemic family therapy.

- Each of the three schools has brought particular techniques to the practice of work with families.

FURTHER READING

Carr, A (2000a) Evidence-based practice in family therapy and systemic consultation: I. Child focused problems. *Journal of Family Therapy*, 22(1), 29–60.

Carr, A (2000b) Evidence-based practice in family therapy and systemic consultation: II. Adult-focused problems. *Journal of Family Therapy*, 22(3), 273–95.

These two articles examine the evidence for the effectiveness of family-based treatments from critical literature reviews and controlled trials, the first in relation to child-focused problems and the second in relation to adult-focused problems.

Vetere, A and Dallos, R (2003) *Working systemically with families: Formulations, intervention and evaluation*. London: Karnac.

In this book the authors review research studies into family therapy and conclude with a critical review of major recent developments in theory and application. Each chapter includes a number of exercises that relate to the ideas presented.

Anderson, H (1997) *Conversation, language and possibilities*. New York: Basic Books.

Drawing extensively on a case study and focusing on post-modern and clinical narratives, this book describes how to create the kind of relationship and conversation with a client that allows the client to access their creativity and develop possibilities.

Wilson, J (1998) *Child-focused practice: A systemic collaborative approach*. London: Karnac.

This is a very accessible and practical book, in which the author discusses traditional and contemporary theories and explains them in the context of how he works with children.

Chapter 10
Brief solution-focused therapy

Irene Lindsay

A C H I E V I N G   A   S O C I A L   W O R K   D E G R E E

This chapter will help you to develop the following capabilities from the **Professional Capabilities Framework**:

- **Professionalism**
  Identify and behave as a professional social worker committed to professional development.
- **Knowledge**
  Apply knowledge of social sciences, law and social work practice theory.
- **Intervention and skills**
  Use judgement and authority to intervene with individuals, families and communities to promote independence, provide support and prevent harm, neglect and abuse.

It will also introduce you to the following standards as set out in the 2008 social work subject benchmark statement.
5.1.1 Social work services and clients.
5.1.4 Social work theory.
5.1.5 The nature of social work practice.
5.5.1 Managing problem solving activities.
5.5.3 Analysis and synthesis.
5.5.4 Intervention and evaluation.

Introduction

We have already discussed two approaches that could be considered to be brief therapies: crisis intervention and task-centred work. Some cognitive behavioural therapies can also be completed within a relatively short time span. In this chapter we will look at another 'brief' intervention, brief solution-focused therapy. In the literature, the terms brief therapy, solution-based therapy and the solution-focused model are used interchangeably. Here, I am referring to the model of brief solution-focused therapy developed and described by De Shazer (1985). De Shazer acknowledged the problems associated with the term 'brief' and suggested using goal achievement rather than time limits to determine termination of work. The method's ability to generate expectations of change, it is suggested, in itself ensures that therapy will be briefer than that used in more traditional therapeutic methods.

This approach originates in constructionist thinking. We will briefly consider what is meant by constructionism and then go on to consider the approach itself.

Social construction

Many sociological theories work from the premise that social reality exists separately from people living it or talking about it. However, social constructionism takes the view that what we believe reality to be comes about only through the social interaction of people. When we attempt to explain reality we inevitably overlook the processes by which reality is constructed. There are no given 'truths'. What we understand as the 'truth' comes about only through our conversations (verbal and non-verbal) with other people. We can start to understand the implications of this if we examine a list of the main ideas associated with constructionism, given by Burr (1995, cited in Milner and O'Byrne 2002).

These include:

- *taking a critical stance towards many taken-for-granted ways of understanding the world;*

- *viewing various ways of understanding the world as relative to periods of history and to culture;*

- *seeing knowledge not as being determined by the nature of things, but as constructed between people as they talk and interact;*

- *an awareness that social action is driven by the social constructions of the time;*

- *since the world is made up of people's interactions, believing that there are no essential 'given' natures to be discovered;*

- *a questioning of realism and the idea of objective truth; and an awareness that the language we use determines the meaning of things, rather than vice versa. Language, rather than being just a medium for expressing ideas, actually determines thought to the extent that truth is the product of language: language constructs social reality.*

(Milner and O'Byrne 2002, p2)

This last point, *language constructs social reality*, is key in brief solution-focused therapy. It means that problems and solutions can be constructed through the conversations that we have with our clients and they with us or themselves. We use language when we think, but language is more than just a neutral vehicle for our thoughts: it is through talking to people that we construct our world. Therefore, through these conversations we can construct a different future and change. By talking, change can occur from *either a difference in how a person views his or her world or by a person doing something different, or both* (George, Iveson and Ratner, 1990, p3, quoted in Parton and O'Byrne 2000, p97).

Solution-focused brief therapy

Most of the other interventions we have discussed in this book take the position that if we can discover the causes of a person's problem, we can find a cure which will remove or lessen the problem. Let us suppose that we have toothache. We go to the dentist who examines our teeth and finds a cavity. The dentist can see that the cause of the problem (pain) is the cavity and so drills and fills; the tooth is fixed; the pain goes away; the problem is solved. Solution-focused brief therapy does not work in the same way. Instead of the focus being on the problem, the focus is on the solution.

Solution-focused therapy came about as a consequence of the work of a team led by De Shazer and Berg, at the Brief Therapy Center in Milwaukee, during the 1980s. The team discovered that clients often made significant positive change following conversations about their preferred future, whether much attention had been paid to the nature of their problems or not. Furthermore, when clients came up with ideas about possible solutions, sometimes these were related to problems and sometimes not. It seemed that the more they focused on problems, the more and greater problems they discovered, but when they focused on solutions, the more solutions materialised. De Shazer, Berg and the team realised that workers could play a part in helping clients focus on solutions – hence *solution-focused* therapy.

O'Connell (2007) draws attention to a number of underpinning assumptions.

- It is not possible to discover objective 'truths' about a client's life. There are many different truths.

- Clients may feel the need to understand the causes of their problems in order to find 'closure' but it is not always helpful and can sometimes delay positive change.

- Exploring problems is a separate process from constructing solutions.

- Clients are rich in skills, qualities and abilities but they and other people may not be aware of this.

- Clients are often already employing these skills, qualities and abilities in a constructive way.

- Clients have definite ideas about how they would like their futures to be.

- It can be more helpful to have a focus on the present and future than on understanding the past. The past is often a source of problems while the future provides a focus for solutions.

- Nevertheless, the past is a territory where the client can find exceptions; that is, times when the problem did not exist or was not so severe.

It would be a mistake to think that this approach ignores the problem. It may seem that the approach moves immediately to a position of finding solutions without knowing anything about the problem. It is important to know what the problem is so that both you and the client know what you are trying to achieve and why. The goal is an absence of the problem or at least a reduction of its effect. Without knowing what the problem is you cannot know that you are going away from it and you will not know when you have reached your destination. Also it would not be appropriate to refuse to allow the client to 'talk out' the problem. The approach, after all, has to be felt by the client to be relevant. Nevertheless, solutions are not to be found in exploring the causes of the problem. The past is considered to be useful only in terms of finding exceptions to the problem.

Finding exceptions

Finding exceptions is an important part of solution-focused therapy and a number of techniques have been devised to help with this process. *Exceptions* (or *micro-solutions*) are occasions when the problem is or was absent or less. Since nothing ever stays the same there will always be times when problems are more or less problematic and so it is always possible to find these exceptions. Parton and O'Byrne (2000) refer to two types of exceptions. *Deliberate exceptions* are exceptions for which the client can take credit. These are deliberately 'talked up', mainly to make the most of their significance as holding the seeds of possible solutions, but also so as to engender in the client a greater sense of self-efficacy. *Spontaneous exceptions*, on the other hand, are exceptions for which the client is not responsible; things that other people have done or which have happened by chance. Nevertheless, these are also important, especially if they are *predictable*. Clients can learn to become better and better at prediction. Being able to predict an exception suggests that it may be more in the hands of the client than first thought. Predicting an exception is likely to lead to behaviour that increases its likelihood (Milner and O'Byrne 2002). Having identified an exception, work begins on turning this micro-solution into a fully-fledged solution with questions like 'How did you do that?'; 'What were the signs that that was going to be a useful thing to do?'; 'What will need to happen for you to do that again?'

CASE STUDY

In a conversation with Aisha, Brenda mentions that Philip is much happier about going to school now as he has been picked for the school football team.

Aisha   *That's brilliant, what did you do to bring that about?*

Brenda   *Oh, I didn't do anything at all; he did it all himself; he's a great little player.*

Aisha   *Did you know it was going to happen? Did you have a clue?*

Brenda   *Well, after our chat about the suspension, he started back at school on a better footing, so things were a bit better and I suppose the teachers thought he deserved another chance, but I didn't know he was going to get picked.*

Aisha   *Well, it sounds as if you started the thing off and it's great anyway. Is there anything you can do to keep his enthusiasm up, so that he stays on the team?*

Brenda   *I was thinking about that. I am going to make a bit of a fuss of him and show plenty of interest in how he is getting on. Oh, and I suppose I'll make sure that he gets support from the family by going to see him play.*

Here Brenda volunteers an exception. Aisha explores Brenda's role in bringing it about and ways of ensuring the change is sustained.

Exception-seeking and constructing change

As with other methods of intervention, the relationship between the client and worker is an essential ingredient in success. We will look shortly at some of the techniques that characterise the approach; however, it is important to recognise that:

Technique does not make a therapist solution-focused. It is the quality of the relationship underpinned by solution-focused values which makes someone genuinely solution-focused.

O'Connell (2007, p389)

The values of solution-focused therapy involve attempting to establish a relationship based on equality in which the client is recognised as the expert on their life. The worker's role lies in creating an environment in which it is possible to facilitate and encourage the client to find their own solutions. This involves active listening, feeding back positively on the client's abilities and successes, but also keeping the conversation to a solution-focused agenda as far as possible. Having recognised the importance of the relationship, we will now look at some exception-seeking techniques.

Pre-session change

Research studies (Weiner-Davis et al. 1987; Lawson 1994) have found that between 62 and 66 per cent of clients reported positive change between making the appointment and turning up for their first session with the therapist, but only if they were asked in a way that suggested that change was expected.

Beyebach et al. (1996, cited in Miller et al. 2002) found that clients who reported pre-therapy change were four times more likely to finish treatment with a successful outcome.

Taking this research on board, De Shazer and his colleagues devised the *pre-session change question* which goes something like: 'Can you please describe to me any ways in which things have improved since you made the appointment?' When the client describes a change that has taken place the worker immediately follows up with a further question such as, 'How did you do that?' Even where the client makes an outright denial of having contributed in any way to the change, the worker can always ask how they will be able to sustain the change. In this way, not only is the partnership launched on a solution-focused agenda but client self-efficacy is reinforced.

Similarly, a study by Reuterlov et al. (2000) found that when asked, 'What is better since the last visit?', 76 per cent of clients reported positive change. Therefore the thinking behind the pre-session change question applies equally to between-session change.

The miracle question

This is a useful technique for by-passing any problem-focused thinking and helping the client to focus on how things would be in the absence of the problem. A usual form would be, 'Imagine when you go to bed tonight, a miracle happens and all the problems which brought you here magically disappear in an instant. Since you are asleep you cannot know that this has happened. When you wake up in the morning, what is the first thing that you notice that tells you that the miracle has taken place?' This is followed by a series of questions which add detail, for example other indicators of the miracle, how other people would be affected. In this way a start is made on constructing a solution without any attention being given to the problem.

The miracle question is helpful in highlighting issues which are of importance to the client, for example, having a stress-free life, having a better marriage, or being able to meet people socially, and also in eliciting what the client wants or expects from their contact with you. Sometimes the client comes up with some unrealistic expectation, enabling discussion between the client and worker as to what it might be possible to achieve realistically.

ACTIVITY 10.1

Note down your answers to the following questions.

- *Imagine that while you are asleep tonight a miracle happens which results in your life becoming exactly as you would like it. What would be the first thing you would notice had changed when you wake up?*

- *What would be the next thing you would notice?*

- *Would other people realise the miracle had happened? What would they notice that would tell them?*

COMMENT

This activity should give you an indication of the future you would like for yourself and also some of the small steps that you need to take to bring that about.

The fast forward question

Similar to the miracle question, but good for people who don't believe in miracles, this question takes a form such as, 'If you were to wind your life forward, like the fast forward on a DVD, how do you see things being in a year/five years/when the situation is much better? What will have changed?'

The fast rewind question

This technique helps the client examine the past for exceptions that might provide the basis for future solutions. 'Using the fast rewind button on your life, go back to a time when the problem was much less. What was different then?' This question also looks for strengths which may help with self-esteem and increase self-efficacy.

Scaling

In this technique workers invite the client to put their situation on a scale. An example of a question would be, 'If, on a scale of nought to ten, zero represents the worst things could be and ten the very best, where would you place yourself, right now?' The question can be used in relation to any aspect that the worker thinks may be important, for example, 'How are you feeling about yourself just now?'; 'How confident do you feel that things will get better?'; 'How well motivated to change do you feel?' The question is followed by a series of others, all designed to identify the possibility of solutions. Let us look at some examples.

- 'How will you notice that you have moved up a point (from four to five)?' This encourages the client to focus attention on observable signs of progress and improvement. It reduces the possibly long journey towards a satisfactory outcome to one small step.

- 'Why have you rated yourself on point four rather than three?' implicitly asks the client to consider positives and is a useful way of giving hope and confidence in what has been accomplished already, as well as potentially identifying a strategy that has worked already.

- 'How far up the scale do you think you will get? How will things be different then?' Like the miracle question this helps to define the desired future and identifies the ways things can be different. It also allows people to aim for seven or eight, rather than ten, making the end goal more attainable. Ten may seem far too unrealistic. It also allows shades of grey, rather than all or nothing, black and white, as in the question: 'Do you think you will stop drinking?', to which the only answers are 'yes' or 'no'.

ACTIVITY **10.2**

Note down your answers to the following questions.

- *On a scale of nought to ten, where do you think you are now in terms of your progress on the social work degree, nought being the pits and ten being the best possible outcome you could hope for?*

- *Why have you given yourself that score rather than a point or two points less?*

- *What would need to happen for you to move up a point?*

- *Where do you think your closest friend would put you on the scale?*

- *Looking back to a month after you started on the course, where were you then?*

- *What has happened since then to change your score?*

> **COMMENT**
>
> *Notice that the first question only establishes how you see your current point on the scale. Whether it is a two or an eight is much less important than the answers you gave to the other questions. You may consider that for you a three is very good or an eight far too low. The remaining questions in turn may have helped you to:*
>
> - *become aware of some things you have achieved recently;*
>
> - *identify some small step that will help you to improve your progress;*
>
> - *check out whether your perception of where you are is correct. It would be interesting to check out your friend's actual answer to the fourth question and discuss the reasons for any difference;*
>
> - *reflect on the progress you have actually made since starting the course;*
>
> - *identify some of the things you have achieved since starting, plus some of the areas of support you have had.*

Coping questions

Where it is impossible to find positive exceptions, for example in working with recently bereaved people, Parton and O'Byrne (2000) suggest using coping questions or 'getting by' questions such as, 'Have you noticed a time when it has been a little easier? What is different then?' or 'This sounds impossible for you. How come you are coping so well?'

All these questions we have discussed can be followed up by questions seeking more elaboration – 'What else?'

Between-sessions tasks and feedback

At the end of each session the worker provides feedback and sets tasks.

A standard format for feedback is:

- giving positive feedback, recognising and valuing what the client has achieved during the session (at the very least the client has participated);

- summarising what has been achieved between sessions;

- linking achievements to goals;

- negotiating between-session tasks.

The tasks usually take the form of one or more of the following.

- If it works keep doing it.

- If it doesn't work don't do it.

- Do something different – doing something different raises the possibility of stumbling across a solution, but, of course, what the client does is most likely to take the form of doing something they think might work.

- Take notice – of when the problem is less, or when someone does something helpful or when they do something they are pleased with. This is useful for people who are struggling to find exceptions.

- Pretend. The worker asks the client to pretend that something has improved. The idea is that there is not much difference between pretending to do something and actually doing it, especially if told not to let anyone else know that you are pretending.

- Predict when some spontaneous exception will happen again. As indicated earlier, predicting exceptions increases the chances of them happening.

CASE STUDY

Aisha visits the family. Brenda is alone. Aisha asks Brenda what differences she has noticed that might indicate that things might be improving. Brenda launches into a series of complaints about all the members of the family. She says that she had hoped that family therapy might have helped but it just seems to have increased the rowing. Aisha says that that must seem like an impossible situation for Brenda and wonders aloud how she manages to cope. Brenda says that she copes mainly by getting out of the house. She goes swimming a lot and she has also joined a keep-fit class. The later part of the evening is quite nice as well, she says, because it is usually just her and the two youngest at home watching television that they all enjoy. Aisha asks again if Brenda has noticed any improvements in her situation and she says that actually she and Sandra have been getting on a bit better. Aisha asks Brenda, 'How did you do that?' Brenda laughs and says, 'Well, I bribed her.' But then goes on to say that actually she and Sandra went shopping and she bought Sandra some badly needed new clothes. While they were out Sandra had asked, 'Are we going to go bankrupt?' Brenda had replied that the business would probably go but that they would all survive and Sandra had seemed quite pleased. There had been no rows between Sandra and Brenda since, although Brian and Sandra had been shouting at each other a lot. Aisha congratulated Brenda on her good work with Sandra, pointing to a number of things she was doing well: looking after herself physically and putting into practice some of the lessons learned about stress management; engaging in appropriate activity with the children; recognising the fashion needs of her teenage daughter and being open with her while showing optimism.

Aisha asked Brenda a scaling question about how optimistic she felt that things would continue to improve. Brenda said five. Aisha asked why not four and Brenda said that five was a better reflection of how she was getting on at an emotional level with the children. Four would mean that she wasn't. Aisha asked what would move Brenda from a five to a six. Brenda said that would be if the children got on better with each other. Aisha asked how she could do that but Brenda said she really didn't know.

Aisha asked the miracle question. Brenda said the first thing she would notice when she woke up was that David wouldn't be in the bed beside her. Aisha said, 'You mean, you would have split up?' Brenda laughed and said, 'No, he'd be up looking for work, instead of nursing his hangover.' Aisha then asked Brenda what the miracle would have changed to enable her to get David back into work mode. Brenda said that maybe it had stopped

Continued

CASE STUDY *continued*

David getting so angry every time she mentioned the business to him and so she would be able to discuss it with him. Aisha asked what she would be doing differently to make a difference to David's anger. Brenda said she would have got David to realise that what was important to her was the family and not the business. It didn't matter to her so long as they could get by. Aisha asked if David knew that now and Brenda said that maybe he didn't and perhaps she should tell him.

Aisha provided Brenda with feedback on the session.

COMMENT

Aisha starts by looking for exceptions since the last visit but Brenda immediately goes into problem mode, so Aisha shifts tack and uses a coping question. This prompts Brenda to talk first of all about getting out of the house but then more positively on to her swimming and fitness sessions, which is exactly what was suggested to her on the stress management course. In a more positive mind frame then she also remembers a pleasant afternoon spent with Sandra, which led to Sandra indirectly expressing some of her worry about what has been happening. Brenda was able to offer her daughter reassurance. Aisha then used the miracle question which suggested one small solution.

ACTIVITY 10.3

Read the case study above and write down an end-of-session feedback statement that you would make to Brenda if you were in Aisha's place. Include some tasks for Brenda for the next period.

COMMENT

Here is one we did earlier (apologies to Blue Peter).

'I thought you did brilliantly today – the way you were able to put a positive slant on things, especially when you were feeling down. It was good to hear that you had made progress with Sandra and were able to get closer to her through the shopping trip. That allowed her to share her worries with you and you were able to reassure her. Spending relaxation time with all the children was an excellent way to get them feeling good about being in this family. The goals you identified some weeks ago included finding support for Sandra and Philip, so that is all important work in that direction.

'Another thing I was impressed with today was how you were able to think about what the future could look like and see ways of talking to David that could remove one of the obstacles to you getting there. That links in well with what you said when we met with the whole family; you said you wanted to be able to communicate better.

Over the next week I wonder if you could notice any more changes that take place. Also I would like you to pretend that you and David are able to talk about the business without getting upset. Would you like to try that?'

Aisha provided positive feedback and set some tasks for Brenda for the period ahead.

To conclude this section it may be helpful for you to learn the EARS acronym.

- **E**liciting from the client when and how things have changed for the better. Things are bound to be better from time to time as nothing stays the same.

- **A**mplifying the changes by 'talking them up' – asking what differences they made for whom and by whom.

- **R**einforcing the client by compliments.

- **S**tarting over again – asking for more examples of change and discussing how they can do more of the same.

(Milner and O'Byrne 2002, p147)

Application to social work practice

Parton and O'Byrne (2000) discuss the changes that have occurred in social work over the past 25 years, pointing to the erosion of the traditional social work role due to a number of factors and the failure to develop theoretical approaches which inform practice, in particular those that reflect the development of social theory associated with constructivism, post-modernity and the role of language in understanding the human condition and social world. Brief solution-focused therapy is one of a number of approaches which does reflect these theoretical developments. This approach, which recognises the potential for positive change resulting from direct worker–client contact, provides something of an antidote in an environment characterised by defensive organisational and proceduralist demands.

Strengths

- This is a client-centred approach; the focus is on attending carefully to the client's story and on finding the client's solutions. It emphasises the need for negotiation with potential clients, not only in ensuring that their individual definition of their problems is elicited, but in ensuring a commitment towards change in specific areas.

- Since the client is doing the work, it reduces risk of dependency.

- Rather than pathologising the client as someone with problems, the focus is on the client's strengths and resources.

- This is an optimistic approach which looks towards a comparatively problem-free future. This and the concern with exceptions are empowering.

- It can be very broadly applied and is useful for dealing with a wide range of problems and goals.

- Depending on the client, the work can be completed over a relatively short period of time. A major advantage of solution-focused work is its claim to represent a cost-effective method of treatment.

- There are also some advantages for the worker. Changes in the concept of welfare referred to earlier have led to feelings of uncertainty and confusion in social workers and a questioning of the value of the effectiveness of social worker interventions. Solution-focused therapy represents an accessible, clearly articulated mode of intervention emphasising change, solution and resolution of problems; a welcome innovation to social workers experiencing a sense of powerlessness in their work.

Limitations

- The concern is with behaviour and perceptions rather than with feelings. Behaviour, perception and feelings are interlinked. If feelings are not attended to, the client's memory may be clouded so that it may not be possible to remember exceptions or imagine a problem-free future.

- Some clients do seem to need to explore their problem fully, in order to move on. People who have experienced trauma, for example, often need to spend some time discussing the event in order to make sense of it for themselves and to come to terms with what happened to them.

- The method is unlikely to be effective with people in crisis, when people have problems accessing their internal and external resources.

- Some clients may have such low self-esteem that they cannot accept that they have any skills, strengths or qualities.

CHAPTER SUMMARY

- Solution-focused therapy draws on the ideas of social constructionism, which argues that there are no given truths, only what we construct through the use of language.

- It is based on ideas that it can be helpful to use conversations with clients to construct solutions to their problems and so it is not necessary to discover the causes of problems.

- It is useful to find exceptions, time when the problem is less or does not exist, as these provide clues about what might be solutions.

- Although a strong client–worker relationship is essential, the approach relies on a number of techniques, such as the miracle question and scaling questions, to help the client find exceptions and to identify small steps that may become solutions.

- Workers may negotiate tasks for the client to undertake between sessions. These tasks form part of a positive feedback given by the worker at the end of each session.

FURTHER READING

Parton, N and O'Byrne (2000) *Constructive social work: Towards a new practice.* Basingstoke: Palgave.
This book explains social constructionism in social work practice and includes a useful description and discussion of solution-focused brief therapy and other constructive social work practices.

Milner, J and O'Byrne, P (2002) *Assessment in social work.* 2nd edition. Basingstoke: Palgrave.
This is a useful text which presents a number of different models of assessment, including the solution-focused approach.

O'Connell, B (2007) Solution focused therapy. In Dryden, W (ed.) *Dryden's handbook of individual therapy.* 5th edition. London: Sage.
This is a detailed chapter on solution-focused therapy with a case study in an edited volume of different individual therapies.

O'Connell, B (2006) Solution focused therapy. In Feltham, C and Horton, H (eds) *The Sage handbook of counselling and psychotherapy.* London: Sage.
This is by the same author as the chapter above but in this he presents solution-focused therapy in a much more summarised form.

Chapter 11

Life story work and life review

Anne Campbell

ACHIEVING A SOCIAL WORK DEGREE

This chapter will help you to develop the following capabilities from the **Professional Capabilities Framework:**
- **Professionalism**
  Identify and behave as a professional social worker committed to professional development.
- **Knowledge**
  Apply knowledge of social sciences, law and social work practice theory.
- **Intervention and skills**
  Use judgement and authority to intervene with individuals, families and communities to promote independence, provide support and prevent harm, neglect and abuse.

It will also introduce you to the following standards as set out in the 2008 social work subject benchmark statement.
5.1.1 Social work services and clients.
5.1.4 Social work theory.
5.1.5 The nature of social work practice.
5.5.1 Managing problem solving activities.
5.5.3 Analysis and synthesis.
5.5.4 Intervention and evaluation.

Once you have met one person with dementia ... you have met one person with dementia.

(Unknown, often attributed to the late Tom Kitwood)

Introduction

This chapter will look at the use of life story work and life review in the care of older people with dementia. However, before we think about the interventions and how they are used in practice, we will consider the definitions of dementia and examine the prevalence of the condition in the UK. Subsequently, the discussion will focus on the inter-relationship and overlap in the interpretations and use of reminiscence, life review and life story work and how these are perceived and used in practice.

You will be invited to consider the detail of a case study which outlines the familial background of a client (Sadie) alongside a synopsis of her current situation. Sadie has been recently diagnosed with Alzheimer's and in the course of your reading you will also be asked to consider which form of dementia care intervention might best suit her needs. You will be provided with explanations of the various formats used in both life story work and life review. In addition, you will be provided with references to useful, pragmatic and theoretical reading material, which will inform your future work in this sector. Guidance and advice regarding how to practically apply the theory and methods of working will enable you to think about how to utilise the learning within your own practice experience. As part of the activity-based work, you will be asked to consider the process and content of structured life review using the Haight Life Review and Experiencing Form (LREF) (Haight 1991), to think about how information may be best gathered and how you might feel when participating in the work with the older person. Finally, you will contemplate the social work skills and values which are essential and integral components of life story and life review work undertaken in the dementia care setting.

Dementia: Definitions

Dementia is a syndrome which collectively describes a number of very specific illnesses, each with a similar and overlapping range of characteristics, symptoms and pathologies which are medically assessed and confirmed. Definitions are variable according to the professional background of the analyst, researcher or expert. However, the International Classification of Diseases ICD-10 (WHO, 2006) provides the most widely recognised medical definition of dementia.

> *Dementia is a syndrome due to disease of the brain, usually of a chronic or progressive nature, in which there is disturbance of multiple higher cortical functions, including memory, thinking, orientation, comprehension, calculation, learning capacity, language, and judgement. Consciousness is not clouded. The impairments of cognitive function are commonly accompanied, and occasionally preceded, by deterioration in emotional control, social behaviour, or motivation. This syndrome occurs in Alzheimer's disease, in cerebrovascular disease, and in other conditions primarily or secondarily affecting the brain.*

(WHO 2006)

While it is recognised that there may be a general pattern of cognitive and functional impairments, dementia will also affect the person on an individual level in terms of the very personal and subjective experience of the progress and pathway of the condition. The individual may experience a combination of the following indications. Memory impairment may be manifest through short-term memory loss initially, with long-term memories from the past remaining most clearly defined for the longest period of time. There may also be difficulty in articulating the words to express thoughts and emotions (aphasia) and this may be accompanied by difficulty in mobility and motor activities (apraxia), for example getting dressed or making a cup of tea. There may also be a level of confusion and disorientation with the failure to recognise family members or the inability to identify everyday objects and symbols (agnosia) (Chapman et al. 2001).

While heath and social care professionals may view the symptoms and characteristics of dementia within the biomedical model, they have increasingly considered the importance of social and psychological factors in relation to the subjective experience of the individual. Indeed, since the 1990s, many authors now agree that the lived experience of the person with dementia must also be viewed within the fluid context of the individual's background, past life experience, current lifestyle, care/living arrangements and familial and social relationships. The complex interplay of socio-historic and current situational factors has a substantial impact on how the underlying biological and neurological changes affect each person (Gibson 2004; Chapman et al. 2001). Symptoms and behaviours are not solely as a result of impaired biological functioning but are as a result of the social environment as well as the individual's perceptions and reactions to symptoms and events (Kasl-Godley and Gatz 2000).

Reminiscence, life story work and life review in dementia care: The interrelationship and overlap

The concepts and practical applications of reminiscence, oral history life review and life history work have engendered much debate and given rise to a range of definitions and uses in work with a number of client groups. Depending on the authors, the definitions may vary, but most agree that reminiscence, life story work and life review and oral history are concerned with 'looking back' and recalling different memories and past events in our lives. In addition, all have interconnectedness in the appreciation of the importance of recollection and consideration of past lives, thoughts and feelings, whether experienced at individual, group or community levels (Murphy 1994).

On a community group level, oral history is concerned with the collective appreciation of past events and the subsequent recording and preservation of those memories. Reminiscence work is seen by Bornat (1993) as moving beyond the objectives of oral history, where the group discusses and records past experiences, to the sharing of these experiences with a view to engendering some level of change in the participants' lives. However, Gibson (1994) states that it is difficult to disentangle the boundaries between oral history and reminiscence, as each can provide both personal and group satisfaction together with the production of a record of mutual experiences and shared past events. Moreover, where Murphy (1994) and Goldsmith (2002) note that reminiscence and oral history are usually delivered within the group setting, Gibson (1994) and Schweitzer and Bruce (2008) articulate that reminiscence may be a private or public activity undertaken by the individual alone or as part of a group.

Gibson (1994) also advises that group reminiscence with individuals from ethnic minorities may be more beneficial than individual life history work. In a number of Eastern and Indian cultures, the personal and collective attitudes to experiencing illness and death are much more publicly discussed and less personal and private than that demonstrated within Western cultures. Indeed, older people from other than Western ethnic backgrounds may look unfavourably on a private one-to-one discussion about their life via a life story or structured life review. When conducting reminiscence, the worker must also recognise the religious background of the participant as they may have beliefs which recognise more than one life, both in the past and in future reincarnations. Therefore, tuning in to the background, ethnic origin and religious beliefs of individuals with a range of beliefs is an essential preparation to the choice and implementation of the intervention.

Prior to any reminiscence intervention, the decision to undertake group or individual work should be informed by:

*   the purpose of the work;
*   the function and objectives of the work;
*   the needs of the client;
*   the professional background and experience of staff;
*   staff resources;
*   accommodation;
*   participants' availability (Gibson 2004, p82).

While individual and group work may be seen as separate interventions they may also be interlinked and used sequentially to afford the client a choice of intervention which best suits their needs. For example, during group work it may become clear that an individual might also benefit from individual work, or conversely work in a one-to-one setting might be used to encourage a person with low self-esteem and social confidence to participate in a group. Furthermore, as a social worker undertaking group reminiscence with older people with dementia, you may find there are times when the work with some individuals may not be appropriate or effective. For example, some individuals, in the early stages of dementia, will have to cope with frightening changes to their cognitive abilities and behavioural functions and thus may experience feelings of anxiety, depression or acute frustration. It may be difficult for the individual to cope with certain memories and they may be happier to fix life events and experiences in a vacuum-packed past. In these practice experiences, it is important to respect the wishes and feelings of the individual who does not wish to participate and also observe and respond quickly to any signs of non-verbal or verbal distress or unease. The alternative would be to explore the possibilities of other forms of intervention such as life story work and the more structured and evaluative life review as advocated by Gibson (1994, 2004); Haight et al. (2003); Schweitzer and Bruce (2008); Murphy (1994).

RESEARCH SUMMARY

There is a paucity of quasi-experimental and experimental research examining the effectiveness of reminiscence work via controlled rigorous methodologies. The current Cochrane Review (Woods et al. 2005) highlights the absence of controlled studies as the authors were able to locate only four randomised controlled trials suitable for analysis. However, the review indicated some significant results. These highlighted that cognition and mood improved four to six weeks after the treatment, care-givers taking part in the group reported decreased 'strain' and individuals with dementia were reported to

Continued

have some improved general behavioural function and cognition. In addition Chiang et al. (2010) considered the use of reminisence with older people without a diagnosis of dementia and found that participants who had received reminisence therapy showed higher levels of sociability, lower levels of depression and greater indications of well-being than their control group participants.

CASE STUDY

Sadie Cartwright is 79 years old and since her husband George passed away ten years ago, she has lived with her youngest daughter, Diane, in a three-bedroom house not far from her son David Cartwright (whose family is profiled in the case study in earlier chapters). Sadie had always been a central member of her birth family and worked hard to keep the family together after the death of her mother when she was 15 years old. She had a part-time job at the local textile factory and worked to supplement her father's income from his job at the local butcher's shop. She also looked after her four younger brothers (ranging in age from eight to 12 years) until she was 25 years old. Sadie felt that this had been a very demanding and difficult responsibility but she was quite proud that they had 'turned out as grand fellas' and that this would have made their mother 'very proud'. She recounted how she had finished work each day at 12.30 p.m. to 'get the soup or stew warmed for the youngsters' when they returned from school at lunchtime. She also recalled how she had spent the remainder of the day doing household chores and then prepared the meal for the boys and her father which was always served at exactly 6.15 p.m. as her father wished. When the boys married and moved away from home she made sure that they kept in contact with each other and she reminded them of all family birthdays and special occasions. Both Diane and David stated that their mother had been the central person and focal point of the family while they were growing up. They also reported that she had disciplined them in a very zealous manner, often with harsh words and a fiery temper, although both felt that she had been a loving, kind and fair parent. Diane also stated that her mother had never been a sociable person and did not care much for social gatherings or parties involving people from 'outside the family'.

Sadie was diagnosed with Alzheimer's approximately eight months ago. Prior to this, over the past 18 months, Diane had noticed that her mother had regularly been misplacing her house keys, repeatedly leaving her glasses and slippers in the bathroom cabinet and then denying that she had done so. In addition, Diane noticed that she had become increasingly withdrawn and very subdued. Sadie appeared to have shunned the prospect of socialising or indeed having any contact with her friends. Recently, Sadie has also begun to talk about her husband, George, almost on a daily basis. Diane reports that she will talk about him as if he is still alive and then becomes very upset when Diane gently reminds her that he passed away ten years ago.

After a long period of behavioural and mood changes, Diane persuaded Sadie to visit her GP. He carried out some blood and urine tests to discount other possible causes of the confusion and administered the Mini Mental State Examination (MMSE), which asks the patient some questions relating to a number of factors including language recall and attention. Usually an MMSE score of 20 to 24 indicates mild Alzheimer's, a score of 10 to 20 shows moderate Alzheimer's, and a score below 10 suggests severe Alzheimer's. Sadie scored 20 on the test and the GP referred her to a consultant geriatrician as an outpatient for further diagnostic tests including a brain scan and detailed assessment which confirmed the diagnosis. The GP then referred Sadie to the local Older People team where she received an assessment of needs to decide which services could be put in place to meet those needs. (If a person with dementia is assessed as being in need of certain services, social services have a duty to provide the services that fall within their eligibility criteria.) The social worker from the team visited Sadie at home several times over a few weeks to conduct the needs assessment.

After the comprehensive assessment had been completed, an individually tailored care plan was compiled to promote Sadie's independence and to enhance her quality of life. The care plan described what services were to be provided at what times and via which agency. One recommendation of the care plan was that Sadie should visit a day centre to participate in reminiscence work three mornings a week. This is implemented by the senior care worker (a qualified social worker) and other care workers in the older person's dementia care team based within the day centre.

From the information in the case study and your reading so far, consider which type of reminiscence work would be best suited to Sadie's needs: group or individual?

Which issues or events as described by Diane influenced your decision to undertake either group or individual work?

Gibson (2004) provides a useful summary of deciding factors in the decision to use reminiscence on an individual or group basis. Individual work should take place where the person has communication, sensory or cognitive difficulties. It should also be used with individuals who are isolated, introverted, anxious, depressed, agitated or aggressive. Individual intervention is also appropriate when the person has experienced a traumatic event or life-changing experience and is reticent to share this in a group environment. Finally, it may simply be that the person does not wish to participate in the group reminiscence activity and prefers to work on a one-to-one basis.

On the other hand, reminiscence in the group setting may be useful when a person with dementia has articulated that they are not comfortable with the intimacy of a one-to-one intervention. Group intervention is best suited to the individual who has an extrovert personality and enjoys the sharing of information in a group environment. This person may also welcome the camaraderie and socialisation afforded by the group setting.

Continued

From the case study, we can note a number of factors which would influence the type of reminiscence intervention to be undertaken with Sadie. From reports by her daughter, Diane, it is clear that before the diagnosis of dementia, Sadie had been quite an unsociable person, preferring to attend small gatherings involving family members only. Diane has also reported that her mother has become increasingly withdrawn and very subdued and has indicated that she no longer wishes to participate in any activities which would involve friends and/or community members. Sadie has also recently become very upset when talking about her husband and increasingly agitated and anxious when she has failed to remember that George passed away ten years ago.

In view of Sadie's episodes of agitation and anxiety and the historical tendency to avoid social situations, the social worker and senior care worker who compiled the care plan together have agreed that Sadie would probably derive greatest benefit from individual life story work or structured life review work. The following section looks at the individual life story with reference to definition, possible formats, contents and process used in the work and considers its use with Sadie while she is attending the day centre.

Life story work

There are many and varied explanations of the definitions and applications of life story work with a range of social work client groups, including those with learning disability, those with family and childcare issues and older people (Ryan and Walker 1997; McKeown et al. 2006). The term was originally synonymous with work involving children and young people, including foster care interventions and family therapy. The life story intervention has been used effectively with children and young people who have a terminal illness or chronic disability or who have experienced anxiety, anger, loneliness or family breakdown (Ryan and Walker 1997).

The benefits of using life story with older people and more specifically in work with older people with dementia have been widely acknowledged by a number of professional experts who work, write and research within the sector (Murphy 1994; Kitwood, 1997a; Murphy and Moyes 1997; Gibson 1994; Marshall 2005; Williams and Keady 2006). Gibson (2004) sees it as a fluid phrase which relates to a number of ways of engaging with people to encourage them to recall and record their personal narratives in an observable format.

RESEARCH SUMMARY

Moos and Bjorn (2006) compiled a systematic literature review, which considered the use of life story work in the institutional care of people with dementia. The authors reviewed 28 evaluation studies which were conducted between 1990 and 2003 and focused on the benefits of life story work, with a specific emphasis on the effects on the person's sense of identity. The research evaluations were divided into three groups according to intended changes in 1) self-esteem and self-integration; 2) quality of life; and 3) behaviour. The studies which showed an 'enhanced sense of identity' had included a thorough treatment

RESEARCH SUMMARY *continued*

of the individual's life story, the regular use of life story in care and the encouragement of the participants' initiatives. The authors concluded that while rigorous and controlled quantitative methodological designs are useful to look at behaviour changes, the qualitative analyses of the use of the life story in daily care should be utilised more widely to provide a more comprehensive and in-depth examination of the benefits of life story work in dementia care.

Pinquart and Forstmeier (2011) conducted a meta-analysis of the effectiveness of reminiscence interventions on psychosocial outcomes for a range of service user groups. The reviews observed larger effects for those receiving life review therapy rather than simple reminiscence and greater improvements for those individuals who had a diagnosis of depression.

Formats used in life story work

There are multiple formats utilised in life story work including written books which may take the form of very structured compositions or those which may adopt a more unstructured, simple or informal format. Gibson (1994) suggests using an A4 loose-leaf binder to which adjustments can be made as the work is compiled over a number of weeks or months. Family trees and genograms may also be used as pictorial representations of the person's family relationships, roles and major events in their lives, which may be presented within a loose-fitting chronological framework. Life story work used with people with dementia may also take the form of sound or video recordings or computer-generated accounts with footage of the past used to illustrate the time frame captured within the work. Innovations in Dementia (2008), an organisation which considers new ways of working with people who have dementia and their carers, encourages the use of information technology in dementia care. Software packages such as *Word* and *PowerPoint* are being used to record the work of reminiscence groups, or document the life stories of individuals, which are then utilised as a basis for reflection and further work. Ryan and Spadafora (2005) also looked at ways of engaging clients via the development of innovative web-based reminiscence tools. The research and development team used digital memory boxes that could be personalised or thematic, to facilitate communication between family members. However, the team also noted that there needs to be development of software and hardware that is more responsive to the specific needs of people with dementia.

Murphy and Moyes (1997) advise that the suggestion of a 'book' format may be unnerving for some clients with its implication of long tracts of narrative and detailed content. The 'book' concept may also carry with it the notion of including everything that has happened in a strict chronological order, when in fact the most memorable (either happy or sad) events are usually included within the recounted narrative in a semi-structured format. Murphy and Moyes (1997) also caution that the 'book' may be perceived as a discrete task which, when finished, may remain on the corner of a shelf precipitating little or no use by workers, family members or the individual. In order to prevent this happening, the worker must be mindful that life story work is an ever-shifting osmotic process which must be revisited to maintain the momentum and enhance the therapeutic outcomes of its use in dementia care.

Content

A range of artefacts, written documents and memorabilia may be used to trigger discussion and, if agreed between worker and client, could be included within a 'memory box' addendum to the written piece. Photographs, school reports, newspaper cuttings, letters, postcards, marriage certificates and visual art can be utilised to trigger specific memories and can also be used to supplement the recorded memories and past events (Murphy and Moyes 1997; Gibson 2005).

Using the appropriate format, the life story may house the following sections: childhood, parents and siblings, adolescence, young adulthood (relationships, family and children, work) middle age, later years, ethnicity, religion, achievements, interests, special skills, personally relevant local stories and memorable holidays and trips (Gibson 2005; Murphy 1994).

Process

The process is planned but may be brief or lengthy, simple or very detailed according to the individual's wishes and needs. Gibson (2005) states that at least six weekly sessions should be used to gather, discuss and organise information. The work may take place with the individual or together with family members or carers, who can often provide very insightful contributions into the individual's life history. Prior to the beginning of the work, Murphy (1994) advises that you must explain the purpose of the interaction to the individual, illustrate with an example (if none is available then use the life story of a grandparent) and underline that it is not a formal process. It is also necessary to outline who might see the book and for what reason (other clients or other workers who may wish to look at the information for ongoing assessment or for the purpose of care planning or review) and obtain the individual's consent to proceed with the life story work prior to commencement of the work. Gibson (2005) also recommends that the worker accompanies the older person on a trip to places of past significance as this is an important method of obtaining past and present information.

Many workers, particularly newly qualified workers or social work students, may feel uncomfortable or unable to deal with the grief or sadness which is often triggered by the life story work. Murphy (1994) underlines that the worker must try to address the expression of negative emotion and support and encourage the client's ventilation of feelings. Gibson (2005) also highlights that there is a small risk that the client may not be able to immediately resolve painful emotions or come to terms with the negative feelings that the recall has precipitated. On such occasions, the inexperienced worker/student should seek advice and guidance from a mentor, onsite supervisor or practice teacher. Moreover, in the very few cases where serious emotional upsets are incurred in either the client or worker, there should be an immediate referral to an experienced and highly skilled mental health professional (Gibson 2005). The following depicts the essential elements of good practice in life story work.

Charter for good practice in life story work

Do tell the individual what you are proposing to do and ask permission to do it

Do try to understand what it would feel like to have all information recorded

Do think about what preconceptions you bring to the situation, for example doubt instead of belief

Do see the life story as an organic activity

Do use triggers when doing life story work and be aware that all five senses have the potential to be stimulated

Do acknowledge sadness and grief when these emotions are expressed

Do offer an environment relatively free of distractions when doing life story work

Do include current material as well as historical details on the individual with dementia

Do remember who owns the book

Do be aware of the variety of ways that the life story book can be used (by the individual with dementia, by the carer, by the family and by the worker)

Do not feel that you need to record everything

Do not let pressure for accuracy overshadow the need to understand the underlying feelings and emotions

Do not see a life story book as a task to be completed

Do not be constrained that photographs are the only way to illustrate a life story book

Do not see life story work as a separate activity; it feeds into and from other work such as reminiscence groups, outings and care planning.

(Source: Murphy 1994, p22)

ACTIVITY **11.2**

You are to compile one section of a life story book with Sadie, focusing on her teenage and early adult years.

Read the case study and write down the main points of the narrative in relation to Sadie's caring responsibilities before the death of her mother.

What did Sadie value strongly, both in her early adult years and also whilst looking after her own children?

COMMENT

From the case study we can see that Sadie looked after her four younger brothers throughout the latter half of her teenage years and through part of her early adult years. She recounted how she had prepared the meals for her brothers and father and maintained the household chores as well as working in the mornings at the local factory. Sadie was obviously a very strong young woman who had focused entirely on the main caring duties and tasks that had naturally been undertaken by her mother before her death. We can see that Sadie would have struggled to maintain her position as a mother, a role which had been inherited at a young age, and she would have had to face many issues and problems as the boys had grown up. As part of the life story book we could probe further as to how this made Sadie feel: did she feel that she struggled simply to cope with the day-to-day tasks and responsibilities of looking after four boys? How did this experience in her teenage years and early adulthood affect her relationship with her own daughters and family members?

Sadie obviously has strong family values and this was formerly demonstrated via a commitment to looking after her brothers within a secure, routine-based and loving family environment. This pattern of positive care-giving was continued with the raising of her own children; both Diane and David described Sadie as a loving mother who was fair but who did provide strict boundaries and a level of discipline in the family.

Another method of working with Sadie, i.e. structured life review, could be employed as an alternative to the less structured life story work described above. Whereas reminiscence is primarily a group activity concerned with remembering and reconstructing past lived experiences, and individual life story work may be viewed as an unstructured, multi-formatted process, life review is concerned with the structured recall of events and past lived experiences with the subsequent analysis and evaluation of the recalled information.

Life review – definition and theoretical context

Life review refers to an intervention usually conducted on an individual basis with an older person in a time-limited and structured fashion. The process may be facilitated by a social worker who has been trained in counselling skills and has developed an empathic and attentive listening style. The purpose of structured life review is to encourage the individual to recount, discuss, revisit and make sense of events and past experiences and develop new and/or more positive perspectives on the past within a therapeutic environment (Gibson 2004).

Haight et al. (2003) emphasise that since the 1990s life review has increasingly been recognised as a therapeutic method of working with older people. As regards working with dementia, reminiscence has traditionally been the method used by health care professionals and carers. However, there is a growing recognition that structured life review may also be used selectively with older people who have dementia (Gibson 2004; Haight et al. 2003). However, Gibson (2004) cautions that consent must be freely given and the client must be able to talk about their life and actively participate in the evaluation of the life story. She also advises that the sessions may often not adhere to the proposed structure (see below) as the individual may switch between life stages or recount the narrative in a repetitive manner making the interpretation and evaluation difficult for the worker and for the older person. Nevertheless, there are many benefits to using structured life review in dementia care. Older people have expressed their enjoyment and pleasure at the work while some have been able to fully participate in the review and evaluate the importance and helpfulness of the sessions (Gibson 2004).

The therapeutic aspect of this method of intervention is also evident, as it encourages the clients to assess and consolidate their life experiences before they enter the phase of the disease when they will no longer be able to participate in cognitive work. Black and Haight (1992) refer to the tapestry of life as experienced by the person with dementia. On the flip side of the tapestry is a mass of tangled threads which bear no meaning or have no form. Conversely, when the picture is turned over a meaningful and clearly visible picture is presented. The tasks and outcomes of recall are likened to the threads which are decoded via the structured life review. It is proposed that the life review intervention will facilitate a more peaceful existence for those who are experiencing the increasingly tangled side of the tapestry as the cognitive decline gains momentum. Through the programme of structured and evaluative work, the threads may be untangled to some extent and the tapestry may be rewoven for a while longer.

Kunz and Soltys (2007) highlight a continuum from reminiscence to life review, moving from the expression of random memories (reminiscence) to a full evaluative review of one's life history with concomitant formal analysis (life review). The latter is in keeping with the theory of psychosocial development as posited by Erikson (1980), whereby the last stage, 'integrity versus despair' (age 60 or over), is asserted as the final developmental challenge. Older people will naturally revisit the different stages as part of the normative life review process when they are aware that they are approaching or experiencing the end of life phase (Butler 1963). As part of this normative life review process, older adults will look at past events, try to solve or come to terms with unresolved conflicts, celebrate or negate lifetime achievements and thus realise either a sense of integrity or despair with their current life phase.

Narrative theories of self have been viewed as methods of understanding who we are via recollections of our past which are then placed within our current familial, social and interpersonal contexts (Surr 2005). A narrative theory of self underlines that our past history and lived experiences should be merged within a holistic continuum by means of ongoing and fluid narratives. Furthermore, current experiences must be placed within the narrative context, and, therefore, stories and memories of the past are revisited to achieve the ever-fluctuating narrative detail. The result is not a recall of every detail and minutiae of the person's life but a recollection of the events, occasions, relationships and experiences which were selected and interpreted by the individual. Surr (2005) also identifies three types of story (from literature) used as a means of maintaining self. Firstly, the development and telling of the life story itself assists us to contextualise the current within the past. Secondly, the 'storied reconstruction' of certain autobiographical events, occasions and epiphanies in our lives assists us to make sense of the present. Thirdly, the reiteration of 'metaphorical stories' create an *interpretive puzzle with no definitive answer* (Surr 2005, p1722). The author further surmises that narrative theory may be used to suggest that life story is crucial to the development and preservation of self.

Process of the structured life review

Haight et al. (2003) advise that the process is divided into eight weeks of one-hour sessions, including one week to introduce and assess the viability of conducting life review, six weeks to review one's life and one week to provide a closing evaluation to the intervention. However, it is also recommended that the length of time used for delivery should be amended according to the needs of the client. The social worker or other trained care worker uses a person-centred counselling approach to underpin the delivery of the life review and experiencing form (LREF) (Haight 1991). The questions in the review cover death, grief, fear, religion, school, hardships, sex, work and relationships over the life course. It is not necessary to ask all questions in the review and the schedule should serve as a guideline only. The form, which has been proven as both a valid and reliable tool, is formatted according to the subsections shown in the box.

Prior to interview, the worker must undertake preliminary tasks with the client, including assurance of strict confidentiality, establishing a contract for work, obtaining permission to tape the life review process, assessing psychological status using tools to gauge depression and life satisfaction at the pre- and post-intervention junctures (see Geriatric Depression Scale (GDS) or Life Satisfaction Index (LSIA)). The following is a sample of questions adapted from Haight (1991). Alternatively, see Appendix G in Gibson 2004, p.301 for the full schedule.

Session one

Childhood

What is the first thing you remember in your life?

What was life like for you as a child?

What were your parents like?

Did you have any brothers or sisters?

Did someone close to you die when you were growing up?

Do you ever remember being very sick?

Did you enjoy being a child?

Session Two

Adolescence

When you think about your life as a teenager, what is the first thing you can remember about that time?

Did you go to school? What did school mean for you?

Did you work during these years?

Tell me of any hardships experienced at this time?

Do you remember feeling that there wasn't enough food or necessities of life as a child or adolescent?

What were the pleasant things about your adolescence?

What was the atmosphere in your home?

Who were you closest to in the family?

Sessions three and four

Adulthood

Tell me the most important events that happened in your adulthood (from 20 years onwards).

What place did religion play in your life?

What was life like in your twenties and thirties?

Tell me about your work. Did you enjoy work?

Did you form significant relationships with people?

ACTIVITY 11.3

Find someone to work with. Look at the questions for the 'Adolescence' section of the Haight's life review and experiencing form (LREF). In your pair, one person should take on the role of the interviewer while the other responds to the questions in an open and honest manner.

Questions for the interviewer

How did you feel when asking the questions?

Were there any that were particularly difficult to ask?

What did you learn about yourself?

What did you learn about the person?

Questions for the interviewee

How did you feel when asked about your personal life?

Was there anything that you feel that you could not have talked about?

Were you open with the interviewer?

Did you feel that he/she was empathic or demonstrated understanding?

What did you learn about yourself?

ACTIVITY 11.4

Sadie was born in a town in Northern Ireland and was raised in a strict religious household until the death of her mother when Sadie was 15. (See the case study for more detail.)

You have asked Sadie a question from the 'Childhood' section of the Haight's life review (1991) pro forma, what was life like for you as a child? She replies as follows.

'When I was a youngster you went to church every Sunday, all holy days, and prayed to St Anthony and St Martin and, oh, St Jude for hopeless cases because I am one [laughs]. I, my mammy and my friend's mammy worked in the shirt factory which was just at the bottom of the street. My father didn't seem to get much work, much like the rest of the men in the town at that time. My mammy was a great seamstress and could run you up a wee dress in no time at all on the treadle sewing machine, although she took the dresses in to work to do the tricky bits. I loved the fact that I always had a different dress from the rest of the girls in the street and I wondered at how quickly she seemed to get everything done ... Nothing was a bother to her. I remember saying that I was feeling down once and she said, 'Sure, in our day you had no time to be feeling that way.' I never said it aloud again even though I felt it as I was growing up. She loved children and there was always the sound and smell of babies in the house ... She always said that she loved her wee boys ... but that she loved me as the number one girl ... I loved her saying that even though I knew I was the only girl ... It made me feel special to be her number one. It just doesn't seem right that a house should be empty of youngsters now and she isn't here either ... I miss her so much these days.'

Summarise the main points of Sadie's narrative.

What points would you probe further on?

Are there any issues which you would feel awkward in addressing?

How would you approach these issues?

What skills would you use?

What values would you employ?

COMMENT

From this excerpt, it is clear that Sadie is recalling her relationship with her mother and remembers the loving, caring environment that she experienced in these formative years. It is also apparent that she felt 'special' as a young girl who loved her home-made clothes, which were so different from those of the other children. She was also very enthused when she talked about her memories of being 'number one girl' in her mother's eyes and this was obviously a memory which influenced her subsequent providing of a caring environment for her brothers when her mother died. These are of course issues which may be comfortable to discuss for both the worker and the client and will most probably engender a substantial level of detail and positivity. However, it may be more difficult for the student to broach comments such as, 'I remember saying that I was feeling down once and she said, 'sure, in our day you had no time to be feeling that way.' I never said it aloud again even though I felt it as I was growing up.' *In order to address the meaning implied in this comment, it is important to think about the professional values which underpin the work and the social work skills required to enhance the interaction.*

In order to undertake meaningful and productive life story work or structured life review, the worker must utilise a range of basic interpersonal social work skills and professional values. The skills base required includes the use of generic communication skills, such as non-verbal skills, attuned listening skills, sensitive questioning and responding skills as well as the specific social work skills of observation, assessment, recording and evaluation. The following are some of the communication skills needed for work with the interventions described in this chapter.

Listening skills and sensitive questioning skills

Try to be completely attentive to what the individual is saying and do not 'rush in' to fill the gaps with a prompt or question. As people with dementia often need time to formulate a response to a question, be prepared to wait for their answer. Respond to the feelings as well as the content of the client's responses and guard against the use of questioning which may be regarded as intrusive (Schweitzer and Bruce 2008).

Skills of understanding

As you listen to the person with dementia articulate their thoughts and feelings, these may at times appear garbled and incomprehensible. The person may refer to incidents that have happened many years ago as if they happened yesterday. Endeavour to understand and interpret what is being communicated; this may be aided by a previous knowledge of their culture, lifestyle and socio-historic context. In addition, there may be times when the person may become agitated and frustrated with attempts to 'reach for words'. Chapman et al. (2001) recommend that the worker should learn the vocabulary that the person uses and also recognise the difference between words articulated which may be based on social pleasantries or learned mantras and those words which require reasoning and word-finding ability. In addition, the worker should take time to learn the meaning underlying the words used. For example, a person may use swear words or emotively charged language in what at first may appear an angry manner but after careful examination it is clear that the person is expressing pleasure and satisfaction.

Adaptability skills

The worker must be willing to alter plans quite quickly and move with the fluctuating needs of the client. In this way, the person is afforded the opportunity to communicate immediately what she or he wishes to say rather than adhering to the specific chosen topic (Schweitzer and Bruce 2008).

Skills of mirroring and reflecting back

Keep the pace of the communication at the same level as displayed by the client, leaving pauses in communication which mirror the person's silent periods. Moreover, if you have difficulty in comprehending the meaning of the person's responses, then reflect back what you think you have heard via the use of phrases such as 'Have I got this right?' or 'Would I be correct in thinking that …?' (Schweitzer and Bruce 2008).

Non-verbal communication skills

Eighty per cent of our communication is non-verbal and is expressed via eye contact, body posture, facial expression and gesture. We respond to non-verbal cues and gauge if we are being listened to through the interpretation of body language as we listen to the spoken word. Buijssen (2005) stresses that the most important non-verbal action, in working with dementia, is the maintenance of eye contact together with the avoidance of negative body posture, such as turning away from the client. Moreover, Buijssen warns that some people with dementia become very fearful if approached or spoken to from behind, because they may no longer be able to assess a situation from one glance. He advises that the worker should explain what is happening in a straightforward and uncomplicated manner.

Social work values in dementia care interventions

Social work does not ascribe to the medical model of dementia as a disease state but rather views the condition as a disability that is exacerbated by negative collective, societal and structural attitudes towards people with dementia. This perspective is at the core of social work intervention in dementia care and differentiates the profession from other allied professions such as nursing or occupational therapy (Parsons 2005). Social workers are committed to challenging the stereotyping, oppressions, discriminations, social exclusion and marginalisation faced by people with dementia and those who care for them. In terms of everyday personal oppressions, how often have you heard a member of your own family or circle of friends being described as 'doting' or 'demented'?; terms which are inherently negative and carry with them images of vegetative states and the pointlessness of trying to talk to 'poor old granddad'.

Professional social work values applicable to person-centred care in dementia include the core values of respecting the uniqueness of the individual, respecting dignity and worth, citizenship, social justice, empowerment and empathy. One of the most basic human needs is to be accepted and valued as a unique person and this need may be protected via the use of reminiscence and life story/review work. Only in a true understanding of the past can the worker begin to understand the unique personhood and concomitant needs of the person in the present (Gibson 1997). Kitwood (1997b) considers empathy as essential for appreciating the uniqueness of the person as the former is essential for understanding what it means to be that person and what it feels like to have lived and currently live their experience. Empathy is not simply about intellect but primarily about feeling and intuition and is only truly achieved with commitment and with skilled communication using some of the techniques described above. Empathy must also be used actively and reflectively within the life history, life review or reminiscence interventions or the work will run the risk of becoming unfocused or delivering unachievable goals.

Furthermore, people with dementia are at risk of losing their autonomy, the personal control that they formerly had over most aspects of their life and of becoming increasingly dependent on others for physical and emotional care and support. While the empowerment of the individual may be viewed as problematic, the worker must not be hampered by the difficulties involved and not be sidetracked by notions that it will not work effectively or that it cannot be achieved at all. Chapman and Marshall (1993) note that the actualisation of empowerment in dementia should take heed of the following points.

- Individuals have the capacity to make their own decisions and act on their own behalf.

- Social workers must recognise that the offer of discussion or intervention may be rejected at any time; the relationship is not unilateral.

- Imbalances of power must be exposed and discussed where relevant and understandable.

- Social workers should obtain and utilise resources to promote individual ability.

(Chapman and Marshall 1993)

CHAPTER SUMMARY

- There are similarities and overlap between the definitions, uses and applications of reminiscence, life story and structured life review in dementia care.

- The biomedical perspective on aging has increasingly been augmented by an understanding of the client's social, situational, familial and current lifestyle factors. Subsequently, there was an examination of the congruencies and differences across the reminiscence, life story and life review continuum.

- The exploration of 'Sadie's story' encouraged you to think about which type of reminiscence work would best suit the work with Sadie and there were a number of issues and events in Sadie's history and current situation which might influence that decision.

- A number of formats can be used in life story work, ranging from simple pen and paper to information technology software.

- An alternative approach is to use structured life review which is time limited and structured. The purpose is to encourage the individual to recount, discuss and revisit and make sense of events and past experiences and develop new and/or more positive perspectives on the past within a therapeutic environment.

- The skills of listening, understanding, sensitive questioning and reflecting, together with the core social work values of respect, empowerment and empathy, are essential in life story work.

FURTHER READING

Gibson, F (2004) *The past in the present: Using reminiscence in health and social care*. Baltimore: Health Professions Press.
The text provides a comprehensive overview of the various forms of reminiscence interventions and how they may be utilised in dementia care and in other areas related to social work practice.

Gibson, F (2005) Fit for life: the contribution of life story work. In Marshall, M (ed.) *Perspectives on rehabilitation and dementia*. London: Jessica Kingsley.
A chapter in an edited collection, this gives a concise synopsis of the formats and content used in life story work.

Goldsmith, M (2002) *Hearing the voice of people with dementia: Opportunities and obstacles*. London: Jessica Kingsley.
This explores the general characteristics of dementia, non-verbal communication and empowerment in dementia care and the utilisation of life story work as a method of intervention.

Haight, B K (1991) The state of the art as a basis for practice. *International Journal of Aging and Human Development,* 33 (1), 1–32.
The journal article outlines the Haight Life Review and Experiencing Form (LREF).

Murphy, C (1994) *It started with a sea-shell: Life story work and people with dementia*. Stirling: University of Stirling.
This is a valuable resource for life story work with dementia as it demonstrates the various modes of use by means of real case studies from practice.

Schweitzer, P and Bruce, E (2008) *Remembering yesterday, caring today: Reminiscence in dementia care: A guide to good practice*. London: Jessica Kingsley.
A practical handbook which makes evidence-based claims; this accurately presents the knowledge distilled from repeated practice.

Chapter 12
Mediation approaches

Huw Griffiths

Introduction

In this chapter we look at mediation as an approach to resolving disputes, in this context disputes about how to make arrangements for the children and other issues such as money and accommodation when couples are separating. However, you will find here useful advice in other situations where negotiation and mediation skills may prove useful.

CASE STUDY

Aisha has continued to work with Brenda, who is now receiving medication and feels that her coping mechanisms have improved. However, her self-esteem remains low and she feels estranged from David since his release from prison. Brenda felt that she had had to cope with a multiplicity of problems caused by David's conviction for fraud. Sandra has now taken against her father and neither she nor Brian will speak to him and have told their mother to 'dump him and get a life'. Philip, in contrast, is pleased that his father is home and wants his dad to continue to take him fishing and to the various tool-hire exhibitions where he can indulge his passion for motorised vehicles. Philip wants his mum and dad to 'just be normal, like before Dad went away'.

Following her counselling sessions, Brenda realised that in fact she was very angry with David and that part of the cause of her depression was the fact that she had always 'scrimped and saved' to keep both household and business financially viable. She has confided in Aisha that she does not trust David any more and suspects that he is gambling again. However, Brenda feels trapped within the marriage but is unsure whether she has the strength to go through a divorce and bring up the children on her own.

Brenda feels an emotional attachment to the family home, having invested a lot of time and energy in presenting it to a high standard. The memories of bringing up three children in a neighbourhood that she loved makes her feel tied to the house and tied to the area. However, following the publicity surrounding David's trial, a number of the neighbours have refused to speak to her, and Philip has been badly bullied at the local secondary school. Brenda is extremely angry with David.

David feels ashamed and embarrassed that his misuse of the company finances was discovered and that Brenda, as a co-director of the company, is now aware of the extent of the financial irregularities, and the accompanying amount of money spent gambling, both online and in casinos. He feels that Brenda is very cold towards him and that the children have taken her side and maybe he would be better 'shot of the lot of them'. He is aware that Philip wants 'business as usual' but wonders whether Philip might be better without him. David is also of the opinion that Aisha is there to support Brenda and that social services are not interested in him and that she is 'typical of these new feminist social workers coming from the Women and Children's Directorate'.

It seems to him that the less depressed Brenda is the more depressed he is and in fact it was easier in prison. He has now started to drink alcohol while alone at night. He believes that if there were a custody contest in relation to Philip's place of residence, the court would favour Brenda.

In her work with the family Aisha picks up many of the feelings that are around. It seems to her that the break-up of the family is becoming a reality. She is aware that all the members of the family are worried and upset. She becomes very concerned about how they will all get through this and is not sure if some form of mediation might be appropriate. However, this is not an area of work with which she is familiar. She certainly doesn't feel sufficiently qualified, experienced or impartial to undertake the task herself.

ACTIVITY **12.1**

Try and think how you would feel, first if you were Brenda and then if you were David. Next consider what would be the impact on you if you were Philip, Brian or Sandra? Make notes against each of these names regarding how they might be feeling.

COMMENT

Each family member in this situation will have a different perspective. What is a solution for one party may be problematic for other parties. It is worth considering that no perfect solution exists, but that the role of mediation is to promote a good enough solution that encourages a perspective that looks to the future rather than the past.

ACTIVITY **12.2**

As a qualified social worker what do you think the challenges would be to your remaining impartial and neutral prior to agreeing to work with this couple? Note down the different challenges.

COMMENT

Social work practice is predicated on a value base that promotes equality and adheres to principles of anti-oppressive practice. As someone practising in a value-neutral manner it is necessary to become mindful of the barriers to anti-oppressive practice. Examples of this to consider are the gender bias of the mediator; class, ethnic or religious differences between the mediator and the individual family members and awareness of any tendency for collusion with one party against another.

Mediation services

Referral to mediation services

A qualified social worker or solicitor who had undertaken an accredited mediation course or was in the process of training would accept referrals. Training to be a mediator under the auspices of the UK College of Mediators would entail regular supervision while co-working child-focused cases. *All issues mediation* involves dealing with issues such as salary, pensions and property assets and these would require additional training.

The desired outcome is a *memorandum of understanding*, which is a written agreement worked out with the mediator in the room, usually with the aid of a flip chart which is then taken to the parties' respective solicitors who eventually will present the written copy to the court. The premise is that the couple retain control over the process, the elements of which then become legally binding when agreed by the court.

If you were David or Brenda, what would be the argument for entering a mediation process? What would be the argument against? List the arguments for and against for each of them.

COMMENT

The principle of 'do no harm' applies. Mediation therefore should not qualitatively make a painful situation worse. Often parties are frightened by the formality of the process; the loss process they are experiencing; the crises that they are in; the fear of the unknown; and the fact that one party may have more to lose than the other (see Acland 1990, pp17–22).

Referral process

Referral to a mediation service is a straightforward process. People like Brenda and David can be referred by:

- self-referral;
- a solicitor;
- the court as directed by a judge;
- a social worker or other professional;
- another family member.

The key issue is the issue of agreement by both parties to attend. In cases of separation and/or divorce, it is quite common for one party to be in favour of mediation and the other party to be resistant to mediation. Often it is the party who feels that they have more to lose who is resistant. The person who has been 'dumped', rather than the 'dumper', may be angry or depressed. Thus the conflict of the relationship is perpetuated through the process of disengagement; in other words a bereavement process is taking place without a death.

ACTIVITY *12.4*

Write down what practical arrangements you would need to make to create an atmosphere of safety and comfort for both David and Brenda.

COMMENT

The primary issue is one of safety; for example, if there is a history or a suggestion of domestic violence, then the question arises, should the mediation process take place at all? How does the alleged victim feel about sitting in the same room as the alleged perpetrator? If agreement to mediation has been reached, should arrangements be put in place to facilitate separate arrival and departure times? It is necessary to allow any party who has experienced domestic violence to leave the session first and this issue should be contracted at the beginning of each session.

The essential practical factors necessary for a successful session may include:

- *a venue that is perceived as neutral;*

- *a room that is quiet and comfortable with an ambient temperature that is neither too hot nor too cold;*

- *a room that is free from interruption by phone and especially mobile phones which should be switched off;*

- *a hot or cold drink, offered on arrival, a jug of water to be provided and a mid-session break offered;*

- *a box of tissues available in the room;*

- *ideally, a separate room available to permit time out should the need arise.*

The intake appointment

Initially, a first individual appointment is offered to assess the suitability of mediation for a particular couple. Mediation may be deemed unsuitable if:

- one party is incapable of effectively engaging in the process, for example because of high levels of domestic violence; addiction to drink or drugs; depression or other significant mental illness;

- one party is engaging in bullying or demeaning behaviour at the expense of the other party;

- one party has initiated a parallel legal process without the knowledge or agreement of the other party;

- a significant child protection issue has emerged that directly affects the sharing of parental responsibility; and/or

- the mediation process is damaging to one party; and/or

- one party is deliberately concealing financial information which prevents an equitable sharing of joint assets.

Options that David and Brenda may choose

Option 1

The idea of mediation appeals because it allows the couple to engage in child-focused mediation to enable them to formally agree on the residence and contact pattern in relation to Philip.

Therefore, following this individual appointment, both parties decide that they would prefer to engage in a *conjoint mediation process*.

Option 2

If the couple cannot agree these issues themselves a *court-directed resolution* would decide the residence and contact pattern in relation to Philip.

Option 3

David and Brenda may also need to share their financial assets and wish to engage in *all issues mediation*, which will decide the equitable division of money and property. All issues mediation will also include the childcare needs of Philip.

ACTIVITY 12.5

Which option would you choose and why? What are the gaps in your knowledge at this stage?

COMMENT

Option 1 *It is clear that all parties entering into, and participating in, a mediation process will experience varying degrees of ambivalence. Thus Brenda and David may change their minds at different points in the process. It is important to separate the issues from the personalities and highlight the fact that, although the children may not be physically present in the room, their interests must be paramount. Depressed, unhappy or angry adults do not always cognitively or effectively function in the most child-centred manner. In other words they have become psychologically absent from their children and, as a consequence of their own distress, may be unable to accurately tune in to the impact of separation on the children and family members. However, the care and well-being of the children also provide issues of commonality, issues upon which a skilled practitioner can refocus the attention of the adult parties. It is quite common, dependent upon the age of the child/young person, that signs of distress will have manifested themselves as the process of separation and divorce progresses to a conclusion, often against the wishes of the child. Asking parents to write separately a brief pen picture of the children/young person often emphasises both a difference in perception and the individuality of family member(s), with the underlying thrust of providing a platform upon which to build a memorandum of understanding.*

Option 2 *Alternatively it may be the case that Brenda is too angry with David to sit in the same room with him and feels that her interests are best served by a court-directed decision.*

Option 3 *Money for some couples is both a symbol and a cause of conflict. However, at the point of division it can prove an insurmountable problem. It could be at this point in the process that David determines that he does not wish to enter into a mediation process on the grounds that he 'has the most to lose'. Secondly, any settlement in relation to pension assets, the equity held in the family home and/or shares, is predicated on principles of openness and honesty. Both parties are legally bound to provide a transcript of assets verified by a professional financial adviser. Similarly, goods that each party acquired prior to being married should be noted, for example Great-Aunt Aggie's Coalport dinner service. Gifts which parties have given to each other can be a source of contention – was it really a gift? It may be that, ultimately, the court determines such issues in the absence of agreement.*

The issue in essence is one of power and control and the mediator's skill is to empower the weaker party. What is potentially damaging is a scenario where the adult financial concerns prevent an agreement in relation to the residence and contact pattern in relation to the children. Any financial settlement would in this case example have to take account of the costs associated with Philip and Sandra entering further or higher education or, arguably, any costs associated with an educational need that Brian might have while under the age of 21.

Pre-mediation stage

CASE STUDY

The family therapy, although helpful at the time, has raised a lot of issues. Similarly, Brenda's treatment by means of medication and counselling has empowered her to the point where she is of the opinion that the marriage has irretrievably broken down. David also feels that it is time for a fresh start and that he has wasted his life coping with Brenda's depression.

Aisha decides to recommend that the couple, following their refusal to attend marriage guidance counselling, attend mediation.

COMMENT

It is important to distinguish between mediation, which occurs when a couple have decided to divorce or separate, and divorce counselling, which takes place when one or both parties are unsure or ambivalent about staying together or separating. It is worth noting that a divorce is the end of a long and painful process and some couples will have already attended couple counselling and/or individual counselling.

CASE STUDY

Purpose of mediation as perceived by David and Brenda

The couple would like to think that they can separate in a civilised manner and preserve what little dignity they have left. Both hope that the end of their own relationship will not damage their continued parental relationship with their three offspring. They hope that mediation will enable them to remain in control of events rather than giving away responsibility to solicitors and ultimately the court.

Brenda is worried about the emotional impact on Philip; money; the upkeep of a place to live; her capacity to earn her own living if she ceases to be a co-director of the family business; whether she is tough enough to negotiate with her ex-partner; and the possible return of her depression.

David is worried about being 'taken to the cleaners' by Brenda and whether it would be better simply to rely on a solicitor fighting his cause for him; his deteriorating relationship with his elder son and his daughter; the practicalities of maintaining a relationship with an increasingly distressed Philip; the sharing of the company's business assets; losing his temper completely; and/or returning to gambling ... or that he might just end it all.

ACTIVITY 12.6

What would be the content of a risk analysis in relation to both Brenda and David? List the areas that need to be explored?

COMMENT

A mediator checklist should consider the following elements.

Mediator checklist

- *Is Brenda's depression sufficiently controlled that she can engage in a negotiation process without disadvantaging herself?*

- *Can Brenda and David face each other in the same room and manage the emotional content of the break-up?*

- *Given David's criminal conviction for fraud, can he be trusted to honestly declare his liabilities and assets and provide verification by the company accountant?*

- *Has Brenda received independent financial advice as to her financial position as a co-director of the family firm?*

- *Who is going to move out of the shared family home? Can one party afford to move out of the marital home?*

- *How will David continue to maintain a relationship with his two eldest children?*

- *Philip, given his age, would be deemed by the court to be Gillick competent and, therefore, how would his views be taken into account?*

- *How will Brenda and David manage their son's distress and agree on a common approach to shared care?*

- *Who will Philip stay with at Christmas; go on holiday with; and which parent will attend parents' evenings at school?*

- *Should Philip and his brother and sister be seen directly by the mediator or can their mother and father represent their views?*

- *Are there any other professionals involved? If so, what is the responsibility of the mediator in preserving confidentiality and the sharing of information?*

- *What are the limits of confidentiality?*

- *Are there any domestic violence and/or child protection issues that will impact on the process?*

Theoretical approaches to mediation

Mediation has been defined as *assisted negotiation* (Acland 1990, p18) by a neutral third party. Moore (2003) elaborates by stating that it is:

> *the intervention in negotiation or conflict of a mutually acceptable third party, with limited or no authoritative decision-making power, and who assists the involved parties to voluntarily reach a mutually acceptable settlement of the issues in dispute.* (p15)

The idea is to facilitate negotiation and reach an agreement that is mutually beneficial to both parties, that is a win/win solution rather than a win/lose outcome. Underpinning this aspirational process is the belief that people have the capacity to find their own solutions if provided with the correct circumstances within a safe enough environment that encourages the sharing of responsibility. The practice dilemma is to be found in establishing a new climate of trust when trust has broken down.

Mediation has also been termed alternative dispute resolution, which is as an alternative to legal remedies within the court system; such a terminology is used widely in both the USA and Australasian literature.

Bush and Folger (1994) stress the transformative power of mediation as a clear example of self-empowerment; however, the authors highlight the fact that the sources of conflict being presented may have their roots in deeper issues than a simple redistribution of assets. Foci that have a particular resonance in dealing with issues of finance, pensions, property and money are simply referred to as all-issues mediation.

Process

Fisher and Ury (1981) deconstruct the method as a fourfold process, namely:

- separate the people from the problem;

- focus upon interests not positions (interests are different from positions. For example, Brenda might have a position that David should not have any contact with Philip but her interest is to prevent further upset being caused for Philip. Interests are easier to find agreement around than positions);

- invent options for mutual gain;

- insist on objective criteria.

Thus the principle in practice is to uncover areas of commonality rather than difference.

ACTIVITY *12.7*

How might these four principles be applied to the case of David and Brenda?

Make a list of what David and Brenda currently have in common?

COMMENT

A useful method of enhancing the elements of commonality is to request that both Brenda and David list their areas of common interest prior to attending the next mediation session. Such an approach places responsibility for problem-solving back with the couple. It acts as a preliminary tuning-in exercise prior to the session and therefore is cost-effective in face-to-face mediator contact as providing an agenda for progress. It also offers hope for the future.

It is often difficult in situations of crisis or high stress for people to separate thinking issues (cognitive) from feeling issues (affective). Therefore, if the couple are questioned as to how they feel, *they may respond differently than if questioned as to what they* think.

175

Power and process

The creativity of mediation is to provide the proverbial level playing field or equal power balance. Thus, if power is unequally distributed, the question has to be posed: how might the mediator empower the weaker party?

People are ascribed power by society in different ways. Feminists would argue that society endows men with more power than women; for example, better career opportunities, greater income and so on. Wealth and power appear as coterminous facets of successful people. The way a person dresses, the accent they have, their ethnic and religious background, sexual orientation and, importantly, their level of education all construct a person's identity. Issues of physical and mental health will also affect a person's capacity to engage in a helping process. A sensitive mediator will need to be able to read or assess a situation in facilitating an atmosphere of trust and safety. Thompson (2006) states that:

> Social work staff need to be sensitive to these issues in order to avoid reinforcing negative and demeaning images and seek opportunities to give positive feedback and enhance self-esteem. (p108)

Egan (2006) highlights the use of the SOLER model as a form of social skills engagement, which is explained as:

S it squarely with an

O pen posture

L eaning forward maintaining

E ye contact with a

R elaxed demeanour. (p76)

What the service user sees and feels in the room is vital to the success or failure of the process as the goal is also being: *aware of your significant thoughts, feelings and actions and of the impact you make on others* (p270).

Self-awareness is vital as service users will be sensitive to the subtleties of the mediator's behaviour.

A major issue in practice is the question of note-taking. Is this unduly officious and will it pose a barrier to communication? How does one maintain eye contact and gather information? The obvious challenge in this area of work is the skill of being able to work with two people as opposed to interviewing one individual.

Thus skills that are used in person-centred counselling are particularly relevant, for example Rogers (1965) utilises the principles of unconditional positive regard, empathy and congruence, operationalised by the means of active listening (see Chapter 2).

However, the following scenarios may take place.

- David is agitated in the first mediation session and interrupts and talks over Brenda.
- Brenda admits to being angrier than she has ever been and shouts at David using swear words.

- The mediation appears to be proceeding smoothly but with Brenda concentrating on writing down every word, much to the annoyance of David. He interprets this action as a threat and wishes to discontinue the session.

- Brenda is monosyllabic, looks at the floor and does not participate. At the mention of Philip requiring a bedroom in the two homes that would be required (following the divorce) Brenda cries silently.

- David states, 'I have no role any more as Philip's dad, he's better off without me and Sandra hates me.'

- Brenda says, 'Unless you give me half the equity in the house and a salary of £30,000 a year I will ensure that you will have no contact with Philip and Sandra.'

ACTIVITY 12.8

How would you respond to each of these points constructively?

What are the mediator options?

COMMENT

It is easier for couples who are in high conflict not to talk to each other but to address all of their communications to the mediator. The skill of paradoxical injunction (see p126) as used in family therapy will take the pressure off the couple to communicate. The natural inclination is also for Brenda and David to talk to each other when asked not to.

People in high conflict with each other are in danger of becoming psychologically absent from their children. Divorce is an adult solution to an adult problem; however, the divorce of parental responsibility is not an option. Therefore, as a method of re-engaging Brenda and David in their parenting role and shifting the focus away from the couple's relationship, various skills may be used. Examples are:

- using a flip chart in the room and asking each party in turn what may be written down with the ultimate purpose of using this material in a future *memorandum of understanding*;

- drawing a family tree on the flip chart and asking the couple to paint a pen picture of their children;

- drawing a family tree and actually sticking photographs on the flip chart;

- representing significant family members in the room by empty chairs;

- using time boundaries to either slow sessions down or focus on the agreed agenda for that particular session;

- summarising what has been achieved in the session and focusing on areas of common agreement, e.g. both Brenda and David wish to continue to actively parent Philip;

- using 'the explicit referee option' where each person is allowed an exact period of equal time;

- basic courtesies such as offering water or a hot drink;

- offering to build in time reviews within the session whereby an agreed break can help provide space at periods of high emotion;

- confronting the couple with the fact that the session is not working and putting the responsibility back to the couple as to whether they wish to continue;

- using third parties to avoid the trauma associated with contact handovers, e.g. using Brian as a staging post whereby Mum or Dad would meet their children at his house;

- using text or e-mail as a method of facilitating communication but without the emotion of a telephone call.

Draft memorandum of understanding

(Marked 'without prejudice')

1. David has agreed to move out of the marital home and will reside in a rented flat until such time as the former marital home is sold.

2. The equity of the marital home will be divided on a fifty-fifty basis on a date specified following Philip's eighteenth birthday.

3. Both David and Brenda will continue to support and parent their two younger children.

4. Sandra wishes to reside with Brenda but is agreeable to meeting her father once a month in town for coffee and possibly shopping.

5. Philip wishes to reside with Dad, but until such time as Dad is able to accommodate him he will reside with Mum and stay with Dad every weekend.

6. The children will choose where to spend the Christmas holidays and David and Brenda will consult via Brian as to what Christmas gifts are purchased by the respective parents.

7. Both David and Brenda will financially support their children in the event of their gaining access to further or higher education.

8. Brenda will receive a salary of £15,000 a year until the business is sold.

9. David agrees to pay an additional monthly figure of £600 per month until Philip reaches the age of 18 years.

10. Brenda as a co-director of the company shall receive 50 per cent of the equity of the value of the business at the point of sale.

11. Estate agents fees, accountancy fees and valuation fees will be borne equally by the couple.

Brenda and David would then take this draft to their respective solicitors who might query some facets of the agreement, which may necessitate further written contact or face-to-face contact with the mediator. Alternatively it may prove easier for the solicitors to negotiate with each other.

ACTIVITY **12.9**

How good are your negotiation skills when faced with a power imbalance?

Choose a friend or colleague and each take the respective role of either traffic warden or driver. Alternate the roles.

You are late to appear as a professional witness in the High Court. You cannot find a parking space anywhere. Other cars appear to be parked on a double yellow line and you manage to park in the only space available but on the double yellow line.

A traffic warden then approaches you.

What skills of negotiation do you employ to avoid getting a ticket? Can you formulate a win/win outcome?

COMMENT

It is a question of how you use your own personality and sense of self-awareness, for example, your tone of voice and use of body language. How do you think the traffic warden experiences you? What empathy can you generate towards an individual performing an unpopular role? What issues of right and wrong are you prepared to acknowledge and/or concede? Is there any legitimate way that the traffic wardens legitimate authority can be questioned? What facts do you need to check out?

Working with cultural, ethnic and religious differences

Conflict will normally exacerbate existing differences within a relationship and the family system(s), some of these points of difference will have their roots in the pre-existing religious, cultural and ethnic origins of the parties (Roberts 2007). Ethnic, religious and cultural issues of difference within the context of a loving relationship would have appeared minor but reconcilable. However, in the context of a separation process these differences will assume a degree of seriousness hitherto denied or unacknowledged. The associated family systems will also endeavour to adapt to the break-up in their respective, if unique, individual ways (Bush and Folger 1994). The parties will bring these perceived and actual perceptions/differences into the mediation process; for example, think of a fine china cup being held up to the light whereby small cracks or fault-lines will become visible and magnified (Mallouli, 2005). Differences and issues that seemed minor during a happy relationship may assume an enhanced importance during the process of separation with a need to manifest defence mechanisms including 'transference and projection' which focus on the opposite culture (see Chapter 1).

ACTIVITY **12.10**

In Activity 12.2 you reflected upon the challenges of remaining impartial and neutral; however, list below the similarities and differences between your own background and that of 'the couple' who you are now working with.

Continued

ACTIVITY **12.10** *continued*

Endeavour to exercise some preliminary empathy in relation to cultures that are different from your own (Brodley and Schneider 2001).

Choose parties where there is a cross-cultural element of major difference from you, for example:

Hindu male–Sikh female;

Traveller female–Settled Male;

Chinese graduate–Scottish tradesperson;

English male with disability–Afro-Caribbean able-bodied;

Welsh speaker–Romanian

Irish Catholic–Scottish Protestant;

List differences in terms of gender, ethnic background, religious affiliation, class, educational background, accent, sexual orientation, able-bodied/disabled …

How might these similarities/differences impact on the respective parties involved in the mediation process?

How are you as the mediator perceived?

Think of a continuum on a scale of 1 to 10, with Distance placed at point 10 and Collusion placed at point 1; now locate yourself in relation to Party 2.

Party 1

1	2	3	4	5	6	7	8	9	10

Collusion   *Distance*

And the same for Party 2.

How might you achieve a balance? What knowledge gaps do you have and how might they be bridged? The idea is to 'power balance'.

Why are you closer to one party rather than the other?

Such a 'tuning-in' or preliminary empathy exercise (Shulman 1992) serves to self-empower the worker and enhance self-confidence.

ACTIVITY **12.11**

Similarly, how might the case scenario of David and Brenda be influenced if David was from Protestant background and Brenda from a Catholic background? How will you address sectarian differences?

COMMENT

It may be that Brenda's fundamental belief system has instilled the belief that divorce per se, is wrong and therefore the best that she can hope for is a 'legal separation'. Thus in fact the couple would no longer constitute a conjoint relationship but in the eyes of the Catholic Church would remain married whilst being separated. Neither party could remarry without the additional procedure of a formal divorce.

It could be that David is accepting of this as a solution. The question is: Does it give him a sense of hope that the couple might at some future unspecified date reunite?

Or alternatively, does this increase his anger that the marriage is not legally over, thus preventing him from 'moving on'?

Correspondingly do these options increase or decrease Brenda's sense of frustration at the ending of her marriage. The 1908 'Ne Temere' ruling by the Vatican highlighted two issues: firstly, that a marriage between a Catholic and non-Catholic would not be recognised by the Church unless married in a Catholic church and it is still common practice for couples to undergo two separate ceremonies in their respective places of worship or registry office. Secondly, the children of that marriage were to be raised within the Catholic tradition (Belfast Telegraph 02/03/12). Or does Brenda wrestle with the guilt of potentially alienating herself from her Church and possibly her family and community? (Cohen 1982) Does she turn or return to her priest for advice? Brenda's existential crises (Roberts 2005) may confuse her thinking in relation to the mediation process, thus generating a sense of ambivalence and uncertainty (McLaughlin 2012). Remember, in times of crises (see Chapter 3) people retreat (or regress) into past areas of primary comfort, for example thinking or dreaming in their language of childhood.

Issues of loss, transition, depression, and abandonment are central to an understanding of bereavement theory. The process of hypocathexis or the 'loosening of the bonds' of affection (like unravelling the threads on a length of string), can take many forms, often characterised by a pervasive sense of ambivalence. Loss is a process which has been deconstructed by numerous authors (Currer 2007; Machin 2009; Rando 1993), but perhaps Kubler-Ross (1969) in her seminal work with leukemic children and their families characterised the process of bereavement as: shock, anger, denial, bargaining and acceptance. Murray-Parkes (2010) in his work with widows of coronary patients highlighted issues of searching and depression.

However, all presume a finite end and therefore some form of positive adaptation and ultimately acceptance. Is this possible in the process of 'uncoupling'?

People undergoing the process of separation and divorce progress through similar stages of 'bereavement', with the exception of not burying the person via a formal, socially acceptable funeral. The salient difference is the lack of an ending and the fact the ex-spouse maybe living with someone else, is happy but continues to act as a parent to the children. Thus he or she is still 'daddy' or 'mummy' to the children but existentially 'dead' to the ex-spouse. Therefore it is not uncommon for one party to become 'stuck' in anger stage whilst the other party has moved to a 'bargaining position' or an 'acceptance' that the relationship is over. Thus court dates, consultations with legal and social professionals take on an added significance which may eclipse the presence of the child(ren). Such a dynamic can in its turn give rise to differing levels of distress, both overt and covert, sometimes with associative negative aberrant behaviour.

A practice example that is becoming more mainstream but for some workers may raise additional challenges is that of same-sex couples who have, following the break-up of the marriage 'come out' as gay (Kleber et al. 1986) and the subsequent impact upon court decisions in relation to contact and residence.

The belief system and associated value base of the mediator is crucial in terms of Rogerian (1965) principles of acceptance as endemic to Key Role 4 within the professional Code of Ethics.

ACTIVITY **12.12**

What particular challenges would this scenario cause you as the mediator?

What is different?

What is similar to the issues generated by the other 'couplings' cited in Activity 12.10?

Children will experience the breakup of their parents' marriage in different ways according to their different ages and stages. Adult professionals are in danger of imposing their own attitudes or perceptions upon the children. The level of adversarial conflict in such situations can be intense, generating strong homophobic attitudes which militate against principles of acceptance and equality. Such negative perceptions are in danger of being internalised by the child often with an accompanying pressure to 'side' with the party who self-ascribes as 'victim' (Amato and Keith, 1991). However, the narrative may read as somewhat different dependent upon the cultural context of the separation. Issues that are deemed to be uncontested on the west coast of the USA may seem insurmountable in a rural area of Northern Ireland.

In contrast children can present attitudes that reflect 'the mature minor test' (Gillick v West Norfolk and Wisbech Area Health Authority 1985), whereby their acceptance of a new situation can be 'matter of fact', tinged with relief that the conflict is diminished, but anxious that 'Mammy will still be "Mammy"' and that '"Daddy" will still be "Daddy"'.

Implications for social work practice

People in distress often act and behave in challenging and unpredictable ways. Divorce and separation could be regarded as crises of adult identity with a profound impact upon the children of the relationship. It is an adult solution to an adult problem whereby parents become enmeshed in their own painful issues. Children are unwitting participants who often feel on the margins of a negative process that impacts upon their daily lives. Parents immersed in their own distress are often unable to view events from the child's point of view. Parents often feel they have parental responsibility but little control over major decisions that affect contact and residence. Children mirror this powerlessness and often manifest their distress in age-appropriate ways. Defence mechanisms may include psychosomatic illnesses; bed-wetting; open aggression to one or both parents and/or a deterioration in standards of academic achievement and behaviour. Some children falsely believe that they are to blame in some manner for the break-up of their parents' relationship. Children and young people can end up taking the side of one parent against another or become pawns in a parental war that is attritional.

RESEARCH SUMMARY

Johnston (1994) in a review of research studies demonstrates that ongoing conflict between parents following divorce is likely to result in problems in parent–child relationships and child emotional and behavioural problems. Children of divorce, especially boys, where there is a high level of conflict over the arrangements for the children, are two to four times more likely to be disturbed emotionally and behaviourally than the national norm. Arrangements that are decreed by courts, rather than agreed by parents, tend to result in poorer outcomes, especially for girls.

On the other hand, outcome studies of mediation indicate that rates of success in reaching agreement range between 40 per cent and 70 per cent (Emery and Wyer 1987; Koch and Lowery 1984; Pearson and Thoennes 1984; Sprenkle and Storm 1983).

Social work intervention in relation to Article 8 interventions (previously referred to as a satisfaction report) under the Children Act 1989 (in Northern Ireland, the Children Order (NI) 1995) is 'after the fact' – that is, some time after the 'de facto' separation has taken place. The report produced by the court officer or social worker is often confined to a minimum number of prescribed visits to the separated parties up to two years after the event. At worst it could be argued that it is merely a 'rubber stamping' of a decision arrived at in a crisis. Similarly, conflictual divorce proceedings are time-consuming and may be perpetuated within a climate of hostility that serves only to place a disintegrating family unit in a 'state of unknowing'. Conflictual contact, or no contact, or limited contact only serves to erode the emotional well-being of the child or young person (Wallerstein and Kelly 1980). The recent publicity emanating from such organisations as Fathers for Justice generates a perception that the courts rightly or wrongly favour mothers' rights over those of fathers. Whatever the merits of the argument the real issue is that of children's rights, thus any proactive engagement, such as mediation, with separating parents at a point of crisis, can only strengthen a family support agenda.

CHAPTER SUMMARY

- Separations are highly charged emotionally and this makes it especially difficult for couples to agree about arrangements for finalising the relationship, especially around children, money and possessions.

- Acrimonious separations can be damaging for children, especially if the conflict is focused on the arrangements for their care and welfare.

Continued

CHAPTER SUMMARY *continued*

- Parents do have the capacity to work their way through these emotions and arrive together at mutually satisfying arrangements.

- Some people need help to realise their capabilities. A range of mediation services is available for people in this position.

- Mediation is complex work, which requires particular qualities, skills and techniques. These are discussed in this chapter.

FURTHER READING

Fisher, L and Brandon, M (2002) *Mediating with families: Making the difference*. Sydney: Pearson Education.

This is a useful resource that provides an overview of family systems and family mediation theory. It contains a number of case studies, practical ways of dealing with issues and references for additional resources.

Pruitt, D and Carnevale, P (1993) *Negotiation in social conflict*. Maidenhead: Open University Press. Although written some time ago this is a valuable book which provides a research-based analysis of negotiation. There is discussion of negotiator strategies and tactics and their impact on the outcomes of negotiation.

Roberts, M (2007) *Developing the craft of mediation: Reflections on theory and practice*. London: Jessica Kingsley.

Drawing on the practice experience of a number of leading mediators, this book discusses individual qualities and approaches, styles and models of practice, which apply in a range of conflict situations.

Chapter 13

Bringing it all together – integrative and eclectic models

Trevor Lindsay

A C H I E V I N G   A   S O C I A L   W O R K   D E G R E E

This chapter will help you to develop the following capabilities from the **Professional Capabilities Framework:**

- **Professionalism**
  Identify and behave as a professional social worker committed to professional development.
- **Knowledge**
  Apply knowledge of social sciences, law and social work practice theory.
- **Intervention and skills**
  Use judgement and authority to intervene with individuals, families and communities to promote independence, provide support and prevent harm, neglect and abuse.

It will also introduce you to the following standards as set out in the 2008 social work subject benchmark statement.
5.1.1 Social work services and clients.
5.1.4 Social work theory.
5.1.5 The nature of social work practice.
5.5.1 Managing problem solving activities.
5.5.3 Analysis and synthesis.
5.5.4 Intervention and evaluation.

Introduction

So far, we have introduced 12 different methods of working with clients. An important question now follows. To what extent can I combine these different methods in my work, drawing on the range of techniques that they offer?

RESEARCH SUMMARY

Norcross and Grencavage (1989) cite nine different studies which indicate that between one third and one half of all American psychotherapists consider themselves to be eclectics. They further identify at least 50 textbooks in which the authors bring together various counselling techniques.

This evidence, together with the fact that there is an international quarterly, the *Journal of Integrative and Eclectic Psychotherapy*, suggests that eclectic and integrative approaches are widely regarded as having validity within the counselling profession. Oddly, comparatively little has been written on the subject within social work. However, before we rush off, happily marrying and blending different methods and techniques in our work, we need to understand a little more. In this chapter, we will look at some of the ways in which methods and techniques have been combined, including one example which provides useful guidance on how you might be eclectic in your practice. The authors in *Social Work Intervention* have used one family for our case studies throughout, applying different methods, as the situation seemed to demand. This has been a deliberate strategy on our part, to try to reflect the reality of practice, where we do not usually adhere strictly to one approach but choose different approaches at different times to deal with different issues.

Already in this chapter, you have been introduced to two confusing terms, *eclectic* and *integrative*. Before we go any further, we need to understand the difference. We cannot do better here than cite McLeod (2003).

> *Eclecticism involves ... selecting the best or most appropriate ideas or techniques from a range of theories or models, in order to meet the needs of the client. Integration refers to a somewhat more ambitious enterprise where the counsellor brings together elements from different theories and models into a new theory or model.* (p217)

Throughout this book, we have been able to cross-reference techniques in use in one method with other methods where they had their origins. When we examine motivational interviewing, for example, we find a number of techniques that we can recognise as having been borrowed from brief solution-focused therapy, for example the miracle question, without any apparent attempt to draw on the underpinning theory (*eclecticism*). At the same time, Miller and Rollnick (2002) define motivational interviewing as *a client-centered, directive method for enhancing intrinsic motivation to change* (p25). In this way, it combines person-centred and cognitive approaches but it cannot be described as integrative as it is not vertically consistent – *client-centred* and *directive* are philosophically and theoretically contradictory concepts. A better example of integration is to be found in cognitive behavioural therapy, which, as we have seen, brings together the two related theories of behaviourism and cognition.

Vertical and horizontal consistency

At this stage, it may help you to consider the concepts of vertical and horizontal consistency. For a method of intervention to be vertically consistent, the theory must follow logically from the underpinning philosophy and the practice must follow in a logical way from the theory without any contradictions between the three. A good example of vertical consistency is Rogers' person-centred model (see Chapter 2). It starts with the philosophy that all people have a natural tendency towards self-actualisation. It moves to a theoretical position that for this to happen the self-actualising tendency must be allowed to express itself in whichever way it can and, therefore, in practice, the worker must do nothing which gets in the way of that and must consequently be non-directive. Although we may draw upon a number of person-centred insights to enhance our relationship with the client, once we become in any way directive we behave in a way that contradicts the philosophy and theory and can no longer claim to be following the approach.

Task-centred work is a practical problem-solving approach that originated in social work practice and in response to research findings. Although it is basically cognitive and behaviourist in its practice, it is not theoretical in its origins and it does not rely directly on any particular philosophical or theoretical understanding. It does not therefore require vertical consistency. It is, however, horizontally consistent since it moves logically through a process of problem exploration, prioritisation, agreement on targets for change, objective setting, task achievement and termination. There are no contradictions here. It would not be horizontally consistent to agree with the client on targets for change without having first prioritised them.

Eclectic approaches do not depend on vertical consistency but must be consistent horizontally. Integrated approaches are both horizontally and vertically consistent.

You may see now that integrating different approaches is a difficult task, since the philosophical and theoretical basis of each of the original approaches must be complementary. Consequently, devising a new method of intervention which draws on two or more existing methods is way beyond the capacity of most social work practitioners, not only in terms of their time and energy but often also in terms of their depth of understanding. After all, in the reality of social work practice we tend to be guided rather than driven by any particular approach: we tend not to apply any particular model with the single-mindedness and knowledge of a counsellor following an approach in which they have been trained and accredited. We can therefore safely disregard integration as an approach for us. What then of eclecticism? Nichols and Schwartz (2001) make a distinction between *eclecticism*, where you draw techniques from a number of methods, and *selective borrowing*, where you mainly follow one particular approach but from time to time employ techniques more usually associated with another. For social work practitioners this approach has some merit.

Eclectic approaches

Lazarus and the multimodal approach

Lazarus (1989, 1997, cited in Dryden and Mytton 1999) was not so much concerned by theoretical underpinnings as interested in what worked for whom and in what circumstances. Having moved from psychoanalysis and person-centred therapy to behaviouralism and then cognitive approaches, Lazarus eventually came to the conclusion that there were seven different dimensions or *modalities*, accounting for every aspect of the human condition, which might require the attention of the therapist. These seven make up the acronym BASIC ID, that is, Behaviour, Affect (emotions), Sensation, Imagery, Cognition, Interpersonal relationships, and Drugs/biology. Depending on the situation, each modality, he believed, could require a separate intervention. This he called the *multimodal approach*. However, Lazarus is a *selective borrower*, sticking mainly to cognitive behaviouralism and blending in some techniques from systems and communications theory.

CASE STUDY

Looking back at the various episodes in the story of the Cartwright family, let us now apply the multimodal approach to the work that Brenda and Aisha have/may have undertaken.

Table 13.1 *Example of Lazarus's multimodal approach in work with Brenda*

Modality	Problem	Intervention
Behaviour	Dealing with Philip's suspension from school	Task-centred work
Affect	Panic	Crisis intervention
Sensation	Tension	Referral to stress management programme (relaxation techniques)
Imagery	Images of family poverty	Positive imagery
Cognition	I am never going to overcome these problems	Dispute unhelpful beliefs
Interpersonal relationships	Family problems	Family therapy counselling
Drugs/biology	Drinks to relax	Motivational interviewing

Adapted from Dryden and Mytton (1999)

Egan's skilled helper model

Egan's skilled helper model (2006) similarly provides a good example of an eclectic approach. Egan was not particularly concerned with the philosophical or theoretical basis of his work either. He liked what the person-centred approach had to say about relationship building, the concept of the unconscious, the challenging practices to be found in cognitive work and the getting-into-action practices of behavioural work. He preferred to select and employ particular skills and techniques based on what would be most efficacious at different stages of the helping relationship. *Clients are not interested in theories; they are interested in outcomes* (p14).

Figure 13.1 *Egan's skilled helper model*

Stage 1: What is going on?	Stage 2: What do I want instead?	Stage 3: How might I get what I want?
1(a) The story (getting the client to tell their story) **Skills:** active listening, reflecting paraphrasing, summarising	2(a) Possibilities (What do I do instead? How will things be when the situation is better?) **Skills:** brainstorming, facilitating imaginative thinking – miracle question, fast forward (Where would I like things to be in a year's time?)	3(a) Action strategies (how many ways are there?) **Skills:** brainstorming
1(b) Blind spots (What is really going on? What is preventing me from seeing myself, my problems, my unused opportunities?) **Skills:** challenging, offering different perspectives, making patterns and connections	2(b) Change agenda (choosing realistic and challenging goals) **Skills:** reflection, paraphrasing, reality checking	3(b) Possible actions (best fit strategies. What will work for me?) **Skills:** reflection, paraphrasing, reality checking
1(c) Leverage (focusing/prioritising. What are the things that will make a difference?) **Skills:** facilitating focusing and prioritising	2(c) Commitment (checking goals are right, finding incentives, resolving ambivalence) **Skills:** exploring costs and benefits, using evocative questions	3(c) Plan (what next and when? Drawing up a map to use on the way) **Skills:** facilitating planning

ACTION: Clients need to act on their own behalf from start to end

---

ACTIVITY 13.1

Examine Egan's skilled helper model in Figure 13.1. Note down the other approaches which coincide with each of the steps (1(a), 1(b), etc.)

COMMENT

We can easily identify a number of similarities between Egan's model and a number of other approaches (whether Egan was aware of borrowing them or not). For example, Stage 1(a) relies on some of the approaches of person-centred work; we can see ideas of the unconscious in 1(b), some aspects of task-centred work appear in 1(c); solution-focused techniques are evident in 2(a); motivational interviewing techniques are put into effect in 2(c).

Egan termed this approach selective eclecticism, *distinguishing it from* random borrowing.

> *Effective eclecticism ... must be more than a random borrowing of ideas and techniques from here and there. There must be some integrating framework to give coherence to the entire process; that is, to be effective, eclecticism must be systematic.*

(Egan 2002, p45)

We can see then that eclecticism is not perhaps the simple matter that we first thought. In fact there are a number of pitfalls. We turn now to Miller *et al.* (2002) for guidance on how we might be appropriately eclectic.

Client-directed, outcome-informed work

> ### RESEARCH SUMMARY
>
> *Lambert and Bergin (1994, cited in Miller et al. 2002, p186) in their literature review concluded that:*
>
> Research carried out with the intent of contrasting two or more bona fide treatments shows surprisingly small differences between the outcome [sic] for patients who undergo a treatment that is fully intended to be therapeutic.
>
> *Rosenzweig (1936, cited in Miller et al. 2002) suggested that effectiveness had more to do with the commonalities between different theoretical or technical approaches than their differences.*
>
> *Based on a large number of studies over a large period of time and varying in client type and research method, Miller et al. (2002, p190) conclude that four main factors account for improvements in people undergoing psychotherapy. These are:*
>
> *extratherapeutic (40 per cent) – factors outside the client–worker relationship;*
>
> *relationship (30 per cent);*
>
> *placebo, hope, and/or expectancy (15 per cent);*
>
> *structure, model, and/or technique (15 per cent).*

These findings are very significant for social work practice and of central interest for this book. They demand restatement.

- One half of any change occurring due to the client–worker engagement is attributable to the quality of the relationship itself.

- The structure, model or technique used is only half as significant as the relationship and is only equal in significance to the placebo effect and client hope and expectation.

Miller et al. (2002), drawing on this research, set out a number of strategies which should lead to positive change.

Extratherapeutic factors

Extratherapeutic factors are any of those aspects of the client's life and environment that contribute to positive change, outside of the client–worker contact, such as the client's own strengths and resources, sources of support and any fortuitous events that occur, such as finding work, moving house, meeting a new friend, winning the lottery. Research studies (Weiner-Davis et al. 1987; Lawson 1994) indicate that, if asked by the worker in a manner that expects a positive answer, between 62 and 66 per cent of clients report positive change prior to the therapeutic intervention commencing (see Chapter 11). Miller et al. (2002) cite a further body of research that shows that improvement between sessions with the worker is the rule rather than the exception. Since factors outside the relationship account for the largest proportion of positive change, it is important that you exploit this phenomenon as fully as possible. For example, you can ask the client to elucidate the part they played in bringing the change about, doing so in a way that presupposes that this is the case. Even if they deny having had such a role, you can ask how they have put the change to good use in their lives and how they will ensure that the positive changes remain in place. Where the client has found a source of support outside the relationship with the worker, you can discuss this with the client, being encouraging and exploring other similar sources of help.

Relationship factors

This is the second largest factor in bringing about positive change. Theorists, such as Hollis and Rogers (see Chapters 1 and 2), established many of the most important ingredients in the formation of a positive helping relationship. Miller et al., however, refer also to research which provides guidelines for enhancing the impact of relationship factors: accommodating the client's view of the therapeutic relationship and accommodating the client's level of involvement.

- **Accommodating the client's view of the relationship** recognises that goals that are both desirable and attainable in the view of the client are more likely to lead to a successful outcome. Furthermore, the client perception of the quality of the relationship is a better indicator of success or otherwise than is the worker's perception (Bachelor and Horvath 1999, cited in Miller et al. 2002). Taken together these findings suggest you are more likely to form a positive helping relationship if you accept the goals that the client views as the most important and accommodate your client's view of a positive relationship.

- **Accommodating the client's level of involvement** involves making sure that there is a good match between the involvement that you expect of the client and what they are prepared to commit to. The motivation of the client is an important factor in the facilitation of positive change and is highly dependent on their interaction with you. Expecting too little or too much of them will inevitably have an adverse effect on their motivation.

Placebo, hope and expectancy factors

These factors are as important in influencing change as is the choice of a method of intervention or technique. Miller et al. (2002) suggest the following strategies to increase the effect of these factors.

- **Having a healing ritual** recognises that rituals in themselves can enhance the effect of placebo, hope and expectancy factors, regardless of whether they themselves are designed to bring about any change. Whether it is telling a client to keep a drink diary, helping them to practise being assertive in role-plays, or greeting them for each session with a handshake, you are engaging in a healing ritual. Healing rituals are common to most cultures and their efficacy has been known for many centuries (Frank and Frank

1991, cited in Miller et al. 2002). The placebo effect is further strengthened when you believe that what you are offering the client will be effective and when you show interest in the results of your interaction with them.

- **Having a possibility focus** involves orienting your work with the client towards their changing in a positive way and/or achieving their goals. Consequently it is preferable to have a focus on having a better future than it is on understanding the past. The act of describing a desired future has the effect of relating the desired future to the present and consequently increasing the reality of bringing it about. A greater sense of control over their lives on the part of clients also increases hope. It is important, therefore, for you to take every opportunity to emphasise your client's sense of control, recognising achievements, however small. In this case, an examination of the past may be useful, in fact, when it takes the form of a search for successes and exceptions to a problem. The client is able to recognise a capacity to control and may be able to identify strategies to bring about the desired future.

Model and technique factors

As we have seen in this chapter the influence of using one particular method or model is not as significant as we may have thought. Nevertheless, it is important and it is useful to have a framework to help with the choice of what method or technique to employ at any particular time or in any particular set of circumstances. Our limited awareness and knowledge of the hundreds of different models available will obviously be a factor. Watson and West (2006) suggest that other important factors include:

- *the assessment of the situation;*

- *the agency context;*

- *the worker's approach and skills;*

- *the service user's ability and supports.* (pp113 and 114)

However, for Miller et al., the focus is on the client alone, making sure that the particular strategy:

> *(1) capitalises on client strengths, resources, and existing social networks;*
>
> *(2) builds on the spontaneous changes that the clients experience while in therapy;*
>
> *(3) is considered empathetic, respectful and genuine by the client;*
>
> *(4) fits with the client's goals for treatment and ideas about the change process;*
>
> *(5) increases hope, expectancy, and sense of personal control.*
>
> (Miller et al. 2002, p194)

Examine this list closely and you will see encapsulated in it many key ideas that we have encountered as we have gone through these chapters.

CHAPTER SUMMARY

- Integrative and eclectic approaches in terms of methods of intervention are alive, well and legitimised in the literature and by research studies.

- Integration involves combining two or more theoretical concepts to arrive at a new theory or approach, whereas eclecticism refers to the use of a number of techniques, regardless of their theoretical origins.

- Vertical consistency involves ensuring that the philosophy, theory and practice of an approach are completely without contradiction. Horizontal consistency requires that there are no contradictions within the practice of an approach.

- Lazarus's multimodal approach and Egan's skilled helper model are examples of eclecticism.

- The most important factors accounting for positive change in helping people are extratherapeutic (40 per cent); relationship (30 per cent); placebo, hope and expectancy (15 per cent) and model or technique (15 per cent). In each of these cases, strategies are available to enhance the positive effect.

FURTHER READING

Coulshed, V and Orme, J (2006) *Social work practice*. Basingstoke: Palgrave Macmillan.
This text provides a summarised version of Egan's skilled helper model.

Egan, G (2006) *The skilled helper: A problem-management and opportunity development approach to helping*. 8th edition. London: Thompson-Brookes Cole.
Here you will find Egan's latest formulation of the skilled helper model. Earlier editions contain slight but not very significant variations.

Dryden, W and Mytton, J (1999) *Four approaches to counselling and psychotherapy*. London: Routledge.
This book contains an accessible chapter on Lazarus's multimodal approach.

McLeod, J (2003) *An introduction to counselling*. 3rd edition. Buckingham: Open University Press.
This contains a comprehensive chapter on issues in eclecticism and integrationism.

Miller, S D, Duncan, B L and Hubble, M A (2002) Client-directed, outcome-informed clinical work. In Kaslow, FW and Leblow, J *Comprehensive handbook of psychotherapy, Volume 4, Integrative/eclectic*. New York: John Wiley.
This text is not easy to find but is worth getting as it provides an excellent overview of the research literature on the outcomes of therapy and then applies these in formulating guidelines for practice.

Appendix 1 Professional capabilities framework

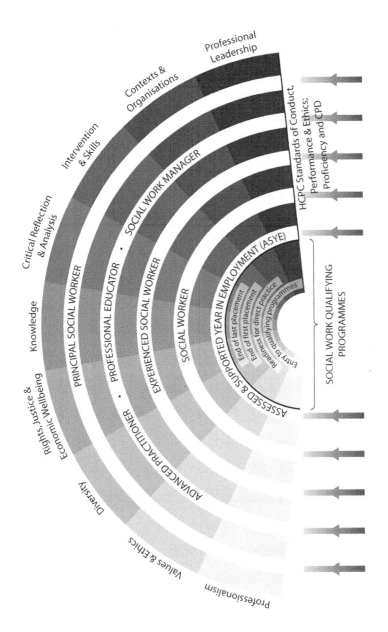

Professional Capabilities Framework diagram reproduced with permission of The College of Social Work

See pages xiii-xiv for the full list of standards.

Appendix 2 Subject benchmark for social work

Subject benchmark for social work

5 Subject knowledge, understanding and skills

Subject knowledge and understanding

5.1 During their degree studies in social work, honours graduates should acquire, critically evaluate, apply and integrate knowledge and understanding in the following five core areas of study.

5.1.1

Social work services, service users and carers, which include:

- the social processes (associated with, for example, poverty, migration, unemployment, poor health, disablement, lack of education and other sources of disadvantage) that lead to marginalisation, isolation and exclusion, and their impact on the demand for social work services

- explanations of the links between definitional processes contributing to social differences (for example, social class, gender, ethnic differences, age, sexuality and religious belief) to the problems of inequality and differential needs faced by service users

- the nature of social work services in a diverse society (with particular reference to concepts such as prejudice, interpersonal, institutional and structural discrimination, empowerment and anti-discriminatory practices)

- the nature and validity of different definitions of, and explanations for, the characteristics and circumstances of service users and the services required by them, drawing on knowledge from research, practice experience, and from service users and carers

- the focus on outcomes, such as promoting the well-being of young people and their families, and promoting dignity, choice and independence for adults receiving services

- the relationship between agency policies, legal requirements and professional boundaries in shaping the nature of services provided in interdisciplinary contexts and the issues associated with working across professional boundaries and within different disciplinary groups.

5.1.2

The service delivery context, which includes:

- the location of contemporary social work within historical, comparative and global perspectives, including European and international contexts

- the changing demography and cultures of communities in which social workers will be practising

- the complex relationships between public, social and political philosophies, policies and priorities and the organisation and practice of social work, including the contested nature of these

- the issues and trends in modern public and social policy and their relationship to contemporary practice and service delivery in social work

- the significance of legislative and legal frameworks and service delivery standards (including the nature of legal authority, the application of legislation in practice, statutory accountability and tensions between statute, policy and practice)

- the current range and appropriateness of statutory, voluntary and private agencies providing community-based, day-care, residential and other services and the organisational systems inherent within these

- the significance of interrelationships with other related services, including housing, health, income maintenance and criminal justice (where not an integral social service)

- the contribution of different approaches to management, leadership and quality in public and independent human services

- the development of personalised services, individual budgets and direct payments

- the implications of modern information and communications technology (ICT) for both the provision and receipt of services.

5.1.3

Values and ethics, which include:

- the nature, historical evolution and application of social work values

- the moral concepts of rights, responsibility, freedom, authority and power inherent in the practice of social workers as moral and statutory agents

- the complex relationships between justice, care and control in social welfare and the practical and ethical implications of these, including roles as statutory agents and in upholding the law in respect of discrimination

- aspects of philosophical ethics relevant to the understanding and resolution of value dilemmas and conflicts in both interpersonal and professional contexts

- the conceptual links between codes defining ethical practice, the regulation of professional conduct and the management of potential conflicts generated by the codes held by different professional groups.

5.1.4

Social work theory, which includes:

- research-based concepts and critical explanations from social work theory and other disciplines that contribute to the knowledge base of social work, including their distinctive epistemological status and application to practice

- the relevance of sociological perspectives to understanding societal and structural influences on human behaviour at individual, group and community levels

- the relevance of psychological, physical and physiological perspectives to understanding personal and social development and functioning

- social science theories explaining group and organisational behaviour, adaptation and change

- models and methods of assessment, including factors underpinning the selection and testing of relevant information, the nature of professional judgement and the processes of risk assessment and decision-making

- approaches and methods of intervention in a range of settings, including factors guiding the choice and evaluation of these

- user-led perspectives

- knowledge and critical appraisal of relevant social research and evaluation methodologies, and the evidence base for social work.

5.1.5

The nature of social work practice, which includes:

- the characteristics of practice in a range of community-based and organisational settings within statutory, voluntary and private sectors, and the factors influencing changes and developments in practice within these contexts

- the nature and characteristics of skills associated with effective practice, both direct and indirect, with a range of service-users and in a variety of settings

- the processes that facilitate and support service user choice and independence

- the factors and processes that facilitate effective interdisciplinary, interprofessional and interagency collaboration and partnership

- the place of theoretical perspectives and evidence from international research in assessment and decision-making processes in social work practice

- the integration of theoretical perspectives and evidence from international research into the design and implementation of effective social work intervention, with a wide range of service users, carers and others

- the processes of reflection and evaluation, including familiarity with the range of approaches for evaluating service and welfare outcomes, and their significance for the development of practice and the practitioner.

Subject-specific skills and other skills

5.2 As an applied subject at honours degree level, social work necessarily involves the development of skills that may be of value in many situations (for example, analytical thinking, building relationships, working as a member of an organisation, intervention, evaluation and reflection). Some of these skills are specific to social work but many are also widely transferable. What helps to define the specific nature of these skills in a social work context are:

- the context in which they are applied and assessed (eg, communication skills in practice with people with sensory impairments or assessment skills in an interprofessional setting)

- the relative weighting given to such skills within social work practice (eg, the central importance of problem-solving skills within complex human situations)

- the specific purpose of skill development (eg, the acquisition of research skills in order to build a repertoire of research-based practice)

- a requirement to integrate a range of skills (ie, not simply to demonstrate these in an isolated and incremental manner).

5.3 All social work honours graduates should show the ability to reflect on and learn from the exercise of their skills. They should understand the significance of the concepts of continuing professional development and lifelong learning, and accept responsibility for their own continuing development.

5.4 Social work honours graduates should acquire and integrate skills in the following five core areas.

Problem-solving skills

5.5 These are sub-divided into four areas.

5.5.1

Managing problem-solving activities: honours graduates in social work should be able to plan problem-solving activities, ie to:

- think logically, systematically, critically and reflectively

- apply ethical principles and practices critically in planning problem-solving activities

- plan a sequence of actions to achieve specified objectives, making use of research, theory and other forms of evidence

- manage processes of change, drawing on research, theory and other forms of evidence.

5.5.2

Gathering information: honours graduates in social work should be able to:

- gather information from a wide range of sources and by a variety of methods, for a range of purposes. These methods should include electronic searches, reviews of relevant literature, policy and procedures, face-to-face interviews, written and telephone contact with individuals and groups

- take into account differences of viewpoint in gathering information and critically assess the reliability and relevance of the information gathered

- assimilate and disseminate relevant information in reports and case records.

5.5.3

Analysis and synthesis: honours graduates in social work should be able to analyse and synthesise knowledge gathered for problem-solving purposes, ie to:

- assess human situations, taking into account a variety of factors (including the views of participants, theoretical concepts, research evidence, legislation and organisational policies and procedures)

- analyse information gathered, weighing competing evidence and modifying their viewpoint in light of new information, then relate this information to a particular task, situation or problem

- consider specific factors relevant to social work practice (such as risk, rights, cultural differences and linguistic sensitivities, responsibilities to protect vulnerable individuals and legal obligations)

- assess the merits of contrasting theories, explanations, research, policies and procedures

- synthesise knowledge and sustain reasoned argument

- employ a critical understanding of human agency at the macro (societal), mezzo (organisational and community) and micro (inter and intrapersonal) levels

- critically analyse and take account of the impact of inequality and discrimination in work with people in particular contexts and problem situations.

5.5.4

Intervention and evaluation: honours graduates in social work should be able to use their knowledge of a range of interventions and evaluation processes selectively to:

- build and sustain purposeful relationships with people and organisations in community-based, and interprofessional contexts

- make decisions, set goals and construct specific plans to achieve these, taking into account relevant factors including ethical guidelines

- negotiate goals and plans with others, analysing and addressing in a creative manner human, organisational and structural impediments to change

- implement plans through a variety of systematic processes that include working in partnership

- undertake practice in a manner that promotes the well-being and protects the safety of all parties

- engage effectively in conflict resolution

- support service users to take decisions and access services, with the social worker as navigator, advocate and supporter

- manage the complex dynamics of dependency and, in some settings, provide direct care and personal support in everyday living situations

- meet deadlines and comply with external definitions of a task

- plan, implement and critically review processes and outcomes

- bring work to an effective conclusion, taking into account the implications for all involved

- monitor situations, review processes and evaluate outcomes

- use and evaluate methods of intervention critically and reflectively.

References

Acland, F A (1990) *A sudden outbreak of common sense: Managing conflict through mediation.* Hutchinson: London.

Action for Advocacy (2011) *Non-instructed advocacy and the IMHA Role: best practice guidance.* Action for Advocacy [online] Available at: **http://static.actionforadvocacy.org.uk/opendocs/a4a_NIA_Best_Practice_Guidance.pdf** (accessed 19 January 2013).

Adler, A (1927) *Understanding human nature.* Oxford: Oneworld Publications.

Amato, P R and Keith, B (1991) Parental divorce and the wellbeing of children: A meta-analysis, *Psychological Bulletin* 110, 26–46.

Anderson, H (1997) *Conversation, language and possibilities: A postmodern approach to therapy.* New York: Basic Books.

BACP (2008) *What is counselling?* Available at: **www.bacp.co.uk/information/education/whatiscounselling.phpl**

Bandura, A (1977) *Social learning theory.* Englewood Cliffs, NJ: Prentice-Hall.

Barkham, M (2007) Methods, outcomes and processes in the psychological therapies across four successive research generations. In W Dryden (ed.) *Dryden's handbook of individual therapy.* London: Sage.

Barnes, D and Brandon, T (2002) *Independent specialist mental health advocacy services in Nottinghamshire.* Durham: University of Durham.

Bateman, N (2000) *Advocacy skills for health and social care professionals.* 2nd edition. London: Jessica Kingsley Publishers.

Bateson, G (1972) *Steps to an ecology of mind: The new information sciences can lead to a new understanding of man.* New York: Ballantine.

Bateson, G (1979) *Mind and nature: A necessary unity.* New York: Ballantine.

Beck, A T (1989) *Cognitive therapy and the emotional disorders.* Hamondsworth: Penguin.

Beckett, C (2006) *Essential theory for social work practice.* London: Sage.

Beidel, D C and Turner, S M (1986) A critique of the theoretical bases of cognitive behavioral theories and therapy. *Clinical Psychology Review*, 6 (2), 177–97.

Beresford, P (2000) Service users' knowledge and social work theory: Conflict or collaboration. *British Journal of Social Work*, 30, 489–503.

Bertalanffy, L (1968) *General systems theory: Foundation, development, applications.* New York: George Braziller.

Beyebach, M, Rodriguez-Morejon, AR, Palenzuela, DL, and Rodriguez-Arias, JL (1996) Research on the process of solution-focused brief therapy. In S Miller, H Hubble and B Duncan (eds) *Handbook of solution-focused brief therapy.* San Francisco: Jossey-Bass.

Black, G and Haight, B K (1992) Integrality as a holistic framework for the life review process. *Holistic Nurse Practitioner*, 7 (1), 7–15.

Bornat, J (1993) *Reminiscence reviewed: Rethinking aging.* Philadelphia: Open University Press.

Bowlby, J (1951) *Maternal care and mental health.* Geneva: WHO.

Bowlby J (1980) *Loss: Sadness and depression. Attachment and loss (vol. 3).* New York: Basic Books.

Boylan, J and Dalrymple, J (2009) *Understanding advocacy for children and young people.* Maidenhead: Open University Press.

Bozarth, J D (1998a) *Person-centred therapy: a revolutionary paradigm.* Ross-on Wye: PCCS Books.

Bozarth J D (1998b) Playing the probabilities of psychotherapy. *Person-Centred Practice,* 6, 33–7.

Bozarth J D (2000) *Non-directiveness in client-centered therapy: a vexed concept.* Paper presented at the Eastern Psychological Association, Baltimore, 25 March 2000. Available at **http://personcentered. com/nondirect.htm** (accessed 10 March 2009).

Brandon, D (1995) *Advocacy: power to people with disability.* Birmingham: Venture Press.

Brandon, D and Brandon, T (2001) *Advocacy in social work.* Birmingham: Venture Press.

Brearley, J (1995) *Counselling and social work.* Buckingham: Open University Press.

Broadhurst, K, Wastell, D, White, S, Hall, C, Peckover, S, Thompson, K, Pithouse, A and Davey, D (2010) Performing initial assessment: identifying the latent conditions of error at the front door of local authority children's services, *British Journal of Social Work,* 40 (2), 352–70.

Brodley, B T (1997) The non-directive attitude in client-centered therapy. *Person-centered Journal,* 4 (1), 18–30.

Brodley, B T and Schneider, C (2001) Unconditional positive regard as communicated through verbal behaviour in client-centered therapy. In J Bozarth and P Wilkins (eds) *Rogers' therapeutic conditions: unconditional positive regard.* Ross-on-Wye: PCCS Books.

Brooke, J (2002) *Good practice in citizen advocacy,* Kidderminster: BILD Publishers.

Brown, A (1992) *Groupwork* 3rd edition. Aldershot: Ashgate Publishing.

Brown, J M and Miller, W R (1993) Impact of motivational interviewing on residential alcoholism treatment. *Psychology of Addictive Behaviors* 7 (4), 211–18.

Buijssen, H (2005) *The simplicity of dementia: A guide for family and carers.* London: Jessica Kingsley.

Bush, R and Folger, J (1994) *The promise of mediation: Responding to conflict through empowerment and recognition.* San Francisco: Jossey-Bass Publishers.

Butler, G (2010) Reflecting on emotion in social work. In C Knott and T Scragg (eds) *Reflective practice in social work.* Exeter: Learning Matters.

Butler, R N (1963) The life review: An interpretation of reminiscence in the aged. *Psychiatry,* 256, 65–76.

Button, J (1997) Safety in numbers: creating safe space in groupwork. *Self and Society,* 25 (2), 4–11.

Caplan, G (1961) *Prevention of mental disorders in children.* New York: Basic Books.

Caplan, G (1965) *Principles of preventive psychiatry.* London: Tavistock.

Carr, A (2000a) Evidence-based practice in family therapy and systemic consultation; I. Child focused problems. *Journal of Family Therapy,* 22(1), 29–60.

Carr, A (2000b) Evidence-based practice in family therapy and systemic consultation; II. Adult-focused problems. *Journal of Family Therapy,* 22(3), 273–95.

Cecchin, G (1987) Hypothesising, circularity and neutrality revisited: An invitation to curiosity. *Family Process,* 26 (4), 405–14.

Cecchin, G, Lane, G and Ray, W (1994) *The cybernetics of prejudices in the practice of psychotherapy.* London: Karnac.

Chapman, A and Marshall, M (eds) (1993) *Dementia: New skills for social workers.* London: Jessica Kingsley.

Chapman, A, Gilmour, D and McIntosh, I (2001) *Dementia care: A professional handbook.* London: Age Concern.

Cherry, S (2005) *Transforming behaviour: pro-social modelling in practice.* Cullompton: Willan Publishing.

Chiang, K J, Chu, H, Chang, H J, Chung, M H, Chen, C H, Chiou, H Y and Chou, K R (2010) The effects of reminiscence therapy on psychological well-being, depression, and loneliness among the institutionalised aged, *International Journal of Geriatric Psychiatry*, 25, 380–8.

Chui, W H and Ford, D (2000) Crisis intervention as common practice. In Stepney, P, and Ford, D (eds) *Social work models, methods and theories: A framework for practice.* Dorset: Russell House.

Cigno, K and Bourn, D (eds) (1998) *Cognitive-behavioural social work in practice.* Aldershot: Ashgate.

Clark, M (2005) Motivational interviewing for probation staff: Increasing the readiness to change, *Federal Probation*, 69 (2), 1–9.

Cohen, N (1982) Same or different: a problem of identity in cross cultural marriages, *Journal of Family Therapy*, 4, 177–99.

Concise Oxford Dictionary (1988) London: Oxford University Press.

Coulshed, V and Orme, J (2006) *Social work practice.* Basingstoke: Palgrave.

Cowburn, M (2006) Constructive work with male sex offenders. In Gorman, K, Gregory, M, Hayles, M and Parton, P (2006) (eds) *Constructive work with offenders.* London: Jessica Kingsley.

Cree, V and Myers, S (2008) *Social work: Making a difference.* Bristol: Policy Press.

Currer, C (2007) *Loss and social work.* Exeter: Learning Matters.

Dallos, R and Draper, R (2000) *An introduction to family therapy: systemic theory and practice.* Maidenhead: Open University Press.

Davies, B (1975) *The use of groups in social work practice.* London: Routledge and Kegan Paul.

Department of Health (2001) *Treatment choice in psychological therapies and counselling: evidence based clinical guideline.* London: Department of Health.

De Shazer, S (1985) *Keys to solutions in brief therapy.* London: Norton.

DiClemente, C C and Prochaska, J O (1998) Toward a comprehensive, transtheoretical model of change: Stages of change and addictive behaviors. In Miller, W R and Heather, N (eds) Treating Addictive Behaviors. 2nd edition. New York: Plenum.

Doel, M (2002) Task centred work. In Adams, R., Dominelli, L. and Payne, M. (eds) *Social work: Themes, issues and critical debates.* 2nd edition. Basingstoke: Palgrave.

Doel, M (2006) *Using groupwork.* London: Routledge.

Doel, M and Sawdon C (1999) *The essential groupworker.* London: Jessica Kingsley.

Douglas, T (1991) *A handbook of common groupwork problems.* London: Tavistock/Routledge.

Douglas, T (1995) *Survival in groups.* Buckingham: Open University Press.

Dryden, W (ed.) (2007a) *Dryden's handbook of individual psychotherapy.* 5th edition. London: Sage.

Dryden, W (2007b) Rational emotive behaviour therapy. In W Dryden (ed.) *Dryden's handbook of individual therapy*, 5th edition. London: Sage.

Dryden, W and Mytton, J (1999) *Four approaches to counselling and psychotherapy*. London: Routledge.

Dryden, W and Scott, M (1988) A brief highly structured and effective approach to social work practice: a cognitive-behavioural perspective. In J Lishman (ed.) *Handbook of theory for practice teachers*. London: Jessica Kingsley.

Duffy, J (2006) *Participating and learning. Citizen involvement in social work education in the Northern Ireland context: A Good practice guide*. Belfast: NISCC, SWAP and SCIE.

Dykas, M J and Cassidy, J (2011) Attachment and the processing of social information across the life span: theory and evidence. *Psychological Bulletin* 137 (1), 19.

Egan, G (2002) The skilled helper: A problem management approach to helping. 6th edition. London: Thompson-Brookes Cole.

Egan, G (2006) The skilled helper: A problem-management and opportunity development approach to helping. 8th edition. London: Thompson-Brookes Cole.

Ehlers, A and Clark, D M (2003) Early psychological interventions for adult survivors of trauma: A review. *Biological Psychiatry*. 53 (9), 817–26.

Ellis, A (1962) *Reason and emotion in psychotherapy*. New York: Lyle Stuart.

Emery, R, and Wyer, M (1987) Child custody mediation and litigation: An experimental evaluation of the experience of parents. *Journal of Consulting and Clinical Psychology*, 55, 179–86.

Erikson, E (1965) *Childhood and society*. 2nd edition. London: Hogarth Press.

Erikson, E (1980) *Identity and the life cycle*. New York: Norton.

Farrall, S (2002) *Rethinking what works with offenders: probation, social context and desistance from crime*. Cullompton: Willan.

Feltham, C and Dryden, W (1993) *Dictionary of counselling*. London: Whurr.

Fisher, L and Brandon, M (2002) *Mediating with families: Making the difference*. Sydney: Pearson Education.

Fisher, R and Ury, W (1981) *Getting to yes: Negotiating agreement without giving in*. Boston: Houghton Mifflin.

Fleet, F (2000) Counselling and contemporary social work. In P Stepney and D Ford (eds) *Social work models, methods and theories: A framework for practice*. Lyme Regis: Russell House Publishing.

Folger J P and Jones T S (1994). Epilogue: Toward furthering dialogue between researchers and practitioners. In Folger, J P and Jones, T S (eds) *New directions in mediation: Communication research and perspectives*. Thousand Oaks, CA: Sage.

Ford, P and Postle, K (2000) Task centred practice and care management. In Stepney, P and Ford, P (eds) *Social work models, methods and theories: A framework for practice*. Dorset: Russell House Publishing.

Freddolino, P P, Moxley, D P and Hyduk, C A (2004) A differential model of advocacy in social work practice. *Families in Society*, 85 (1), January/March, pp 119–28.

Freud, A (1966) *The ego and the mechanisms of defence*. New York: International Universities Press.

Frude, E, Honess,T and Maguire, M (1994) *CRIME-PICS II*, Cardiff: Michael and Associates.

Geldard, K and Geldard, D (2004) *Counselling adolescents.* 2nd edition. London: Sage.

Gibson, F (1994) *Reminiscence and recall: A guide to good practice.* London: Age Concern.

Gibson, F (1997) Owning the past in dementia care: creative engagement with others in the present. In Marshall, M (ed.) (1997) *State of the art in dementia care.* London: Centre for Policy on Ageing.

Gibson, F (2004) *The past in the present: Using reminiscence in health and social care.* Baltimore: Health Professions Press.

Gibson, F (2005) Fit for life: The contribution of life story work. In Marshall, M (ed.) (2005) *Perspectives on rehabilitation and dementia.* London: Jessica Kingsley.

Gillick v West Norfolk and Wisbech Area Health Authority (1985) UKHL 7 (17 October 1985).

Golan, N (1978) *Treatment in crisis situations.* New York: Free Press.

Goldsmith, M (2002) *Hearing the voice of people with dementia: Opportunities and obstacles,* London: Jessica Kingsley.

Gorman, K, O'Bryne, P and Parton, N (2006) Constructive work with offenders. Setting the scene In Gorman, K, Gregory, M, Hayles, M and Parton, P (2006) (eds) *Constructive work with offenders.* London: Jessica Kingsley.

GSCC (2002) *Code of practice for social care workers.* London GSCC.

GSCC (2010a) *Code of practice for social care workers.* London: GSCC.

GSCC (2010b) *Code of practice for social care workers and code of practice for employers of social care workers. London: GSCC.*

Haight, B K (1991) The state of the art as a basis for practice. *International Journal of Aging and Human Development,* 33 (1), 1–32.

Haight, B K, Bachman D L, Hendrix, S, Wagner, M T, Meeks, A and Johnson, J (2003) Life review: Treating the dyadic family unit with dementia. *Clinical Psychology and Psychotherapy,* 10, 165–74.

Haines, K and Drakeford, M (1998) *Young people and youth justice.* Basingstoke: Palgrave Macmillan.

Haley, J (1973) *Uncommon Therapy: The psychiatric techniques of Milton H. Erickson, M.D.* New York: WW Norton.

Harding, T and Beresford, P (1996) *The Standards we expect: what service users and carers want from social services workers.* London: NISW.

Harper, R and Hardy, S (2000) An evaluation of motivational interviewing as a method of intervention with clients in a probation setting, *British Journal of Social Work,* 30, 393–400.

Hayes, H (1991) Clarification of three schools. *ANZJ Family Therapy,* 12 (1), 27–43.

Henderson, R (2006) Defining non-instructed advocacy. *Planet Advocacy,* 18, pp5–7.

Henderson, R (2007) *Non-instructed advocacy in focus.* Available at **www.aqvx59.dsl.pipex.com/ What_is_non_instructed_advocacy.pdf** (accessed 19 January 2013).

Heron, J (1989) *Six category intervention analysis.* Guildford: University of Surrey.

Hodge, J (1985) *Planning for co-leadership: a practice guide for groupworkers,* University of Newcastle.

Holder, H., Longabaugh, R, Miller,W R and Rubonis, A V (1991) The cost-effectiveness of treatment for alcoholism: A first approximation. *Journal of Social Studies on Alcohol,* 52 (6), 517–40.

Hollis, F (1964) *Casework: a psychosocial therapy.* 2nd edition. New York: Random House.

Holmes, J (2002) All you need is cognitive behaviour therapy? *British Medical Journal,* February 2, 324 (7332): 288–94.

Hopmeyer, E and Werk, A (1993) A comparative study of four family bereavement groups. *Groupwork.* 6 (2), 107–21.

IASSW (2012) *Definition of social work.* **http://ifsw.org/policies/definition-of-social-work/** (accessed 19 Jaunuary 2013).

Innovations in Dementia (2008) *A new way of working with people with dementia.* Available at **http://news.elderworld.com/2008/12/innovations-in-dementia-new-way-of.html** (accessed 12 February 2009).

Israelstam, K (1998) Contrasting four major family therapy paradigms: Implications for family therapy training, *Journal of Family Therapy.* 10, 179–96.

James, R K and Gilliand, B E (2001) *Crisis intervention strategies.* 4th edition. Belmont, CA: Wadsworth.

Jaques, D (2006) *Learning in groups: A handbook for improving groupwork.* London: Kogan Page.

Jehu, D, Klassen, C and Gazan, M (1985/86) Cognitive restructuring of disturbed beliefs associated with childhood sexual abuse. *Journal of Social Work and Human Sexuality,* 4, 49–69.

Johnson L, and Yanca, S (2001) *Social work practice.* Boston, MA: Allyn and Bacon.

Johnston, J R (1994) High conflict divorce. *The future of children,* 4 (1) 165–82.

Jones, E. (1993). *Family systems therapy.* Chichester: Wiley.

Jung, C (1963) *Memories, dreams, reflections.* London: Collins.

Kasl-Godley, J and Gatz, M (2000) Psychosocial interventions for individuals with dementia: An integration of theory, therapy, and a clinical understanding of dementia. *Clinical Psychology Review,* 20 (6), 755–82.

Kelly, G A (1955) *The psychology of personal constructs, Volumes 1 and 2.* New York: W W Norton.

Kendall, K (2004) Dangerous thinking: a critical history of correctional cognitive behaviourism. In Mair, G (ed.) *What matters in probation.* Cullompton: Willan.

Kenny, L and Kenny, B (2000) Psychodynamic theory in social work: a view from practice. In P Stepney and D Ford (eds) *Social work methods and theories. A framework for practice.* Lyme Regis: Russell House.

Kitwood, T (1997a) *Dementia reconsidered: the person comes first.* Maidenhead: Open University Press.

Kitwood, T (1997b) The Uniqueness of persons in dementia . In M Marshall (ed.) (1997) *State of the art in dementia care.* London: Centre for Policy on Ageing.

Kleber, D J, Howell, R J. and Tibbits-Kleiber, A L (1986) The impact of parental homosexuality in child custody cases: a review of literature, *Bulletin of the American Journal of Psychiatry and Law,* 14, 81–7.

Klein, M (1932) *The psychoanalysis of children.* London: Hogarth Press.

Knei-Paz, C (2009) 'The central role of the therapeutic bond in a social agency setting clients' and social workers' perceptions, *Journal of Social Work,* April 2009, 9, 2, 178–98.

Koch, M P and Lowery, C R (1984) Evaluation of mediation as an alternative to divorce litigation. *Professional Psychology: Research and Practice,* 15, 109–20.

Kroese, B S (1998) Cognitive-behavioural therapy for people with learning disabilities. *Behavioural and Cognitive Psychotherapy,* 26, 315–22.

Kubler- Ross, E (1969) *On death and dying.* New York: Macmillan.

Kunz, J A and Soltys, F S (2007) *Transformational reminiscence: Life story work.* New York: Springer.

Lawson, D (1994) Identifying pretreatment change. *Journal of Counseling and Development,* 72, 244–8.

Lietaer, G (1984) Unconditional positive regard. In Levant, R F and Sklien, J M (eds) *Client centered therapy and the person centered approach.* New York: Praeger Publishers.

Lietaer, G (1990) The client-centered approach after the Wisconsin project: A personal view on its evolution. In G. Lietaer, J. Rombauts and R Van Balen (eds) *Client-centered and experiential psychotherapies in the nineties.* Leuven: Leuven University Press.

Lietaer, G (1993) Authenticity, congruence and transparency. In D Brazier (ed.) *Beyond Carl Rogers.* London: Constable.

Lindsay, T and Danner, S (2008) Accepting the unacceptable: the concept of acceptance in work with the perpetrators of hate crime. *European Journal of Social Work,* 11(1), 43–56.

Lindsay, T and Orton, O (2011) *Groupwork practice in social work.* 2nd edn. Exeter: Learning Matters.

McGoldrick, M and Gerson, L (1985) *Genograms in family assessment.* New York: W W Norton.

MacKinnon, L K and James, K (1987a) The new epistemology and the Milan approach: Feminist and socio-political considerations. *Journal of Family Therapy,* 13 (2).

MacKinnon, L K and James, K (1987b) The Milan systemic approach: Theory and practice. *Australian and New Zealand Journal of Family Therapy,* 8 (2), 89–98.

McKeown, J, Clarke, A, and Repper J (2006) Life story work in health and social care: systematic literature review. *Journal of Advanced Nursing,* 55(2), 237–47.

McLaughlin, H (2008) What's in a name: 'client', 'patient', 'customer', 'consumer', 'expert by experience', 'service user' – What's next? *British Journal of Social Work.* Advance Access published online on February 21, 2008. **bjsw.oxfordjournals.org/content/39/6/1101.full.pdf+html** (accessed 20 January 2013).

McLaughlin, P (2012) *Mixed Emotions – Real stories of mixed marriages.* Belfast: Northern Ireland Mixed Marriage Association, 28 Bedford Street, Belfast BT2 7FE.

McLeod, J (2003) *An introduction to counselling.* 3rd edition. Maidenhead: Open University Press.

McMurran, M (ed.) (2002) *Motivating offenders to change: A guide to enhancing engagement in therapy.* Chichester: Wiley.

McNally, R J, Bryant, R A and Ehlers, A (2003) Does early psychological intervention promote recovery from posttraumatic stress? *Psychological Science in the Public Interest,* 4 (2), 45–79.

Machin, L (2009) *Working with loss and grief: a new model for practitioners,* London: Sage.

Mair, G (2004) Introduction: what works and what matters. In Mair, G (ed) *What matters in probation.* Cullompton: Willan.

Mallouli, C (2005) *Miniskirts, mothers and muslims.* New York: Monarch.

Marsh, P and Doel, M (2005) *The task-centred book.* London: Routledge/Community Care.

Marshall, M (ed.) (2005) *Perspectives on rehabilitation and dementia.* London: Jessica Kingsley.

Martins, M M, Viegas, P, Mimoso, R, Pauncz, A, Tóth, G, Hiiemäe, R, Harwin, N and Cosgrove, S (2008) *The power to change: how to set up and run support groups for victims and survivors of domestic violence.* Bristol: Women's Aid Federation of England. Available at: **www.womensaid.org. uk/domestic-violence-articles.asp?section=00010001002200370001&itemid=1841** (accessed 20 January 2013).

Maslow, A H (1943) A theory of human motivation. *Psychological Review*, 50, 370–96.

Mearns, D (1994) *Developing person-centred counselling*. London: Sage.

Mearns, D and Thorne, B (2007) *Person-centred counselling in action*. London: Sage.

Meichenbaum, D (1977) *Cognitive behaviour modification*. New York: Plenum.

Meichenbaum, D (1985) *Stress inoculation training*. New York: Pergamon.

Mencap and the Challenging Behaviour Foundation (CBF) (2012) *Out of sight: stopping the neglect and abuse of people with a learning disability*. Available at **www.mencap.org.uk/sites/default/files/documents/Out%20of%20sight_report_0.pdf** (accessed 13 August 2012).

Millar, J (2008) Social policy and family policy. In Alcock, P, Erskine, A and May, M, *Student's companion to social policy*. Oxford: Blackwell.

Miller, S D, Duncan, B L and Hubble, M A (2002) Client-directed, outcome-informed clinical work. In F W Kaslow and J Leblow (eds) *Comprehensive handbook of psychotherapy, Volume 4, Integrative/eclectic*. New York: John Wiley.

Miller, W R (1983) Motivational interviewing with problem drinkers. *Behavioural Psychotherapy* 11 (2), 147–72.

Miller, W R and Rollnick, S (2002) *Motivational interviewing: preparing people for change*. 2nd edn. New York: The Guilford Press.

Miller, W R, Taylor, C A and West, J C, (1980) Focussed versus broad spectrum behavior therapy for problem drinkers, *Journal of Consulting and Clinical Psychology*, 48 (5), 590–601.

Milner, J and O'Bryne, P (2002) *Assessment in social work*. 3rd edition. Basingstoke: Palgrave.

Minuchin, S. (1974) *Families and family therapy*. London: Tavistock.

Mitchell, J and Lynch, R S (2003) Beyond the rhetoric of social and economic justice: Redeeming the social work advocacy role. *Race, Gender and Class*, 10(2), 8–26.

Moore, C W (2003) *The Mediation Process: Practical strategies for resolving conflict*. 3rd edition. San Francisco, CA: Jossey-Bass.

Moos, I and Bjorn, A (2006) Use of the life story in the institutional care of people with dementia: a review of intervention studies, *Ageing and Society*, 26 (3), 431–54.

Munro, E (2011) *The Munro review of child protection: final report: a child-centred system*. Norwich: The Stationery Office (TSO).

Murphy, C (1994) *It started with a sea-shell: Life story work and people with dementia*. University of Stirling.

Murphy, C and Moyes, M (1997) Life story work. In M. Marshall (ed.) *State of the art in dementia care*. London: Centre for Policy on Ageing.

Murray-Parkes, C M (2010) *Bereavement; studies of grief in adult life*. 4th edition. London: Penguin.

Myer, A, and Conte, C (2006) Assessment for crisis intervention. *Journal of Clinical Psychology*, 62 (8), 959–70.

Nathan, J (1997) Psychoanalytic theory. In M Davies (ed.) *The Blackwell companion to social work*. 3rd edition. Oxford: Blackwell.

Nelson-Jones, R (2005) *Introduction to counselling skills*. 2nd edition. London: Sage.

Nezu, A M, Nezu, C M and Perri, M G (1989) *Problem-solving therapy for depression: theory, research, and clinical guidelines*. New York: Wiley.

Nichols, M P and Swartz, R C (2001) *Family therapy: concepts and methods.* 5th edition. Boston, MA: Allyn and Bacon.

NHS (no date) *Managing someone's legal affairs.* Available at: **www.nhs.uk/CarersDirect/ moneyandlegal/legal/Pages/MentalCapacityAct.aspx** (accessed 20 January 2013).

Norcross, J C and Grencavage, L M (1989) Eclecticism and integration in counselling and psychotherapy: Major themes and obstacles. *British Journal of Guidance and Counselling,* 2 (1), 227–47.

O'Connell, B (2006) Solution-focused therapy. In Feltham, C and Horton, I (eds) *The Sage handbook of counselling and psychotherapy.* 2nd edition. London: Sage.

O'Connell, B (2007) Solution-focused therapy. In Dryden, W (ed.) *Dryden's handbook of individual therapy.* 5th edition. London: Sage.

OPAAL (2009) *Speaking up to safeguard, lessons and findings from the Benchmarking Advocacy and Abuse Project, 2008–09.* Stoke-on-Trent: OPAAL.

Palazzolli, M, Boscolo, L, Cecchin, G and Prata, J (1978) *Paradox and counter paradox.* New York: Jason Aronson Inc.

Palazzolli, M, Boscolo, L, Cecchin, G and Prata, G. (1980) Hypothesising, circularity and neutrality: Three guidelines for the conductor of the session. *Family Process,* 19 (1), 3–12.

Parker, J (2007) Crisis intervention: A practice model for people who have dementia and their carers. *Practice,* 19:2, 115–126.

Parker, J and Bradley, G (2010) *Social work practice: Assessment, planning, intervention and review.* 3rd edition. Exeter: Learning Matters.

Parsons, M (2005) The contribution of social work to the rehabilitation of older people with dementia: Values in practice. In Marshall, M (ed.) (2005) *Perspectives on rehabilitation and dementia.* London: Jessica Kingsley.

Parton, N and O'Byrne, P (2000) *Constructive social work: towards a new practice.* Basingstoke: Palgrave.

Payne, M (2005) *Modern social work theory.* 3rd edition. Basingstoke: Palgrave Macmillan.

Pearson, J, and Thoennes, N (1984) *Final report of the divorce mediation research project.* 90-CW-634. Madison, WI: Association of Family and Conciliation Courts, Research Institute.

Pierson, J and Thomas, M (2010) *Dictionary of social work; the definitive A to Z of social work and social care.* Maidenhead: Open University Press.

Pinquart, M and Forstmeier, S (2011) Effects of reminiscence interventions psychosocial outcomes: A meta-analysis, *Aging and Mental Health,* 16 (5), 541–58.

Pinsof, W M and Wynne, L C (1995) The efficacy of marital and family therapy: An empirical overview, conclusions, and recommendations. *Journal of Marital and Family Therapy,* 21, 585–613.

Pinkerton, J and Campbell, J (2002) Social work and social justice in Northern Ireland: Towards a new occupational space, *British Journal of Social Work,* 32, 723–37.

Prochaska, J O and DiClemente C C (1982) Transtheoretical therapy: Towards a more integrated model of change. *Psychotherapy: Theory, Research and Practice,* 19, 276–88.

Prochaska, J O. and DiClemente, C C (1986) Toward a comprehensive model of change. In W R Miller and N Heather (eds), *Treating addictive behaviors: processes of change.* New York: Plenum Press.

Pruitt, D and Carnevale, P (1993) *Negotiation in social conflict.* Maidenhead: Open University Press.

Ramesh, R (2012) Winterbourne View abuse: last staff member pleads guilty. *The Guardian* 7 August 2012.

Rando,T A (1993) *Treatment of complicated mourning.* Champaign, IL: Research Press.

Rapoport, L (1970) Crisis intervention as a mode of brief treatment. In Roberts, R W and Nee, R H (eds) *Theories of social casework.* Chicago: University of Chicago Press.

Reid, W J and Shyne, A W (1969) *Brief and extended casework.* New York: Columbia University Press.

Reimers, S, and Treacher, A (1995) *Introducing user friendly family therapy.* London: Routledge.

Reuterlov, H, Lofgren, T, Nordstrom, K, Ternstrom, A and Miller, S D (2000) What is better? A preliminary investigation of between-session change. *Journal of Systemic Therapies.* 19 (1), 111–15.

Richmond, M E (1922) *What is social casework?* New York: Russell Sage Foundation.

Roberts, A (ed.) (2005) *Crisis intervention handbook: Assessment, treatment and research.* 3rd edition. Oxford: Oxford University Press.

Roberts, M (2007) *Developing the craft of mediation: Reflections on theory and practice.* London: Jessica Kingsley.

Rogers, C R (1957) The necessary and sufficient conditions for therapeutic personality change. *Journal of Consulting Psychology*, 21 (2), 95–103.

Rogers, C R (1961) *On becoming a person: A therapist's view of psychotherapy.* London: Constable.

Rogers, C R (1965) *Person to person: The problem of being human.* Harper-Row: New York.

Rogers, C R (1967) What psychology has to offer to teacher education. *Teacher education and mental health – Association for Student Teaching.* Cedar Falls: State College of Iowa, 37–57.

Ryan, E and Spadafora, P (2005) *Facilitated life story writing by individuals with dementia for conversational remembering boxes.* Ontario: Sheridan Elder Research Centre.

Ryan, T, and Walker, R (1997) *Life story work.* 3rd edition. London: BAAF.

Schweitzer, P and Bruce, E (2008) *Remembering yesterday, caring today: Reminiscence in dementia care, a guide to good practice.* London: Jessica Kingsley.

Scott, M J and Dryden, W (2003) The cognitive therapy paradigm. In R Woolfe, W Dryden and S Strawbridge (eds) *Handbook of counselling psychology.* 2nd edition. London: Sage.

Seddon, J (2000) *Counselling skills in social work practice.* 2nd edition. Maidenhead: Open University Press.

Sharry, J (2001) *Solution focused groupwork.* London: Sage.

Sheldon, B (2000) Cognitive behavioural methods in social care; a look at the evidence. In Stepney, P and Ford, D (eds) *Social work models, methods and theories.* Lyme Regis: Russell House Publishing.

Shulman, L (1992) *The skills of helping; individuals, families and groups.* 3rd edition. Itasca, IL: Peacock.

Smith, D (1996) Psychodynamic therapy: the Freudian approach. In Dryden (ed.) *Handbook of individual therapy.* London: Sage.

Sprenkle, D H and Storm, C L (1983) Divorce therapy outcome research: A substantive and methodological review. *Journal of Marital and Family Therapy*, 9, 239–58.

Stepney, P and Ford, D (2000) *Social work models, methods and theories: A framework for practice.* Dorset: Russell House Publishing.

Sullivan, M A, Harris, E, Collado, C, and Chen, T (2006) Noways tired: Perspectives of clinicians of colour on culturally competent crisis intervention, *Journal of Clinical Psychology*, 62 (8), 987–99.

Surr, A (2005) Preservation of self in people with dementia living in residential care: A socio-biographical approach. *Social Science and Medicine,* 62 (7), 1720–30.

Thompson, N (2006) *Anti-discriminatory practice.* 5th edition. Basingstoke: Palgrave Macmillan.

Thompson, N (2009) Practising social work: Meeting the professional challenge. Basingstoke, Palgrave Macmillan.

Thorne, B (2007) Person-centred therapy. In W Dryden (ed.) *Dryden's handbook of individual therapy.* 5th edition. London: Sage.

Trevett, A (ed.) (2001) *Taking their side: fighting their corner; 16 stories demonstrating the difference independent advocacy makes to the lives of people with dementia.* London: The Dementia Advocacy Network. Available at: **http://dan.advocacyplus.org.uk/data/files/Taking_their_side/FINAL_COPY_ TAKING_THEIR_SIDE_MARCH_2012.pdf** (accessed 20 January 2013).

Trevithwick (2005) *Social work skills: A practice handbook.* 2nd edition. Maidenhead: Open University Press.

Trotter, C (1996) The impact of different supervision practices in community corrections. *Australian and New Zealand Journal of Criminology,* 29 (1), 29–46.

Trotter, C (2006) *Working with involuntary clients: A guide to practice.* 2nd edition. London: Sage.

Truax, C B and Carkhuff R R (1967) *Towards effective counseling and psychotherapy.* Chicago: Aldine.

Vetere, A, and Dallos, R (2003). *Working systemically with families: Formulations, intervention and evaluation.* London: Karnac.

Wahab, S (2005) Motivational interviewing and social work practice, *Journal of Social Work,* 5 (1), 45–60.

Wallerstein, J S, and Kelly, J B (1980) *Surviving the breakup: How children and parents cope with divorce.* New York: Basic Books,

Walrond-Skinner, S (1976) *Family therapy: The treatment of natural systems.* Routledge and Kegan Paul.

Watson, D and West, J (2006) *Social work process and practice: Approaches, knowledge and skill.* Basingstoke: Palgrave Macmillan.

Watzlawick, P, Beavin, J B, and Jackson, D D (1967) *Pragmatics of human communication; A study of interactional patterns, pathologies, and paradoxes.* New York: WW Norton.

WEA North West (2011) *Being a good advocate.* Available at: **nw.wea.org.uk/learning/projects/ resources/resources.php** (accessed 20 January 2013).

Weiner-Davis, M, De Shazer, S, and Gingerich, W J (1987) Building on pretreatment change to construct the therapeutic solution. *Journal of Marital and Family Therapy,* 13 (4), 359–63.

Wells, S (2006) *Developments in dementia advocacy: Exploring the role of advocates in supporting people with dementia.* London: WASSR.

Whitaker, D S (2001) *Using groups to help people.* 2nd edition. Hove: Brunner-Routledge.

White, M and Epston, D (1990) *Narrative means to therapeutic ends.* New York: WW Norton.

Williams, M (1966) Limitations, fantasies and security operations of beginning group psycho-therapists, *International Journal of Group Psychotherapy,* 16, 150–62.

Williams, S and Keady, J (2006) The narrative voice of people with dementia, *Dementia* 5 (163).

Wilks, T (2012) *Advocacy and social work practice.* Berkshire: Open University Press.

Wilson, J (1998) *Child-focused practice: A systemic collaborative approach*. London: Karnac.

Wilson, K, Ruch, G, Lymbery, M and Cooper, A (2011) *Social work: An introduction to contemporary practice*. 2nd edition. Essex: Pearson.

Woods, B, Spector, A, Jones, C, Orrell, M and Davies, S (2005) Reminiscence therapy for dementia. *Cochrane Database of Systematic Reviews* 2005, Issue 2. Art. No.: CD001120. DOI: 10.1002/14651858. CD001120.pub2.

World Health Organisation (2006) *International statistical classification of diseases and related health problems 10th Revision (ICD-10 2006 online version)* Available at: **www.who.int/classifications/apps/icd/icd10online2006/** (accessed 30 December 2008).

Index

Added to the page number, 't' denotes a table.